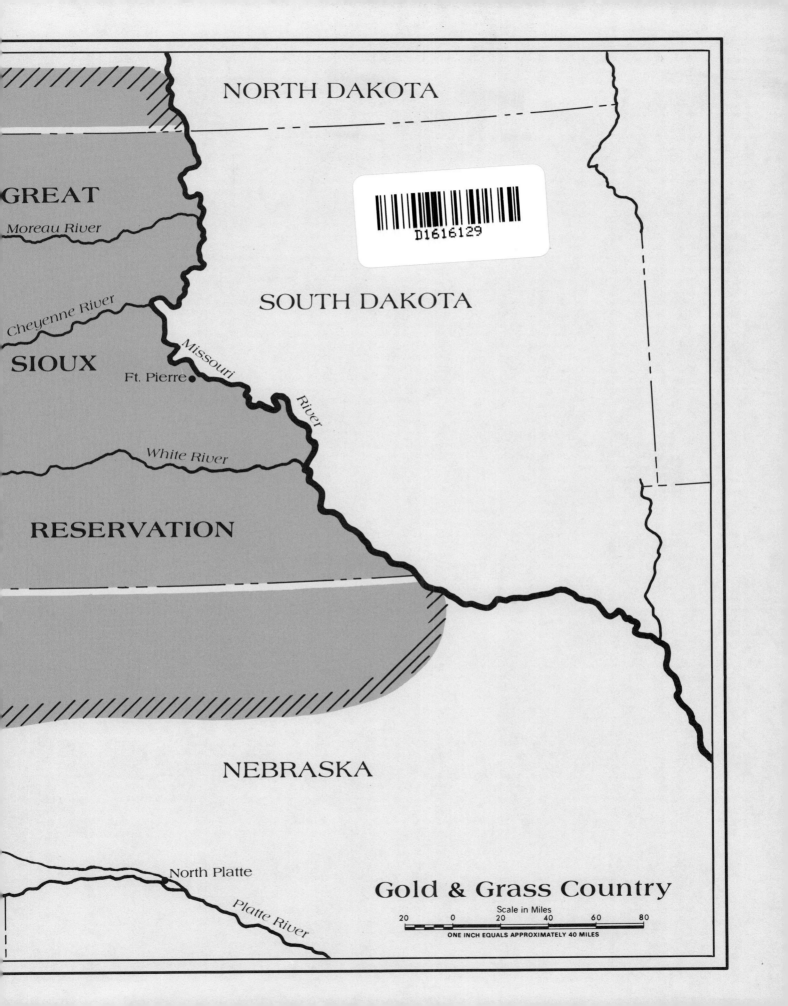

NORTH DAKOTA

GREAT

Moreau River

Cheyenne River

SIOUX

Missouri

SOUTH DAKOTA

Ft. Pierre •

River

White River

RESERVATION

NEBRASKA

North Platte

Platte River

Gold & Grass Country

Scale in Miles

20   0   20   40   60   80

ONE INCH EQUALS APPROXIMATELY 40 MILES

PAUL FRIGGENS

GOLD&GRASS
The Black Hills Story

PRUETT **P** *PUBLISHING COMPANY*
Boulder, Colorado

First Edition
1 2 3 4 5 6 7 8 9
Printed in the United States of America

Library of Congress Cataloging in Publication Data

Friggens, Paul, 1909-
    Gold andGrass.

    Bibliography: p.
    Includes index.
    1, Black Hills (S.D. and Wyo.) — History. 2. Frontier
and pioneer life — Black Hills (S.D. and Wyo.) I. Title.
F657.B6F85   1983   978.3′9   83-2855
ISBN 0-87108-648-4

The author is grateful to the following publishers for permission to quote: *Reader's Digest* for excerpts from three of my own articles: "From Russian Peasant to American Pioneer" (Copyright, July 1949); "Free Land!" (Copyright, May 1963); "America's Shrine of Democracy" (Copyright, August 1972); *The American West* for reprinting "The Curious Cousin Jacks" by the author (Copyright, November/December 1978); Charles Scribner's Sons for quote from "Old Deadwood Days" by Estelline Bennett (Copyright, 1935); University of Nebraska Press for passages from "History of South Dakota" by Herbert S. Schell (Copyright, 1961); *Outdoor Life* for excerpt from "Before the Railroad Came" by Charley Zabel and J. L. Beardsley (Copyright, August 1933); Farm Journal, Inc. for reprinting "The Fourth I Remember Best" (Copyright, July 1949); Vanguard Press, Inc., for excerpts from author's chapter in "The Black Hills," edited by Roderick Peattie (Copyright, 1952); Homestake Mining Company for excerpts from "Homestake, the Centennial History of America's Greatest Gold Mine" by Bronson and Watkins (Copyright, 1977); *Custer County Chronicle* for selection from "The Job" in Badger Clark's *Skylines and Woodsmoke*; Westerner's International for selections from "A Cowboy's Prayer," in Badger Clark's *Sun and Saddle Leather* (Copyright, 1962 by Westerners International, P.O. Box 3485 Tucson, AZ 85722). The quote from Teddy Blue, at top of page 157 is from *We Pointed Them North* by E. C. Abbott and Helena Huntington Smith (Copyright, 1939, Farrar & Rinehart).

Acknowledgements

This is a vastly better book than it might have been, thanks to the generous encouragement, counsel and input of many people. In particular, I am indebted to: Walter B. Mahony, Jr., longtime friend and *Reader's Digest* editor, who kindly urged me "onward and upward" after appraising my early drafts; Gladys Doty, Professor Emeritus of English, University of Colorado, who helpfully discussed and critically read the entire manuscript; Dr. Herbert S. Schell, distinguished South Dakota historian, who gave me both scholarly advice and renewed confidence after reviewing the Black Hills history section of the book; Neil C. Mangum, ranger/historian at Custer Battlefield National Monument, who guided me through Custer's controversial "Last Stand"; Don C. Clowser, Deadwood, for his helpful book, "Dakota Indian Treaties"; James B. Dunn, Director, Homestake Public Affairs, Homestake Mining Company, for history of America's greatest gold mine; Helen Hoyt, Rapid City Public Library; Carol Davis, Sturgis Public Library, and Dora Jones, Special Collections Librarian at Black Hills State College, and for the Leland D. Case Library for Western Historical Studies at Black Hills State College, for help on the life of Annie D. Tallent; *Rapid City Daily Journal*; South Dakota State Historical Society and Shebby Lee for research on Badger Clark; Adams Memorial Museum, Deadwood, for the story of the Thoen Stone and Potato Creek Johnny; Leonel Jensen, Rapid City, for family homesteading material.

For expert and invaluable photographic assistance, I am indebted to: Elinor M. Gehres, Western History Department, Denver Public Library; National Archives, Washington, D.C.; Mrs. Bonnie Gardner, Photo Curator, South Dakota State Historical Society; Mrs. Marjorie Pontius, Deadwood Public Library and Centennial Archives; Deadwood Chamber of Commerce; Homestake Mining Company; Coffrin's Old West Gallery, Miles City, Montana; National Park Service, Mount Rushmore National Memorial; Mark A. Young, South Dakota Department of Economic and Tourist Development; Western History Research Center, University of Wyoming.

Contents

Part Four

To my wife Myriam, South Dakota ranch girl, homesteader's daughter, history-lover and critic, who so knowledgeably and tirelessly shared in the birth of this book.

Prologue

To begin with, this is not a scholarly book heavy with footnotes. It is a journalist's endeavor to write for the general reader a human, accurate and interesting account of the Indian wars, the gold rush, the pioneering and struggle that led to settlement of the Black Hills of South Dakota—a place I love.

My roots run deep in the Black Hills. Here my courageous parents pioneered about the time of the tragic Battle of Wounded Knee and the last days of the Sioux Nation. Here I was delivered into the world by a horse-and-buggy doctor. Here I walked three miles to a crude but wondrous country school that first opened to me a window on the world. Here I grew up just in time to know some memorable characters—the *last* of the old Indian fighters, the *last* of the old Texas Trail drivers, the *last* of the grizzled old prospectors. And visiting wide-open, wicked old Deadwood, I've often climbed to famed Mount Moriah Cemetery—Boot Hill—where, incongruously, my grandparents are laid to rest close by that notorious pair, "Wild Bill" Hickok and "Calamity Jane" Cannary.

I've had a lifelong love affair with the Black Hills. Raised on a ranch on Lower False Bottom Creek near the pioneer settlement of St. Onge, I looked up every day to the lofty, pine-crested hills, rising heavenward from the rolling prairie. I gazed at those hills at dawn and at dusk, in sunlight and in storm, all through the changing seasons. And always with a feeling of wonder and mystery and delight.

I've climbed the craggy peaks of the Black Hills, explored their crystal caves, driven their scenic canyons, picnicked in their parks, fished in their rippled trout streams, poked around their eerie ghost towns, descended a mile or more underground in the Homestake—America's greatest gold mine—and gloried at the heart-stirring sight of four American presidents enshrined on rugged Mount Rushmore.

These are the Black Hills that I treasure and love; and it seems to me that despite the abundance of writings about them—some superficial, some superb—there is a need for a new telling of their absorbing story.

Simply stated, it is a saga of *gold* and *grass*. "There's gold from the grass roots down, but there's more gold from the grass roots up," a scout with the U.S. government survey party exploring the Hills in 1875 sagely observed. Nature was lavish with its nutritious species of grasses which grew abundantly in the foothills and valleys of the Black Hills and on the surrounding plains. These great grasslands teemed with millions of brownish-black buffaloes until the westward movement following the Civil War and the white man's invasion of the Indians' heartland. This invasion almost wiped out the buffalo, simultaneously threatening to destroy the red man's livelihood and nomadic way of life.

While the Indians greatly valued the grasslands because they nurtured the buffalo, which in turn nurtured their people, the whites eagerly desired the region for another reason. The Black Hills and adjacent land offered some of the finest livestock grazing on earth; and here on these seemingly illimitable grasslands was free open range and a world of wealth waiting to lure cattle barons and settlers alike. With discovery of this bonanza, the hell-for-leather American cowboy was soon driving his bawling herds of Longhorns a thousands miles up the Texas Trail to graze this sea of grass; and with this impetus and demand, farming and ranching in the Black Hills region began.

So the first prize was grass. The second was gold.

Discovery of this hidden treasure by Gen. George Armstrong Custer's military expedition to the Black Hills in 1874 sparked one of the West's great gold rushes and intensified the struggle between Indians and whites. The struggle grew all the more involved and embittered because the Indians considered the Black Hills sacred. Recognizing their claim, the U.S. government, under the Treaty of Laramie in 1868, permanently set aside this holy ground "for the absolute and undisturbed use and occupation" of the Sioux Nation. Then, finding gold, white men ruthlessly retook and raped the Hills for their riches. This clearly illegal act, together with other shameful injustices against the Indian, led to the famed Battle of the Little Bighorn, in which "Yellow Hair" Custer and his entire command were annihilated by the Sioux and the Cheyenne.

Thus I choose to title the book *Gold and Grass*. It opens with a journalist's eye-view of early Black Hills history. It continues with the saga of my pioneer family's valiant struggle to settle a bit of the sacred soil of the Sioux. It closes with a gallery of memorable Black Hills characters.

Where are these lovely mountains located, how were they formed, and why are they called the Black Hills?

Thrusting up abruptly some 3,500 feet above the surrounding Great Plains, the Black Hills lie in the southwest corner of South Dakota and extend into northeast Wyoming. Viewed from a satellite in outer space, this 100-by-60-mile great elliptical dome of igneous rock, covered with blue-green pine and spruce, stands out as a verdant island in a billowing sea of tawny grass. The Black Hills are among the oldest mountains in the world and, rising to 7,242 feet at Harney Peak, they are the highest east of the Rockies in North America. Unlike the rugged ranges of the Rockies or the gentle folds of the Appalachians, however, they are not wrapped in a maze of mountains, but stand alone.

The Black Hills first started to form about two *billion* years ago, it is believed. Then sometime between 30 and 60 million years ago, the molten igneous rocks within were extruded upward in a massive upheaval that lifted them above a great salt sea which then covered the ancient land. Folded over, faulted, subjected to tremendous pressures and complex chemical changes lasting eons of time, these mountains in a few places formed precious gold ore.

The Indians named the mountains. The Teton Sioux, who conquered other tribes living in the area, and then occupied it—probably about the time of the American Revolution—called the region "Paha-Sapa," meaning "the hills that are black." But they are not really *black*, even though their forested slopes appear bluish-black in the late afternoon shadows; and they are definitely not *hills*.

From a distance, the mountains sometimes loom dark and somber, like a threatening thunderstorm. Small wonder then, that the Plains Indians looked on them as awesome and sacred ground. According to legend, strange rumblings could be heard in the hills on a clear, calm day—sounds that the primitive red men interpreted as the voice of the thunder god. Indeed, the Indians reverenced the Black Hills as the abode of *Wakantanka*, the Great Holy, and they regarded the mysterious mountains as the center of the universe. So, devoutly, these nomadic people made annual pilgrimages of worship to Paha-Sapa, where they fasted in solitude and trance, smoked their medicine pipes, saw visions and communed with the Great Holy. The towering landmark, Bear Butte, near Sturgis, formed by magma thrusting up 1,200 feet above the surrounding plains, was a favorite place of worship for the Cheyennes, Mandans and Sioux.

This is the gold-and-grass country of my book. When one flies over this breathtaking region today, bountiful with its fields of waving grain, the green-carpeted irrigated farms, its rolling ranchlands and immense mineral riches, one cannot help reflecting that this was once a part of the West considered fit only for savages and wild beasts—utterly worthless. Until the mid-1800s, the general public held only the vaguest ideas about the wide-open lands between the Missouri River and the Rocky Mountains. They considered the vast, unknown area an uninhabitable wasteland and mapmakers wrote it off as the "Great American Desert." The white man had yet to discover the wondrous beauty and boundless riches of the Black Hills.

Similarly, I fear a host of Americans today, including many now living in this storied area, have yet to discover the exciting history and colorful lore of the Black Hills. It has been my purpose, in writing this book, to remedy that situation.

Paul Friggens

The West that Nobody Wanted

What do we want with this
worthless area, this region
of savages and wild beasts,
of shifting sands and whirlwinds
of dust, of cactus and
prairie dogs? To what use
could we ever hope to put
these great deserts and these
endless mountain ranges?"

—Attributed to Daniel Webster,
speaking of the then unknown
and forbidding American West
in the 1840s.

PART ONE

The War for the Gold-and-Grass Country

Acquiring horses from the Spaniards, the Plains Indians adopted a radically new way of life, following the buffalo. Darting in and out of the milling herds, the hard riding horsemen hunted the bison with bow and arrow or lance for the food, clothing and shelter they provided. — *National Archives.*

Overleaf. Imagine a 1,000-man cavalcade with cavalry, artillery, about 1,000 horses, together with 600 mules drawing 110 wagons, followed by 300 beef cattle for fresh meat. There was even a 16-piece band! This was Gen.G. A. Custer's impressive military expedition that crossed the plains to the Black Hills in 1874, starting the gold rush and invading the Sioux's sacred domain. — *By Illingsworth. National Archives.*

Whites invade the Indians' heartland

You have come into my country without my con-
sent and spread your soldiers all over it . . .
You have put us in misery . . . We want you to
take away the forts so that all the game will
come back and we will have plenty to eat.
—Chief Iron Shell's plea at Ft. Laramie

On an ominous day in August 1865, a band of Plains Indians was making its accustomed pilgrimage to worship in their sacred Black Hills and to commune with Wakantanka, the Great Holy. Suddenly, from the pine slopes, they looked down on an alarming sight. Out of the dust emerged two blue-coated columns of Uncle Sam's Indian-fighting army skirting the northwest rim of the Hills.

Never had the red men seen so many "pony soldiers" as the 2,000 troopers now parading across lush Redwater Valley, and moving on to the Belle Fourche River. Riding under starred flags, wheeling Gatling guns that glinted in the sunlight, the uniformed cavalrymen seemed formidable indeed to the watchful, apprehensive Indians. A great, white-topped supply train of 140 six-mule wagons, followed by a strong cavalry guard, brought up the columns' rear.

Summoned from their Nebraska garrison in the Platte River Valley and from Fort Laramie in Wyoming, the two columns of about 600 and 1,400 men each, under Colonels Nelson Cole and Samuel Walker, had linked up as prearranged on the Redwater and were now advancing westward to rendezvous with other troops in the Powder River country of Wyoming. Their mission: to clear a large section of the northern Great Plains of Indians in order to build forts and a safe wagon road for travel to the newly discovered goldfields at Virginia City, Montana Territory.

The appearance of this hostile cavalry in the Indians' heartland was disquieting evidence that the 300-year-old battle between white men and red, for the American continent, had now reached this remote western frontier. Ultimately, the white man's invasion of the northern Great Plains would climax in a war involving the Indians' ancestral way of life, possession of the sacred, fabulously rich Black Hills, and the fate of the great Sioux Nation itself.

At stake in this coming conflict was the Indians' beloved buffalo-hunting country. Imagine the illimitable grasslands that were once the red man's sole domain. Extending from Mexico to Montana, they flourished with literally hundreds of species of forage, of which short, sturdy, sod-forming buffalo grass was king. A highly adaptable, palatable perennial, buffalo grass thrived under severe drouth conditions, furnished yearlong grazing and was dominant over vast areas of the Great Plains from the Texas Panhandle to the Dakotas.

Thus this immense sea of native grasses was a natural habitat for the bison or buffalo, which roamed in huge herds of probably 5 to 10 million or more head. At one time, an estimated 60 million of the great lumbering animals dotted the western plains. Slow-gaited, clumsy, poor-sighted, buffaloes were a perfect target for bow and arrow, and they provided the Plains Indians with an inexhaustible supply of beef.

With arrival of the Spaniards in the Southwest in the 1540s, the Indians acquired, by trade and by theft, the horse, which transformed this primitive, nomadic people into formidable warriors and the hard-riding horsemen of the plains. Each year, the red men joined in spectacular buffalo hunts. Riding their wiry ponies bareback, the daring horsemen darted in and out of the great milling herds, killing with bow and arrow or lance before they secured firearms. Sometimes the Indians stampeded the animals over a steep cliff, at the bottom of which the buffaloes piled up badly crippled, so they could be easily dispatched. Even today piles of buffalo bones are found at some of these "buffalo jumps" or slaughter sites.

Fleet-footed and mobile, the plains horsemen became far-reaching hunters and they developed a culture and way of life intimately linked with the buffalo. The buffalo followed the grass and the Indian followed the buffalo. Indeed, they lived together and the great shaggy herds furnished the tribes with food, clothing and shelter, undergirding their entire economy. The buffalo filled an important place in their religious life as well.

The buffalo supplied the first Americans with their principal food, meat, which they roasted, dried as jerky or pounded into pemmican, a high-protein meal for warriors. From the buffalo hide the Indians fashioned shirts, leggings, moccasins, warm winter robes and blankets. Buffalo skins served to cover their teepees and a single hide could be made into a bullboat. From the buffalo paunch, resourceful tribesmen made a cooking pot and from the intestines, sinews and small bones they made various utensils, tools and implements. Buffalo skins were used as a shield in battle, a shroud in death, and as a "canvas" on which to paint pictographs of Indian life. When wood was scarce on the plains, dried droppings or "buffalo chips" were good fuel.

Small wonder then that the Indians revered the buffalo, and held religious ceremonies honoring the beast. They also joined in the buffalo dance to celebrate the blessings of home, fertility and family and to give thanks to Wakantanka, the Great Spirit. The buffalo provided both material and spiritual sustenance.

Some of the biggest herds roamed the region in and around the Black Hills. It was ideal hunting country, and here the proud, fiercely independent Sioux carried on their primitive way of life: hunting, fishing, dancing, feasting, warring on weaker tribes and trekking with their pony-drawn travois and families to worship in their sacred Paha-Sapa. But the untroubled days of the Plains Indians commenced to fade with the westward movement. First, it was the intruding emigrant wagons on the Oregon, Overland and Mormon trails; next, the railroaders building the transcontinental Union Pacific. Spotting U.P. surveyors when they first appeared in the Platte Valley, Chief Red Cloud warned: "We do not want you here. You are scaring away the buffalo."

Still the whites flocked to the alluring West: the railroaders bringing the "iron horse" to puff across the prairies; the gold-seekers pitting the good earth; hordes of settlers building noisy towns and filling up the great, open countryside. The invading whites, who commonly spoke of "the only good Indian" as a "dead Indian," showed scant regard for the Indians' ancestral hunting grounds or their solemn treaties with the government in Washington. Boldly encroaching on the natives' ancient domain, they wantonly killed or drove off the wild game and buffalo, as Chief Red Cloud had feared.

Even worse, were the professional hunters like "Buffalo Bill" Cody, who killed a record 69 bison in one day to feed the hungry Kansas Pacific Railroad tracklaying crews. Paid hunters slaughtered thousands of animals each week. About this time, a process was perfected in the East to tan buffalo hides. Sold for leather, they brought three dollars apiece, and business boomed. Now new hordes of buffalo hunters swarmed over the Great Plains, and in 1872-73 alone the railroads hauled over one million hides. Buffalo hunting also became a popular sport, and so-called "sportsmen," shooting from the car windows of slow-moving trains, killed thousands more buffalo. All told, this appalling slaughter decimated the great herds, so that by the late 1870s buffalo numbers had dwindled to about 13 million. By the turn of the century, fewer than 1,000 head would remain!

Deprived of the indispensable buffalo that supplied their food, clothing and shelter, the red men faced starvation and doom and they struck back. They attacked tracklayers, telegraph stations, white settlements, and clashed sporadically with the army. Promptly, Washington dispatched reinforcements to safeguard the trespassers, to build forts; and in an appeasing effort to preserve order, the government even signed new "peace" treaties with a few scattered tribes. But they proved impossible to enforce and so tension and conflict mounted.

Near the present lovely little town of Lingle, Wyoming, in the North Platte Valley, history buffs today visit the marked site of the Grattan Fight. Here on August 19, 1854, Lt. John Grattan of Fort Laramie rode into an Indian village with 28 soldiers and an interpreter to arrest an Indian accused of shooting an ox in an emigrant train. When the chief refused to surrender his tribesman at once, Grattan threatened to use force.

"If you shoot," warned the chief, "we will kill all your men."

"Fire!" commanded the hotheaded officer, who was quickly surrounded by the Indians and shot down with five of his men. The others were killed as they tried to escape.

The so-called "Grattan Massacre" inflamed the military, and the War Department dispatched tough, Indian-fighting Gen. William S. Harney (for whom Harney Peak in the Black Hills is named) up the valley of the North Platte to punish the "savages" and make the Oregon Trail safe for further travel. Setting a fearsome example, Harney, on September 3, 1855, surrounded an Indian village near the Oregon Trail, ruthlessly cut down 85 men and took some 70 Indian women and children prisoners. Following this murderous attack, large numbers of Cheyenne and Sioux retreated to the still remote and safer country around the Black Hills.

Flaunting the army's might, Harney pursued with 600 troops in a bold march through the Sioux country to the Hills and then on to the Missouri River. He was spoiling for a fight, but failed to draw the enemy into battle. Instead, the alarmed Indians gathered at one of their favorite places of worship, volcanic Bear Butte, near the present town of Sturgis, where their chiefs had called an urgent council of the Great Sioux Nation. By

Shooting them for their hides, meat, and for sport (hunting even from train windows), whites wantonly slaughtered millions of buffaloes on the Great Plains. In a few years they had decimated the great herds and destroyed the Indians' livelihood and way of life.—*National Archives.*

A fiercely proud, independent people, the Dakota Sioux migrated from the forested East to become teepee-dwelling nomads of the Great Plains. Their beaded bucksking clothing, with eagle feathers to crown the warriors, was sheer artistry.— *National Archives.*

now, the aroused red men had begun to realize their peril. Over council fires, they carefully appraised their situation: the powerful enemy with frontier forts and dashing cavalry obviously bent on their submission, if not destruction, and they took a courageous step. The tribes vowed to resist any and all aggression against their homeland and their sacred Black Hills. They were to continue this fierce resistance during the next 20 years.

All this set the stage for eventual war over the gold-and-grass country. It was fueled by repeated clashes with the military. In retaliation for the infamous Sand Creek or Chivington Massacre in southeast Colorado in 1864, which wiped out an entire native village of some 500, including women and children, the Indians ravaged the South Platte Valley, burning, looting and killing. But wary of the army's growing might, these tribesmen also fled to the northern plains. One band of hostiles, together with their families, trekked north over 400 miles across the snowy prairies in frigid winter weather, skirted the Black Hills and moved on to the Powder River country. Their march, says an authority, "ranks as one of the greatest exploits in western history."

The year 1865 turned out to be the "bloody year of the plains." At this time, the U.S. government began building and fortifying the Bozeman Trail (named for enterprising John Bozeman who blazed it) as a wagon road from Fort Laramie by way of the Powder River to newly discovered goldfields at Virginia City, Montana. With this menacing act, the heretofore remote and undisturbed northern plains were now vitally affected. The Bozeman Trail cut through the heart of the Indians' domain, driving out the buffalo or exposing them to slaughter, and thus threatening to destroy the red man's livelihood and nomadic way of life.

Determined to protect their threatened hunting grounds and the sacred Black Hills, the Indians rallied to the call of the fiery, 43-year-old Sioux chief, Red Cloud, who cried out in anguish: "Whose voice was first sounded on the land? The voice of the red people who had but bows and arrows. But now when the white man comes into my country, he leaves a trail of blood behind him." Commanded by Red Cloud, one of the ablest military tacticians ever to challenge the whites, the Indians intercepted the first construction troops on the Bozeman Trail that summer and held them prisoner for two weeks. Angered and humiliated, the government endeavored to negotiate with Red Cloud, but he boycotted its councils and continued to attack work crews, wagon trains, stagecoaches and lonely telegraph stations along the frontier.

To build and fortify the Bozeman Trail, the army in 1865 put in command an aggressive officer, Gen. Patrick E. Connor, who arrogantly proclaimed that all Indians "must be hunted like wolves," and did so.

Connor led about 3,000 men on a march to subdue the rebellious Cheyenne and Sioux. But his Powder River campaign proved a costly fiasco, and the 2,000 cavalrymen under Colonels Cole and Walker, who had marched some 400 miles from the Black Hills to join him, nearly perished. Lost in the wild country, sick and short of rations, the green, mutinous troops had to slaughter their pack mules to survive. Scurvy broke out among the troops and the ragtag soldiers were in no condition to fight when at last they linked up with General Connor's main column. In stealthy hit-and-run fighting that summer, the Indians were victorious; and they seized vast booty, including horses and mules, carbines, valuable army supplies—and took many scalps!

The following year, 1866, Red Cloud, together with another rising young warrior named Crazy Horse, executed a daring coup that further humiliated the military. Known as the Fetterman Massacre, it involved Capt. William J. Fetterman, a brash, young army officer at Fort Phil Kearny, who had boasted, "Give me eighty men and I would ride through the whole Sioux Nation." On the frosty morning of December 21, Captain Fetterman dispatched a small wood-cutting detail that was lured into an ambush by the Indians. But it was only a feint to decoy reinforcements from the fort. Riding to the rescue with 80 men (by chance, the same number he had bragged would wipe out the whole Sioux Nation) Fetterman was surrounded by hundreds of howling warriors and within minutes he and his entire command were annihilated. Exultant, the Indians then stripped the bodies of the much-prized new army rifles and clothing and scalped the dead. Red Cloud's warriors roamed the Powder River country at will, harassing the military posts and attacking unwary troopers and wagon trains headed for the Montana goldfields. At last, weary of fighting Red Cloud's war, the U.S. government was compelled to give up guarding the Bozeman Trail. Uncle Sam's vaunted Indian-fighting army had been bested and wanted peace.

Sending out a treaty commission, headed by William Tecumseh Sherman of Civil War fame, the government in Washington summoned the Plains Indians to an historic council during the spring and summer of 1868 at old Fort Laramie, located near Lingle, Wyoming. Here, hundreds of Indian teepees dotted the green Platte River Valley; and huddled under a great army field tent, the council began its historic deliberations. The Indian chiefs and white commissioners held a surprisingly frank exchange. The Indians complained bitterly that the whites had trespassed on one of their last hunting grounds, killing and driving out the buffalo, and they demanded that the three forts on the Bozeman Trail be abandoned and the road closed. "You have driven away our game and

Fiery Red Cloud, a chief of the Oglala Sioux. His successful war against the U.S. Army led to the Treaty of Laramie that was to permanently seal off the sacred Black Hills from settlement.—*National Archives.*

Fort Phil Kearny, one of the hated posts on the Bozeman Trail that the Indians forced the army to abandon.—*Harper's Weekly, Western History Department, Denver Public Library.*

"Give me eighty men and I would ride through the whole Sioux Nation," boasted a brash army captain. But Capt. Fetterman and his entire command were annihilated. The Fetterman Massacre pictured in *Harper's Weekly*, 1867.—*Western History Department, Denver Public Library.*

"Guarding the Supply Train." Artist Frederick Remington portrays Uncle Sam's Indian fighting army sent to clear the Great Plains for the white man.—*Copy from print loaned by Library of Congress. National Archives.*

Making their accustomed pilgrimage to worship in their sacred *Paha Sapa*, these Teton Sioux families were camped near the Black Hills about the time of the gold rush.—*Centennial Archives, Deadwood Public Library.*

Pioneer photographer Alexander Gardner pictures Dakota Indians ferrying across the North Platte River to join the Treaty Council at Ft. Laramie in 1868.—*South Dakota State Historical Society.*

our means of livelihood until now we have nothing left," was the repeated complaint.

In turn, the white commissioners spoke openly and General Harney amazed the chiefs with his candor. "We know very well that you have been treated very badly for years past," Harney conceded. "You have been cheated by everybody, and everybody has told lies to you, but now we want to commence anew. You have killed our people and taken enough of our property and you ought to be satisfied. It is not the fault of the great Father in Washington. He sends people out here that he thinks are honest, but they are people who cheat you badly. We will take care that you shall not be treated so any more." Gen. John B. Sanborn spoke and warned the chiefs bluntly: "We do this and offer you peace to save your nation from destruction. If you continue at war your country will soon be overrun by white people, military posts will be located on all the rivers; your game and yourselves will be destroyed."

Following long, hard bargaining, the conferees at length drafted the Treaty of Larmie—one of the most remarkable documents ever agreed to by Indians and whites. Seeking to end the warfare sparked by invasion of the whites, the government promised to set aside a vast 45,000-square mile tract (about the size of Pennsylvania) in Dakota Territory *"for the absolute and*

undisturbed use and occupation of the Sioux Nation." Designated as the Great Sioux Reservation, the land would encompass all of present-day South Dakota west of the Missouri River, and most important to the Sioux, it would include the coveted Black Hills. These shining mountains, so familiar to the nation today as the location of the Mount Rushmore National Memorial, enshrining four American presidents, were guaranteed to be kept inviolate and permanently sealed off from settlement.

To further mollify the inflamed tribesmen, the government set aside a huge illdefined "unceded Indian territory," stretching roughly from the Bighorn Mountains to the Black Hills. The treaty stipulated that "no white person or persons shall be permitted to settle upon, occupy or even pass through this territory without the Indians' consent." And here the tribes would be free to hunt buffalo and wild game as of old. Moreover, the government promised to protect the Indians "against the commission of all depredations by people of the United States." The whole amazing treaty, with its astounding concessions, was a stunning victory for the powerful Red Cloud and his people, for never before had an Indian chief so defied the Great White Father in Washington and exacted such promises.

Seeking peace, Gen. William Tecumseh Sherman and white commissioners parley with Indian chiefs at Ft. Laramie in 1868. Outcome was the Treaty of Laramie, sealing off the Black Hills from settlement and setting aside the Great Sioux Reservation, but it was soon violated.—*National Archives.*

Above. Like all Plains Indians, the strong Sioux women maintained a portable home in their secure, comfortable teepees, crowded with hide bedding, cradleboard for baby, cooking pots, supplies of food, fuel and household gear. — *National Park Service Photo. Left.* Sitting Bull, the revered Hunkpapa Sioux leader and medicine man who refused to be confined to a dreary reservation and fled instead with his people to Canada. He remained there for four years. — *Western History Department, Denver Public Library.*

In the end, the army agreed to abandon its three military posts—Fort C. F. Smith, Phil Kearny and Reno—and cease further efforts to maintain the Bozeman Trail. Still Red Cloud refused to join the peace parley or sign the treaty. Instead, he stood that fall with his people on a hill near the Bozeman Trail jubilantly observing Fort Phil Kearny as it was abandoned and the army moved out. Then swooping down with his gloating warriors, he put the torch to the hated fort, burning it to the ground. In triumph, he moved on to watch the evacuation of Forts C. F. Smith and Reno, which were also burned. Satisfied at last that his people had won their righteous cause and could continue their ancestral way of life, the proud Red Cloud finally consented to travel to Fort Laramie where in November 1868, he was the last Indian chief to sign the historic treaty.

While the 17-article Treaty of Laramie was in many ways a surprising victory for the Sioux, it nevertheless exacted a tremendous price which apparently the Indians did not fully comprehend at the signing. In return for abandoning the hated frontier forts, closing the Bozeman Trail and forever sealing off the sacred Black Hills from settlement, the United States now required these proudly independent and nomadic people to peacefully settle down on the empty prairies of the Great Sioux Reservation and live like "civilized" whites.

The government, in its infinite wisdom, had blueprinted every detail. For those who would abandon the chase and commence farming, Washington agreed to furnish "one good American cow and one good well-broken pair of American oxen." The government promised the reservation Indians plows to break the virgin sod, seed to plant, food until crops were raised and a white man to teach them farming. For each agency set up throughout the huge sprawling reservation, a doctor, carpenter, blacksmith, miller, engineer and teacher would be assigned. All children between the ages of 6 and 16 would be required to attend school and learn English. Among other promises, the government agreed to feed all Indians so that no one would starve, and it pledged each year, for 30 years, to clothe every Indian family: "For males over 14, a woolen suit, flannel shirt, hat and a pair of homemade socks: For females over 12, flannel skirt, pair of woolen hose, twelve yards of calico and twelve yards of cotton domestics: For boys and girls such flannel and cotton goods as needed, together with a pair of woolen hose for each."

In this detailed, bureaucratic fashion, the Treaty of Laramie attempted to plot the way for one of the most traumatic events in American history: the forced removal of probably 20,000 to 30,000 Sioux from their wild, free life on the plains to a humbling fate as confined, regimented wards of the U.S. government. Defying the United States, however, several thousand rebellious Sioux refused even to move to the reservation and continued to roam outside its boundaries. Chief Crazy Horse and his band remained in the Powder River country. Likewise, the charismatic medicine man and bellicose Sioux leader, Sitting Bull, chose to roam the "unceded Indian Territory" between the Bighorns and the Black Hills rather than surrender his people to a life like the white man's on the dreary reservation. Eventually, Sitting Bull would lead hundreds of his Hunkpapa Sioux to temporary refuge in western Canada.

Eager to keep the peace and promote the westward movement, the U.S. Senate promptly ratified the Treaty of Laramie and President Andrew Johnson officially proclaimed it on February 24, 1869. But fateful events were still to come and, far from keeping the peace, the hard-won Treaty of Laramie would soon be violated and the war for the crucial buffalo-hunting country begun. The overt cause: GOLD!

Unearthed near Spearfish in 1887, this Thoen Stone, with crudely scrawled message telling of gold seekers being killed by Indians in 1833, may have been the first evidence of gold discovery in the Black Hills.—*Centennial Archives, Deadwood Public Library.*

Custer finds gold in Holy Wilderness

Who first discovered gold in the Black Hills? So far as is known, it might have been a party of six white men and an Indian who were first to find the precious yellow metal. A mystifying stone, inscribed with their names and a pathetic account of their tragic ending, was found one day in 1887 by two pioneer settlers, Ivan and Louis Thoen, while building a house at the foot of Lookout Mountain overlooking the present scenic city of Spearfish. The Thoen brothers unearthed a flat piece of sandstone with this crudely scrawled message:

came to these hills
in 1833   seven of us
De Lacompt   all ded
Ezra Kind   but me
G W Wood   Ezra Kind
T. Brown   Killed by Ind
R. Kent   beyond the
Wm King   high hill got
Indian Crow   our gold June
                    1834

On the reverse side of the stone was carved their last dramatic words:

Got all of the
gold we could
carry   our ponys
all got by the Indians
I hav lost my gun
and nothing to
eat and indians
hunting me

Visitors today may see a replica of the Thoen Stone at the Adams Memorial Museum in Deadwood (the original is kept in a vault), or view an historic marker with a reproduction set high on a hill above Spearfish Valley. But whether or not the stone is authentic is still being debated by scholarly authorities. The Thoen Stone may be the first evidence of discovering gold in the Black Hills, but rumors of other gold finds abounded through the years. Ascending the Missouri River and crossing the plains in 1839, the Jesuit missionary Father Pierre Jean De Smet reportedly found gold in the Black Hills but kept it a secret. It was rumored that Indians had brought out nuggets, and from the recovery of long-rusted old

pieces of pick and shovel, a skeleton and other artifacts, it would appear that someone had prospected here long ago. As for more positive evidence, Dr. F. V. Hayden, noted geologist who skirted the region in 1859, recognized ore-bearing rocks and noted grains of gold glinting in the streams gushing from the mountains.

As the West was opened to settlement following the Civil War, there were fresh rumors of gold in the Black Hills, and gold-hungry miners and adventurers clamored to enter the region. Indeed, Dakota Territory newspapers boldly encouraged exploration of the Hills for gold and other valuable minerals, arguing that the "savage" Indians were wasting the potential wealth of one of the richest sections in America. "What shall be done with these Indian dogs?" asked the influential Yankton *Press and Dakotaian* in an editorial. "They will not dig gold or let others do it. . . . They are too lazy and too much like mere animals . . . to have the exclusive control over a tract of country as large as the whole state of Pennsylvania or New York, which they can neither improve or utilize." At the same time, political pressure mounted in Washington to throw open the area, even though it had now been permanently ceded to the Sioux, and as a consequence, the 7th U.S. Cavalry, under Lt. Col. George Armstrong Custer, was ordered to make a reconnaissance of the Black Hills. Although Custer's mission was primarily to locate the site for a large military post to control the Indians, it was also to confirm rumors of gold.

Riding out of Fort Abraham Lincoln (located on the Missouri River near Bismarck, North Dakota) to the stirring strains of an army band, the flamboyant Custer headed for the Black Hills with a 1,000-man military expedition on July 2, 1874. It consisted of 10 companies of cavalry with about 1,000 horses, 2 companies of infantry, Indian scouts, a corps of scientists, experienced miners, a photographer, newspaper correspondents and a black woman who cooked for Custer. The whole detachment was supplied by 600 mules drawing 110 wagons, followed by 300 beef cattle for fresh meat. "This was one of the largest, most complete and best-equipped expeditions ever launched on the frontier in time of peace," says South Dakota historian Herbert S. Schell. "There was even a military band." The approved cost: $2,500!

Marching some 250 miles across the scorching plains, the military expedition entered the Black Hills in late July and began exploring the mountains of solid

A panoramic view of Custer's camp at Hidden Wood Creek. By Illingworth during the 1874 Black Hills expedition.—*National Archives.*

"Our First Grizzly, killed by Gen. Custer and Col. Ludlow." By Illingworth during the Black Hills expedition of 1874.—*National Archives.*

quartz, shining mica schists, rippling trout streams and flowered meadows. Noting the lush grass country, Custer reported: "In no portion of the United States, not excepting the famous blue-grass region of Kentucky, have I ever seen grazing superior to that found growing wild in this hitherto unknown region." Reaching a site near the present city of Custer, South Dakota, the cavalry camped, and here on August 2, 1874, two miners with the expedition, Horatio N. Ross and Willis McKay, washed gold from the glistening sands of French Creek. Following further exploration, Custer sat down in his tent to pen a field report to the Adjutant-General, Department of Dakota, St. Paul, in which he related:

> It will be understood, that within the limits of the Black Hills we were almost constantly marching, never halting at any one point for a longer period than one day, except once and that was near Harney's Peak, where we remained for five days.... Enough, however, was determined to establish the fact, that gold is distributed throughout the extensive area within the Black Hills. Gold was obtained in numerous localities in what are termed gulches.... No large nuggets were found; the examination, however, showed that a very even, if not a very rich distribution of gold is to be found throughout the entire valleys.

Custer's field reports confirmed gold in the Black Hills and the news electrified the nation. Newspaper correspondents with the expedition dispatched more sensational accounts, and on August 27, 1874, the Chicago *Inter-Ocean* carried a story headlined:

Gold!

*The land of Promise—Stirring
News from the Black Hills
The Glittering Treasure Found
At last . . . A Belt of Gold
Territory Thirty Miles Wide
The Precious Dust Found in the
Grass Under Horses' Feet—
Excitement Among the Troops*

Exciting news, indeed! Custer's discovery triggered one of America's greatest gold rushes and only a few weeks later, on October 6, 1874, the first history-making party of gold-seekers—26 men, one woman and a nine-year-old boy—started from Sioux City, Iowa, in their covered wagons to illegally enter the Black Hills, now permanently sealed off from the whites. Suffering great hardship and one death, crossing the frigid plains and Badlands in winter, the exhausted members of the Gordon party arrived at French Creek on December 23, where they promptly erected a crude stockade for shelter from the severe

weather and protection from the Indians. They found some gold during the winter, but the following spring the entire party was evicted from the region by the 7th Cavalry, under orders to keep the Hills inviolate. Intercepting a second gold-hunting expedition crossing Nebraska, the army burned most of the wagon train and arrested the leaders. Undaunted by the news, however, still other prospectors eluded the troops and slipped into the region.

Meanwhile, back East, newspapers were now screaming "Gold!" on page one and gold fever was sweeping the country. Following failure of a number of leading eastern financial firms, Black Friday of September 1873 had plunged a large part of the nation into bankruptcy and panic, and the depression that followed was one of the worst in American history. The prospect of a new gold rush, therefore, brightened the outlook for the economy, and by the winter of 1875, an estimated 4,000 to 5,000 fortune-hunters had flocked to the southern Hills to pan gold. They started a mining camp called "Stonewall," named for the celebrated confederate hero, Gen. Stonewall Jackson, but later changed the name to honor General Custer. The burgeoning camp boomed and its first post office was a spacious cave in the rocks where the homesick gold-seekers gathered to sort out their own meagre mail. Miners swarmed around French Creek and nearby valleys panning for gold and by March 1876, Custer City was a thriving "metropolis" with some 6,000 population and famed the country over.

That was Custer City's big boom period. "But alas!" says an early-day mining account, "the fond hopes of the enthusiastic citizens were turned to ashes by the discovery of gold galore in Deadwood Gulch, which resulted in one of the most remarkable hegiras ever experienced in the West. The gilded reports of rich gold strikes in the northern Hills in a few brief days had done its deadly work, and the proud city, with its great expectations and lofty hopes, was practically abandoned. Only fourteen souls remained!"

Deadwood Gulch got its name from the tangle of debris and dead wood left on the hillsides from earlier forest fires, and the scene of the "gold galore" discovery was a remote placer camp hedged in by towering granitic walls and a pine forest. The gulch in 1876 was a primitive, forbidding wilderness, but braving the deep snows and the bitter cold, thousands traveled there to strike it rich. With spring that year came heavy rains, followed by a Chinook wind that melted the deep winter snows, and the motley horde of gold-seekers stampeding into Deadwood Gulch slogged through a filthy, impassable bog. Attracted by glowing accounts of "gold at the grass roots," the hopefuls flocked from everywhere—Connecticut to California—and from all walks of life. Soon the gold rush reached a fever pitch, and at Cheyenne, Wyoming

Territory; Sidney, Nebraska; Bismarck, Yankton and Fort Pierre, Dakota Territory, wagon trains were hurriedly outfitted to travel 250 to 400 miles to the Black Hills. Reported *Leslie's* magazine that year, "hotel keepers find it profitable to keep up the excitement and marvelous stories of lucky finds are put into circulation." For a time the army tried to keep out the flood of gold-seekers, but it was an impossible task.

Arriving at the new El Dorado by bull-train, pack mule, oxcart and even afoot, the frenzied miners crowded into Deadwood and nearby gulches to stake out their rival "discovery" claims. Usually, these were strips of ground extending from rim to rim across the gulch and for 300 feet along a stream, in this case Deadwood and Whitewood creeks. Setting up their sluice boxes and rockers in the streams, the miners washed the gravel from the creek beds and the fine, heavier gold, passing through riffles in the troughs, settled to the bottom and was recovered. Crude though it was, placer mining might yield from $25 to $150 a day, and infrequently a fortune. The Wheeler claim in Deadwood gulch produced $50,000 and a few others did nearly as well, causing such excitement that by winter of 1876 literally miles of ground along the creeks had been staked out and worked.

The Black Hills gold rush was not only illegal, but a hazardous venture and the Indians, seeing the desecration of their "Holy Wilderness," were a constant menace. Slipping into the high hills, they lay in wait with their newly captured Winchester army rifles to pick off unwary miners working in the gulches below. Soon, the placer miners posted sentries and guns were kept handy. There were other hardships in the primitive wilderness, and thousands that first year roughed it in tents, caves, sapling lean-tos and brush huts, while a fortunate few were able to hastily throw up log cabins for shelter. Many rushed to the Hills equipped with only a few cooking utensils and a woolen blanket or two. The miners lived on "sowbelly," beans, flapjacks, coffee and dried fruit, relieved by occasional wild game or a tough piece of meat from slaughtered skin-and-bones oxen. Before long, an enterprising businessman had started up a sawmill and the first false-front stores and saloons arose, jumbled together mining-camp fashion. The demand for rough lumber boomed and huge pine trees were hewn out of the forest, leaving the slashed hillsides barren, eroded and ugly.

They came by the thousands that memorable year of '76. Miners, merchants, butchers, bakers, doctors, lawyers, saloon keepers, con men, cutthroats and ladies of the evening swarmed into Deadwood Gulch for quick riches. "An interesting procession pulled out of Cheyenne for the Black Hills gold fields," the Cheyenne *Daily Tribune* reported early in 1876.

Members of the town's lower social strata—

"Madames," tinhorns—turned out en masse to bid a riotous farewell. The procession was composed of three wagons, loaded with whisky, bar fixtures, faro layouts, roulette wheels, and other supplies and paraphernalia essential to the operation of a combined saloon and gambling place in the parlance of the period called "Dance Hall."

Perched upon this cargo were the other essentials—gamblers and "Girls." There were eight of the former, 14 of the latter. Proprietors of the outfit cannily reckoned there would be a better chance to make a fortune in the Hills with gals and games than thru sluicing for gold in the gulches. The "Girls" waved gaily to all and sundry as they shook the dust of Cheyenne from their slippers as the prelude to shaking the "dust" from the miners in the Hills.

The new arrivals slept in shifts, food was scarce and sanitary conditions in this wild, chaotic camp were appalling. Frequently, the bull-trains or freighting wagons were mired hub-deep in mud, tying up the solitary trail or "main street" up the gulch for hours. Altogether, probably 10,000 people (some sources estimate as many as 25,000) stampeded into congested Deadwood Gulch, while hundreds more fanned out into nearby mining camps—Central City, Gayville, Galena, Black Tail, Grizzly Gulch, Gold Run, Rockerville, to name a few. Hard-pressed for living space, the newcomers began building their log cabins and wooden houses on the terraced hillsides. Business was booming, and in April 1876, enterprising pioneers officially laid out the wide-open town of Deadwood on land which still rightfully belonged to the Indians. The townsite was soon lined with saloons, gambling houses, dance-halls, a huge log theatre with sawdust floor and canvas roof, low-down dives and brothels side by side.

Writing in Frank *Leslie's Illustrated Newspaper*, a reporter described the gold rush capital:

Deadwood is a city of a single street, and a most singular street it is. The buildings which grace its sides are a curiosity in modern architecture, and their light construction is a standing insult to every wind that blows. Paint is a luxury only indulged by the aristocracy. . . . Wells are dug in the middle of the street and every manner of filth is thrown into them. The city is honeycombed with shafts running down into the bowels of the earth from every yard. A keen-eyed, money-grubbing set of men makes up the population, but they are far from the bloodthirsty scoundrels the average newspaper correspondent would make them out to be.

And here on the dusty, milling streets of Deadwood walked the notorious gunman, James Butler "Wild Bill" Hickok; and the carousing "Calamity Jane" Canary. There were a host of other colorful

Ordered to evict all whites from the Black Hills, General George Crook's soldiers arrived at the Gordon Stockade hastily built by the first party of gold seekers on French Creek in December, 1874.—*South Dakota State Historical Society.*

Crossing the plains and Badlands in winter, these history making gold seekers—the Gordon party—illegally entered the Black Hills in late 1874. The following spring they were arrested, transported to Ft. Laramie and released.—*South Dakota State Historical Society.*

This was Deadwood Gulch in 1876—a forbidding wilderness and filthy, impassable bog. With the booming demand for rough lumber, the pine forests were rapidly cut down leaving the slashed hillsides barren, eroded and ugly.—*Centennial Archives, Deadwood Public Library.*

They strike it rich! Custer's discovery triggered one of America's great gold rushes, and thousands, like these placer miners panning the streams at Rockerville, flocked to the Black Hills.—*Western History Department, Denver Public Library.*

characters from "Deadwood Dick" to "Preacher Smith." The miners carried their gold dust around in buckskin bags and squandered it recklessly on liquor, women and gambling. Since there was as yet no legal government, the raw frontier community maintained a kind of rough justice of its own—sometimes with vigilante committees. Most of the fights were over disputed mining claims, but robberies, saloon brawls and killings were frequent. Of the thousands who surged into the Black Hills, sadly only a handful struck real paydirt. A dozen or more of the richest claims yielded from $40,000 to $150,000. Some miners sluiced the streams for a fair reward, but most worked for $3.50 to $5 daily wages. From all sources, the Black Hills in 1876 produced over $1.5 million in gold, selling around $20 per ounce in those preinflationary times.

But living was sky-high—flour cost $60 per 100 pounds—and life was precarious. Frequently, miners were ambushed on the outskirts of Deadwood by Indians. Smallpox, the dread scourge of frontier towns, swept the gulch and at famed Mount Moriah Cemetary today the sunken graves of countless victims pit the steep hillsides. Fire and flood also ravaged the mining camp. Then abruptly, within three or four years, the rich placer diggings petered out, and Deadwood's days of glitter and glory were largely over. Meanwhile, quartz gold had been discovered three miles up the gulch on the present site of Lead, South Dakota, and that booming new mining town was born. Still other

hard-rock mining camps mushroomed and the long-term mineral development of the Black Hills began. Hearing one day in 1875 about the Custer military expedition, a pair of enterprising prospectors, Fred and Moses Manuel, left the Helena, Montana, diggings for the Black Hills. Finding no luck near Custer, they prospected in the northern Hills, where with their partner Hank Harney, they discovered a rich outcropping of ore on April 9, 1876, on what is now known as the awesome "Open Cut" in Lead. Sinking their discovery shaft into the mountain, the brothers took out $5,000 the first spring. Their claim turned out to be the famed Homestake Ledge or "lead" (pronounced "leed") which launched the fabulous Homestake—America's greatest gold mine and one of the richest in the world.

Thus thousands of fortune-hunters unlawfully invaded the Black Hills, and as the Indians sorrowfully complained, had desecrated their "Holy Wilderness." Even worse, the government of the United States, bowing to public pressure, had withdrawn the army and opened the region in spite of its solemn promise to keep the Hills inviolate "for the absolute and undisturbed use and occupation of the Sioux Nation." That was the pledge to the Indian chiefs in the Treaty of Laramie, but now it was broken, and there would be bloodshed.

"We want no white man here," raged the Sioux leader, Sitting Bull. "The Black Hills belong to me. If the whites try to take them, I will fight."

With news of Custer's sensational discovery, thousands of frenzied gold seekers stampeded into the "Holy Wilderness" to stake out their rival claims, scar the land with their ugly diggings, rape and plunder the Black Hills as evidenced here in Deadwood Gulch.—*National Archives.*

The Rape of the Black Hills

The Black Hills gold rush flagrantly violated the Treaty of Laramie and brought the long-smoldering struggle between white man and red to the brink of war. It climaxed a long list of shameful injustices against the Indians. Ever since they had been forcefully removed to the reservation seven years before, the hungry, demoralized Sioux had complained bitterly about lack of promised supplies, food that made them sick, even starvation, and they sought removal of corrupt Indian agents who were getting rich through scandalous fraud and theft. For the disillusioned Sioux, the Treaty of Laramie already had proven a pyrrhic victory. On the other hand, the government vigorously protested the frequent depredations of the bellicose Sitting Bull, Crazy Horse and other "hostiles" who continued to roam outside the reservation in utter defiance of the United States.

So now, with discovery of gold and the rape and plunder of the Black Hills, the whole question of U.S. Indian policy in the West had reached a crisis. Both sides were inevitably headed toward a showdown, with disastrous consequences. The widespread feeling among whites was that the Black Hills should never have been ceded to the "savages" in the first place. Typifying the current sentiment was the comment of Mrs. Annie D. Tallent, first white woman to enter the Hills, with the illegal Gordon party in 1874. Mrs. Tallent was elated that the "gold-ribbed Black Hills were to be snatched from the grasp of savages, and given over to the thrift and enterprise of the pioneer, who would develop their wonderful resources and thereby the interests of the whole country."

Lamentably, however, there were very few who considered the rightful interests of the Indians, and the whites now confidently expected the Sioux to relinquish their claims to the rich region. "After all, from the white man's viewpoint, the Black Hills were of little use to the Sioux except as a source of lodgepoles and for an occasional hunt in the foothills," notes the South Dakota historian, Dr. Schell. "But to the Indians the Black Hills were sacred and keeping them undefiled had a deep spiritual significance."

No longer able to seal off the new Eldorado and keep the Black Hills inviolate, the government desperately determined to lease or buy the region. But "One does not sell the earth upon which the people walk," Chief Crazy Horse spoke feelingly for his people. The Indians vehemently protested violation of the Treaty of Laramie and invasion of their holy ground; and the government, in an effort to placate them, invited a delegation of chiefs to visit the Great White Father in Washington. But President Ulysses S. Grant, who had campaigned on a policy of subduing the "hostiles" in favor of white settlement, was scarcely a receptive host. He gave the chiefs scant satisfaction, and hinted that should the Sioux continue to clash with the whites over the Black Hills, the Indians should relinquish their claims and consider being removed to Indian territory in Oklahoma. Seriously affronted, the chiefs refused to parley with minor Washington officials and demanded to return home instead to confer with their fellow tribesmen.

Caught now in an extremely untenable position, the U.S. government hastily dispatched a Sioux Commission, headed by Senator William B. Allison of Iowa, to visit the various Indian agencies on the Great Sioux Reservation and discuss holding a grand council on the thorny Black Hills question. On September 20, 1875, after much haggling over where to meet, the Grand Council convened near the Red Cloud Agency on the White River in northwestern Nebraska, and it was a tense occasion indeed.

There, pitching their teepees on the parched brown prairies, an estimated 15,000 to 20,000 inflamed Sioux had gathered in force to show their determination to deal resolutely with the federal government. The Indians appeared divided into two parties: a large group who would part with the Black Hills for a huge price; and a smaller, more militant group who were opposed to selling their sacred Paha-Sapa at any price whatsoever.

The U.S. commissioners, assembled under a huge tarpaulin for shade, were guarded by troops of the 7th Cavalry. But the Indians resented the intimidating presence of the military. Addressing the whites, Spotted Bear protested: "It looks bad to see the troops around the council while we are trying to make a treaty. My tribe wants a good deal for the Hills and we don't want the white people to steal them before we sell them."

Opening on this note of distrust and suspicion, the Grand Council, moreover, faced an impossible task. Realizing that the gold-hungry whites could never be dislodged from the Black Hills, the commissioners at first attempted to secure mining rights in the region. "We ask if you are willing to give our people the right to mine in the Black Hills, as long as gold or other valuable metals are found," Chairman Allison addressed the Indians. He promised a "fair and just sum" and said "when the gold and other valuable minerals are taken away, the country will again be yours to dispose of in any manner you wish."

The bargaining began and the government offered to lease the mining rights for $400,000 a year. But Spotted Tail and some of the other wily chiefs, who had visited the gold diggings, saw that the white man was profiting handsomely and were not about to lease for a pittance. "When the white men have a good thing, they get rich out of it," said one of the chiefs, Little Bear. "Now our people want to get rich out of the Black Hills and want back pay for all that has been taken out of the hills by whites."

The assembled chiefs were determined to drive a hard bargain, and certainly they would never lease for a preposterous $400,000 a year. Mopping their brows in the September sun, the conferees haggled over terms, but the Indians demanded huge sums and other conditions for granting mining rights. Moreover, they insisted that the Hills must be returned to them once the gold had run out. The commissioners were outraged and threatened to end negotiations. As a last resort, the government endeavored to buy the Black Hills outright. The commissioners offered a paltry $6 million, which the Indians scornfully rejected. In place of a cash settlement, Red Cloud proposed as payment that the United States agree to feed, clothe and house seven generations of Sioux.

The charismatic Red Cloud, who had soundly defeated the army and forced the government to sign the Treaty of Laramie in 1868, realized by now the Indians could no longer stem the tide of white invasion, and he turned to shrewd bargaining and skillful negotiation for his people. He became a powerful politician. Now, rising before the U.S. commissioners, the sad-eyed Sioux leader spelled out his demands.

"For seven generations to come I want our Great Father to give us Texas steers for our meat," Red Cloud began his appeal. "I want the Government to issue for me hereafter, flour and coffee, and sugar and tea, and bacon, the very best kind, and cracked corn and beans, and rice and dried apples, and tobacco and soap and salt and pepper for the old people. I want a light wagon with a span of horses and six yoke of working cattle for my people. I want a sow and a boar, and a cow and bull, and a sheep and a ram, and a hen and a cock for each family."

Speaking with emotion, the statesmanlike Red Cloud continued: "I am an Indian, but you try to make a white man out of me. I want white man's houses at this agency to be built for Indians. I have been into white people's houses, and I have seen nice black bedsteads and chairs, and I want that kind of furniture given to my people. I thought I had some interest in this sawmill here, but I find I have not. I want the Great Father to furnish me a sawmill which I can call my own. I want a mower and a scythe for my people. Maybe you white people think that I ask too much from the Government, but I think those hills [Black Hills] extend clear to the sky—maybe they go above the sky, and that is the reason I ask so much. . . . I know it well, and you can see it plain enough that God Almighty placed those hills here for my wealth but now you want to take them from me and make me poor, so I ask so much that I won't be poor."

The government considered Red Cloud's price sky-high indeed and promptly rejected the proposal. Then it was Spotted Bear's turn to speak, and he staggered the commissioners with his final demands. Said the chief: "Our Great Father has a big safe, and so have we. The Hills are our safe. . . . We want seventy million dollars for the Black Hills!" He went on to say that white men put their money out at interest, and the Sioux wanted to profit in the same way.

Incensed at these "outrageous" demands, the U.S. commissioners ended three days of fruitless bargaining and broke off negotiations altogether. The commission in its report concluded:

It was plain from the beginning that no agreement could be reached. . . . We do not believe that the Indians' temper or spirit can or will be changed until they are made to feel the power as well as the magnanimity of the Government. . . . They can never be civilized except by the mild exercise, at least, of force in the beginning. This generation will not voluntarily sustain themselves and the Government [which already had spent some $13 million feeding and settling the tribes] has only before it the alternative of perpetually supporting them as idlers and vagabonds, or using such power as may be necessary to enforce education in English, in manual labor, and other industrial pursuits upon the youths of the tribes, male and female, thus preparing the coming generation to support itself and finally to become citizens of the United States.

With failure of the Grand Council either to lease, buy or settle the Black Hills question, Washington in effect abrogated the Treaty of Laramie. President Grant then ordered the military to withdraw from guarding the Hills, and miners, merchants, freighters and every citizen (all of whom were illegally occupying the ceded land) were warned to arm themselves and travel at their own risk. The battle for the Black Hills had entered an explosive stage.

Greatly complicating matters were treaty violations on both sides. While the Sioux justly charged the government with trying to take back the Black Hills, the military was busy chasing marauding Indians outside the reservation who continued to attack settlements, travelers, freighters and railroad surveyors. As these wild bands grew in strength and numbers, the government mapped plans to halt their defiance and force them onto the Great Sioux Reservation.

Abruptly, in December 1875, the U.S. Commissioner of Indian Affairs issued an ultimatum, ordering all Indians to move to their respective agencies on the Great Sioux Reservation by January 31, 1876, or be classed as "hostiles" and treated by the military accordingly. A few days before Christmas, swift native runners were dispatched from the agencies to carry the ultimatum to the defiant Powder River bands. But it was a cruel, heartless order, and no Indian would leave his snug wigwam and, with his squaw pulling the tent-pole travois and all their belongings, attempt to cross hundreds of miles of snowbound prairies without food or shelter in mid-winter. The couriers who had gone out from the agencies, now battled blizzards and were unable even to locate some remote tribes. Still other recalcitrant Indians brazenly ignored the ultimatum, so that by the January 31 deadline, thousands of Sioux still roamed the Powder River country outside of ceded territory and were declared to be "hostiles."

Now Uncle Sam's Indian-fighting army took charge; and in Chicago, Gen. Philip H. Sheridan, commanding all troops in the Missouri country, boldly decided on a winter campaign that would catch the hostiles off guard in their camps, and bring them to heel. Summer was warfare time for the Plains Indians, who were now immobilized in winter's cold and snow. Accordingly, Sheridan ordered his department commanders, Brig. Gen. George Crook in Omaha and Brig. Gen. Alfred H. Terry in St. Paul, to prepare their fighting forces for an early invasion of the enemy country. Confident that it could easily defeat the few hundred warriors in scattered winter camps, the army set forth early in March on the attack.

General Sheridan didn't reckon, however, with the severe weather and the thousands of hostiles still roaming in the Bighorn and Powder River regions. Blizzards quickly bogged down General Terry's two columns, while early in March General Crook pushed up the Bozeman Trail in deep snows and sub-zero cold to attack a winter camp of the Sioux and Cheyenne Indians. The surprised Indians were driven from their warm lodges, but quickly rallying, they waged a fierce counterattack that forced General Crook to retreat to Fort Fetterman. By now, it was apparent the military had badly miscalculated, and instead of fighting an estimated 3,000 or fewer Sioux, the army would be forced to round up vastly more "hostiles" for removal to the reservations.

Sobered by the magnitude of its task, the army reorganized its forces in April and May and General Sheridan prepared to launch a three-pronged summer offensive. Col. John Gibbon would lead his "Montana Column" from Fort Ellis down the Yellowstone River; General Crook would move north from Fort Fetterman; and out of Fort Abraham Lincoln on the east would march the "Dakota Column" under its colorful 7th Cavalry commander, Lt. Col. George Armstrong Custer. It would be one of the greatest military campaigns ever waged on the Great Plains.

With the plunder and rape of the coveted Black Hills, the bitter struggle for the gold-and-grass country flared into all-out war; and the approaching fateful Battle of the Little Bighorn would become, as one historian has noted, "the most memorialized single event in American history."

Marching up the Yellowstone, Brig. Gen. Alfred H. Terry intended to trap the Indians in a pincers movement. But reaching the Little Big Horn battlefield on June 27, belatedly discovered Custer's annihilation. — *South Dakota State Historical Society.*

Determined to round up the wild, defiant Indian bands and force them onto the Great Sioux Reservation, Gen. George Crook was instead attacked by Sioux and Cheyenne warriors and forced to retreat on the Rosebud. — *South Dakota State Historical Society.*

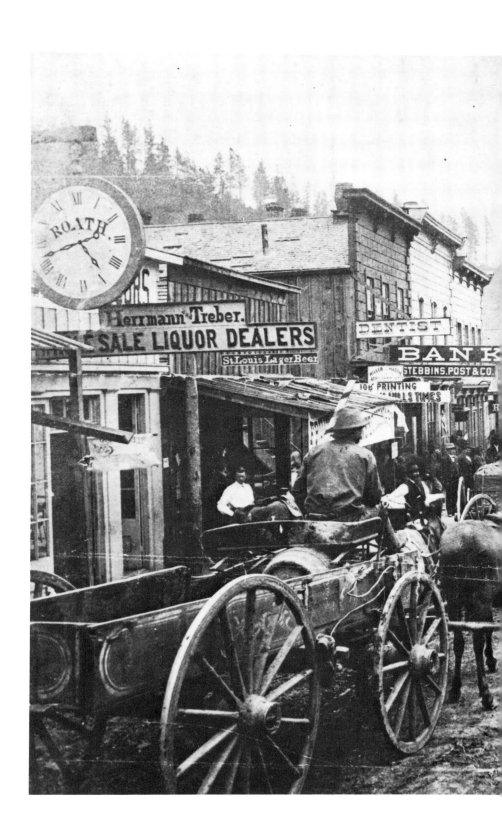

Deadwood's littered, nearly impassable Main Stret teemed with activity as the mining camp boomed. Banks handled $100,000 a day. People slept in shifts. Miners carried their gold dust around in buckskin bags and squandered it recklessly on liquor, gambling and women. — *Nebraska State Historical Society.*

Deadwood in 1876: "A city of a single street . . . with every manner of filth and honeycombed with shafts running down into the bowels of the earth from every yard." Photo by S. J. Morrow.—*National Archives.*

By early 1876, new mining camps, such as this one at Gayville, were mushrooming in the northern Hills. Denuding the pine-crested hills for their logs, the miners crowded the gulches with their crude cabins. Many lived in tents.—*National Archives.*

Gold mining in the Black Hills was a hazardous venture and to protect against claim jumpers and robbers, armed guards like this one were posted in a mining camp near Deadwood.—*Stanley J. Morrow Collection, W. H. Over Museum, University of South Dakota.*

Left. Wearing her fringed buckskin outfit, the carousing hellion and muleskinner, "Calamity Jane" Cannary quickly became a brazen character even for wide-open old Deadwood. *Below.* Riding into the Black Hills with Calamity Jane during the summer of 1876, gunman and gambler "Wild Bill" Hickok was later shot and killed in Deadwood's Number Ten Saloon. His old friend, Colorado Charlie Utter, stands by his newly dug grave. — *Centennial Archives, Deadwood Public Library.*

Since there was as yet no legal government, the Black Hills maintained a kind of rough justice of its own. Robberies, saloon brawls and killings were frequent, requiring Deadwood's first jerry-built jail pictured here.—*Morrow photo. South Dakota State Historical Society.*

They came by the thousands, these hopefuls, traveling by bull train, pack mule and oxcart, even as late as 1889 when this Grabill photo was taken.—*South Dakota State Historical Society.*

Sealed off forever from settlement by the Treaty of Laramie, the sacred Black Hills were occupied, mined and scarred like this a few years later. At top (left), in this panoramic view of upper Deadwood Gulch, lies Terraville; Central City (upper right) and Black Tail (lower right).—*Centennial Archives, Deadwood Public Library.*

Custer Hill, overlooking the Little Big Horn, appears much the same today as it did that fateful June 25, 1876, except for these clustered markers, placed where 52 soldiers fell to the Sioux and Cheyenne.—*National Park Service Photo.*

"Come on—Big Village—Be quick."

In all history, no single battle has so intrigued people with its mystery and controversy as Custer's immortal "Land Stand" on a haunting Montana field of blood over a century ago.

As a boy, I listened wide-eyed while my mother talked about Charles Windolph, last white survivor of the Battle of the Little Bighorn. He was her neighbor when she lived in Lead, and she knew him well. Windolph didn't serve under Custer's immediate command, but with Capt. Frederick Benteen's battalion, with which he fought valiantly against the "hostiles" that fateful day. For risking his life to carry water from the river to the dying and wounded of his battalion, he was awarded the Congressional Medal of Honor.

One day when I was a high school student, Mother took me to see the white-haired old Indian fighter who greatly awed me. He gave me his autographed photo and related how, under a burning Montana sun, he joined the troopers detailed to gather the bodies of General Custer and more than 200 of his men scattered over the battlefield. He said that Custer's body had not been touched except for a bullet hole in his left temple and another hole in his chest. He recalled that the body of Custer's brother, Tom, lay close-by, and like some of the other trooper's bodies had been stripped and horribly mutilated.

This was my earliest introduction to the "Custer Massacre," and years later I was fortunate to visit Windolph again. He lived to be 98. I was a western history buff by now and had discovered the amazing world of Custeriana. The battle is depicted in nearly a thousand prints and paintings alone, together with a flood of books, scholarly studies and sensationalized, highly inaccurate movies. One reason for this astounding interest is that no white soldier in Custer's immediate command lived to tell the tale, and we are eternally challenged by the enigma and the unknown about this deadly struggle. Another factor was Custer's colorful and controversial personality. "He was something different to every man—either a reckless, egotistical fool, or a model of honor and bravery," says one authority.

A handsome, dashing West Pointer, who graduated at the foot of his class in 1861, Custer, ironically, forged a meteoric career during the Civil War and became an American idol. At the age of 23, he was the youngest general in the Union Army. The "boy general" was temporarily reduced in rank with reorganization of the military after the Civil War, but in 1866 he was named a lieutenant-colonel of the newly formed 7th Cavalry Regiment. The bold young officer led the 7th Cavalry in ruthless campaigns against five tribes of Plain Indians, and on November 27, 1868 he celebrated his greatest victory at the Battle of Washita in western Oklahoma. Attacking at dawn, with bugles blaring and guidons streaming, he surprised and destroyed the snow-covered winter camp of Black Kettle's Cheyennes, killing more than 100 men, women and children and taking 60 female and juvenile prisoners.

The impetuous Custer had married lovely Elizabeth Bacon of Monroe, Michigan in 1864 and on one occasion boldly left his field command and traveled nearly 300 miles to visit his devoted wife "Libbie." For this and other offenses, he was court-martialed, found guilty and suspended without pay and rank for one year. But the yellow-haired cavalryman came back to command the 7th Cavalry and make history.

Precisely, what happened that historic June 25, 1876? Was Custer foolhardy and a "glory-hunter," as some critics charge? Did he disobey orders, use poor judgement and thus sacrifice his command? Did he have poor intelligence?

Custer students never cease to argue. Even after repeated military courts of inquiry, formal reports, interviews with Indians who fought in the battle and years of exhaustive study, there are comparatively few facts that can be learned from the epic encounter, and much of what really happened will never be known. However, we can fairly reconstruct the general story and trace how it came about.

Ignoring Washington's ultimatum, thousands of "hostile" Sioux and Cheyenne failed to return to their reservation by the government's January 31 deadline, and on February 1, 1876, the matter was dropped in the War Department's lap. The following spring and summer, the army undertook one of the major military campaigns on the Great Plains. The plan, as earlier

Dashing, gold-bedecked Gen. George Armstrong Custer, one of the most controversial figures in American history. He inspired either love or hate, never indifference. — *Western History Department, Denver Public Library.*

indicated, called for General Crook's force from Fort Fetterman in Wyoming; Colonel Gibbon's command from Fort Ellis in Montana; and General Terry's troops from Fort Abraham Lincoln (with Custer) to converge on the main body of the Indians then concentrated in southeastern Montana under the leadership of Sitting Bull, Crazy Horse and other war chiefs. On June 21, Terry and Gibbon met at the confluence of the Yellowstone and Rosebud rivers (about 35 miles west of Miles City) to plot battle strategy. Hoping to trap the Indians in the Little Bighorn Valley, Terry had ordered Custer and the 7th Cavalry up the Rosebud to approach the Little Bighorn from the south. Terry himself would accompany Gibbon's force back up the Yellowstone and Bighorn to approach from the north in a pincers movement.

It was a jaunty, confident command that Custer led out of Fort Abraham Lincoln on May 17, 1876, as the army band played the regimental battle march "Garry Owen" and "The Girl I left Behind Me." Looking every inch the colorful cavalryman, the buckskinned Custer wore his broad-brimmed gray campaign hat and scarlet cravat, but he had cut his long, yellow hair. Following a fatiguing forced march across the scorching plains, during which his men subsisted on a ration principally of hard bread, bacon, coffee and

sugar, Custer led his weary bluecoats up the Rosebud in southeast Montana on June 22, where the Indians were strung out in probably the greatest encampment ever seen on the Great Plains. Teepees covered the valley for miles below while thousands of ponies grazed the tablelands above. Here the great chiefs—Gall, Crazy Horse, Crow King and Low Dog, among others—from both Sioux and Cheyenne tribes, had gathered their people in a single village. There were altogether probably 10,000 to 12,000 Indians of whom perhaps 2,500 to 4,000 were warriors. The braves were in a fighting, triumphant mood for earlier on June 17, a combined force of Sioux and Cheyenne warriors had attacked General Crook while he was halted on the Rosebud and had forced him to retreat. Now the renowned leader and medicine man, Sitting Bull, had a prophetic vision in which he saw great numbers of white soldiers being wiped out in a mighty battle. It was a good omen.

Custer, who had once boasted that his fighting 7th Cavalry alone could whip all the Indians on the Great Plains, definitely located the "hostiles" on the sultry Sunday morning of June 25. Probably because of the smoke and dust arising from the great camp, however, he badly underestimated the real size and strength of the Indian fighting forces spread out over the broad Greasy Grass Valley, as the Indians called it. But it was too late in any event, for Indian scouts had already discovered his approach. Now Custer made the crucial decision to attack at once before the enemy could elude the army.

Apparently, Custer acted on false assumptions. The military had estimated that perhaps 800 warriors were assembled along the Little Bighorn instead of many thousands. Moreover, it was assumed they would break and scatter if attacked, which was the customary Indian strategy. "Rarely, unless absolutely certain of victory, did the Plains Indian stand and fight," says historian Robert M. Utley. "Usually, he faded into the hills and easily eluded his slow-moving pursuers. Thus military planning focused mainly on how to catch the quarry rather than how to defeat him once caught. . . . The possibility that the warrior force might unite in one place was not seriously considered."

But now Custer confronted a huge village of at least 10,000, including old men, women and children, whom the warriors were bound to defend. Expecting to engage only a few hundred, however, Custer confidently divided his regiment of about 700 men into three battalions. One battalion of three companies under Capt. Frederick W. Benteen was dispatched to scout the bluffs to the south. At the same time, a battalion of three companies under Maj. Marcus A. Reno and one of five companies under Custer marched along opposite banks of a small creek to attack the huge village.

A devoted couple: Custer and his wife Elizabeth, at home in Fort Lincoln about 1875. Once he boldly left his field of command and traveled 300 miles to visit his beloved "Libbie," for which he was disciplined.—*National Park Service Photo.*

Ordered to cross the river and attack, Reno advanced down the sagebrush covered valley and struck the upper end of the camp located in the cottonwoods. Met by withering fire, outflanked by the defending warriors, he retreated in disorder to the river and took up defensive positions on the bluffs beyond. Here he was soon joined by Benteen, who had hurried forward after receiving written orders from Custer to join him. About three o'clock, Benteen was handed Custer's last message, hastily scrawled by his Adjutant W. W. Cooke: "Come on—Big Village—Be quick—Bring Packs. P.S. Bring Pack."

Hearing heavy firing on the bluffs, Benteen and Reno moved out troops to join Custer, but they were attacked by a large force of Indians and compelled to withdraw to their original position on the bluffs overlooking the Little Bighorn. Burdened with dead and wounded, the Benteen-Reno forces picked a good position and dug in. They scooped out rifle pits and trenches with spades, knives, tin cups, mess kits and, miraculously, held out. Although only about five miles away, they were not to learn of Custer's grim fate until two days later.

Vivid accounts of the battle by Indians who fought in it tell us how Custer's gallant command was surrounded and utterly destroyed. Last seen on that tragic afternoon of June 25, the courageous Custer was waving his campaign hat in encouragement as he boldly charged down the bluffs to attack the great village—only about 225 men pitted against thousands of warriors, riding fleet-footed ponies and armed with both arrows and Winchester rifles. "The finest natural cavalry the world has ever known," the military called these Great Plains horsemen. Led by Crazy Horse and Gall, wave after wave of these screaming warriors charged across the bluffs and ravines of the Little Bighorn to cut off Custer from his objective and defend their village. Surrounded and trapped, he must have quickly dismounted and retreated to a ridge, where about 50 of his troopers gathered around him. Shooting their horses to make hurried breastworks against the hail of arrows and bullets, the desperate remnants of Custer's battalion made their heroic "Last Stand."

Two Moon, a chief of the Northern Cheyenne, dramatically tells of the fierce battle: "The shooting was quick, quick. Pop-pop-pop very fast. Some of the soldiers were down on their knees, some standing. . . . The smoke was like a great cloud, and everywhere the Sioux went the dust rose like smoke. We circled all around him—swirling like water round a stone. We shoot, we ride fast, we shoot again. Soldiers drop and horses fall on them."

Charging repeatedly, the Cheyenne and Sioux closed in for the annihilation. It wasn't long. How long, nobody knows. Probably one terrible hour or less. Creeping through sagebrush and gullies, the Indians attacked Custer from all sides. At the height of the fighting, they stampeded the remaining cavalry horses and a few captured by women in the village still carried extra ammunition in their saddle bags. On the heels of the stampede, the Indians must have hurled their final savage attack. Custer was completely outnumbered and overwhelmed. Moreover, his beleaguered

The old Indian fighter, First Sergeant Charles A. Windolph, about 1880. The last white survivor of the Battle of the Little Big Horn, he fought with Captain Frederick Benteen's battalion and was awarded the Congressional Medal of Honor. — *Author's Collection.*

bluecoats were handicapped by jammed and dirty cartridges which they had to pry out to reload their singe-shot rifles. So swift, so merciless was the attack that no U.S. soldier was left alive. "Yellow Hair" lay dead among his men on the grassy ridge above the Little Bighorn. "The blood of the people was hot and their hearts bad, and they took no prisoners," an Indian who fought in the battle recalled. Thus it happened on that historic day in June 1876, the U.S. military suffered one of the most crushing defeats in American history. All told, on June 25 and 26, more than 260 soldiers and attached personnel of the army met defeat and death, while the Indian losses were no more than 100 dead. As Sitting Bull testified years later, "There were no cowards on either side."

Having wiped out "Yellow Hair," the victorious Sioux and Cheyenne warriors returned that night to their encampment where they sang and danced under the garish light of huge bonfires. It was not a victory celebration, but a sad farewell for their dead and wounded. At dawn, on the morning of June 26, a body of Indians attacked the besieged and wounded Benteen-Reno forces, cut off from the river and famished for water. But unable to dislodge them from the ravine where they were dug in, they gave up at last and withdrew. Late in the afternoon that day, the Indians fired the prairie grasses and trailed off in an immense

procession toward the distant Bighorn Mountains. They had good reason to move: fear of Terry and Gibbon's force in the valley, lack of food and ammunition to continue the fight.

Meanwhile, as planned, the 450 troops of Generals Terry and Gibbon had been moving up the Yellowstone to join Custer. The objective was to trap the Indians between the two forces, and compel them to fight. But belatedly reaching the Little Bighorn battlefield, reeking of death on that June 27, the cavalrymen sadly learned of Custer's annihilation. Most of the bodies had been scalped, and a few mutilated. The bodies, including Mark Kellogg, a special correspondent of the *Bismarck Tribune*, were temporarily buried in shallow graves with markers wherever identification was possible. Several wounded cavalry horses were found and destroyed. However, Comanche, Capt. Myles Keogh's horse, wounded in seven places, was transported to Bismarck and nursed back to health. Comanche lived until 1892.

Leaving the battlefield, carrying Benteen and Reno's wounded on mule litters, the entire command moved down the valley to the mouth of the Little Bighorn, where it reached the steamer *Far West* on the morning of June 30. After ferrying General Gibbon's troops across the Yellowstone, Capt. Grant Marsh started his 710-mile journey down the treacherous, snag-filled Missouri to Fort Abraham Lincoln. He made the journey in a record-breaking 54 hours, landing at Bismarck at 11:00 P.M. on July 5, 1876. Immediately, a small group of officers hurried to break the tragic news to the white-faced wives. Years later, the general's devoted "Libbie" wrote of the tragedy in her book, *Boots and Saddles*: "This battle wrecked the lives of twenty-six women at Fort Lincoln and orphaned children of officers and soldiers joined their cry to that of the bereaved mothers. From that time, life went out of the hearts of the 'women who weep' and God asked them to walk alone and in shadow." Mrs. Custer survived her husband by 57 years.

Immediately, the news was flashed to a shocked nation, then celebrating its centennial in July 1876. Telegrapher J. M. Carnahan sat at his key for 22 hours, sending off the news of battle and list of dead and wounded. He worked another sleepless stint of 60 hours telegraphing newspaper dispatches. The "Custer Massacre" was bannered in headlines across the country and has continued to fascinate people and stir controversy to this day.

What did—and did not—happen that tragic June day in '76 is still being hotly debated and argued, and every year now, the Custer experts flock to the battlefield on the Little Bighorn to fight "Yellow Hair's" last hours all over again. Did he stand right here? Was he last to die? Did he commit suicide rather than be killed or taken alive by Sioux and Cheyenne

These proud, independent Sioux warriors, photographed at Standing Rock Agency in 1877, were typical o those who fought Custer, dealing the U.S. Army a crushing defeat at the Little Big Horn.—*National Park Servic Photo.*

Found near death on the battlefield with seven arrow and bullet wounds, Capt. Keogh's horse, Comanche, was the U.S. Army's only survivor of this battle. Nursed back to health, Comanche lived until 1892.—*South Dakota State Historical Society.*

A year after the battle, Capt. Keogh's reconstituted Company I returned to the battlefield to reclaim officers' bodies and rebury those of enlisted men. Capt. Keogh's marker stands where he fell.—*National Archives.*

Carrying wounded troopers and the tragic news of Little Big Horn, the steamer Far West made the 710-mile treacherous journey from the mouth of the Bighorn to Bismarck in a record-breaking 54 hours.—*National Park Service Photo.*

warriors? And what happened to Custer's body? Today Custer Battlefield National Monument attracts some 250,000 visitors a year, including Indians who bitterly protest this monument in the name of the despised "Yellow Hair"—a loser. It's about an hour's drive—about 65 miles—either from Sheridan, Wyoming, or Billings, Montana, to the battlefield where a visit is a memorable experience. Except for the white marble headstones—where tomahawked and tortured troopers fell—the grassy, windswept battlefield looks about the same as it must have appeared that bloody day so long ago. At the crest of the ridge where Custer fell, a granite monument stands over the mass graves of some 220 soldiers, scouts and civilians. Custer is buried at West Point.

There is no monument to the Indian victors. Though they had won the fateful battle, they would eventually lose the war to preserve their independent, nomadic way of life, and they would give up their sacred Black Hills. The Battle of the Little Bighorn was the last stand of the beleaguered Sioux even as it was Custer's "Last Stand."

The Painting that Put Custer in Saloons and Schools

If you are confused and unclear about the so-called "Custer Massacre"—and most people are—you can fault the souped-up old movies you see on television, and you might also lay some blame on a St. Louis brewer who capitalized on the historic battle. Here's the story:

Ten years after the event, an Ohioan, Cassily Adams, painted a showy canvas for the St. Louis Arts Club; and an admiring saloon keeper promptly bought *Custer's Last Fight*. In turn, the Anheuser-Busch brewery acquired the saloon keeper's art treasure on a $35,000 debt, and commissioned a German artist, F. Otto Becker, to modify the scene suitably for advertising. Becker had a flair for the melodramatic and his lithograph pictures a sabre-slashing Custer in the thick of battle, surrounded by dying blue-shirted troopers, a curious buckskinned figure who appears to be looking on and Indians scalping the dead. The

flamboyant Custer wears a short buckskin jacket, flaunts an enormous red neckerchief and his long red hair falls in ringlets down his neck. The depiction is wildly overdrawn as Custer had closely shorn his yellow hair with a horse clippers before leaving Fort Lincoln.

The brewery distributed some 150,000 copies of the Becker-modified lithograph across the country, placed it in saloons, schools and even managed to hang it in the Kansas statehouse. Years later, Anheuser-Busch presented the $35,000 original canvas to the 7th U.S. Cavalry Regiment and it hung at several army posts. In 1934 the painting was discovered in abandoned Fort Grant, Arizona. Badly cracked and torn, the Adams canvas was restored with WPA funds and hung in the officers' club at Fort Bliss, Texas. During a fire at the club on June 13, 1946, *Custer's Last Fight* was destroyed.

"Custer's Last Fight," Cassily Adams' wildly overdrawn painting that a St. Louis brewery bought for $35,000, lithographed and put into saloons and schools.—*Western History Department, Denver Public Library.*

Decreeing that all children between the ages of 6 and 16 would be required to attend school and learn English, the U.S. government built Indian schools like this one at Pine Ridge Agency.—*Grabill photo, 1891. South Dakota State Historical Society.*

The last days of the Sioux Nation

The news of the "Custer Massacre" on the Little Bighorn stunned and shocked the nation, then celebrating its centennial in July 1876, and it rocked the government. "Wipe out the savages!" was the cry in Washington. Back in the booming mining camp, Deadwood, a special edition of the newspaper, the *Black Hills Pioneer*, carried the "horrible news," and a hurried miners' meeting promptly offered a bounty of $50 per head for every dead Indian. Their alarm would soon be justified. Following their smashing victory over Custer, the Sioux staged a series of stealthy attacks and ambushes in or near the Hills, picking off miners, freighters, settlers and a sky pilot, "Preacher Smith," first missionary to the Black Hills.

Custer's spectacular 1874 expedition had started the Black Hills gold rush. In turn, violation of the Laramie Treaty brought on the war for the gold-and-grass country; and now this war had resulted in one of the most humiliating military defeats in American history. Curiously, Custer had written in *My Life on the Great Plains*, published in 1874, "If I were an Indian, I often think that I would greatly prefer to cast my lot among those of my people who adhered to the free open plains, rather than submit to the confined limits of a reservation, there to be the recipient of the blessed benefits of civilization, with the vices thrown in without stint or measure."

But now there was no sympathy for the Indians fighting to save their ancestral way of life. The annihilation of Custer's command had outraged the country and the public demanded swift retribution. The humiliated army wanted revenge, too. In response, Washington hurriedly dispatched heavy military reinforcements to the Sioux country to punish and put down the victorious Indians. Throughout the summer and fall, troops under Generals Crook and Terry scoured the Powder River and Bighorn areas, hunting for the elusive "hostiles." But they were now widely scattered into small bands for protection and were difficult to catch. His troops out of rations, ragged and almost starving in September 1876, General Crook at last gave up the pursuit of Sitting Bull, who then escaped across the border into western Canada with some 400 Hunkpapa Sioux. The Indians had burned off the prairie grass and Crook's cavalry horses, starved and exhausted, were dropping by the scores. In desperation, he ordered a forced march to the Black Hills to replenish supplies at Deadwood. For 11 days, the miserable troops marched in a cold, drenching rain.

More worn-out horses died and the famished soldiers fought savagely over their meat to keep alive—the "Horsemeat March," it was called.

Crook and his ragged army were almost in sight of the distant Black Hills when they encountered a small force of Indians under Crazy Horse and other chiefs camped in the picturesque, pine-clad Slim Buttes (now Harding County). The Indians were huddled in their teepees during a driving rainstorm when Crook attacked at dawn. Fighting their way out, they stoutly resisted. Chief American Horse was killed and both sides suffered casualties. Following the battle of Slim Buttes, General Crook burned the village and buried his dead, ordering the whole column to trample over the soldiers' graves as he broke camp to conceal their location from the "hostiles." As the Indians retreated, Crook captured their priceless supply of dried meat, which his half-starved soldiers hungrily devoured. He then resumed his dreary march, crossed the flooding Belle Fourche River and entered the Black Hills, where he had been ordered to protect the miners from Indian attack.

With this relentless campaigning, the army endeavored to round up the thousands of defiant Indians still roaming between the Bighorns and the Black Hills and to force them back onto the Great Sioux Reservation. But the wary red men continued to elude the troops and the army had scant success.

Meanwhile, Custer's defeat and death had given an outraged Congress just the opportunity and excuse it was looking for to reclaim the Black Hills; and on August 15, 1876, it swiftly retaliated for the victory at Little Bighorn. Congress enacted the Sioux appropriations bill providing that no further funds would be voted for rations, unless the Indians agreed to relinquish all title to the Black Hills. The government sent out a new treaty commission to the reservation with the ultimatum. An "agreement" was drafted giving up the Black Hills to the whites, and the Sioux chiefs capitulated. Already dispossessed of their arms and ponies when they entered the reservation, the Indians now had no choice but to sign or starve.

In bitterness and utter despair, the Sioux chieftains affixed their marks to the new treaty in October 1876, and Congress ratified it on February 28, 1877. Thus the Sioux sadly signed away their incredibly rich Black Hills: Paha-Sapa, sanctuary of the Great Spirit and center of the universe. As a final crushing blow, the government forced the Sioux to give

His troops hungry and fatigued, his cavalry horses exhausted and dying, Gen. George Crook abandoned pursuit of the hostile Sioux to make his "Starvation March" to the Black Hills in September, 1876. Using tents improvised from wagon frames, he camped in this field near Whitewood, Dakota Territory.—*National Archives.*

Burning off the prairie grass, the Indians starved Crook's cavalry horses and they dropped by the dozens. Then these ravenous soldiers shot their mounts for something to eat.—*Morrow photo. South Dakota State Historical Society.*

Drenched in an 11-day downpour and desperate for food, Gen. Crook's soldiers fought over horsemeat on their "Starvation March" to replenish supplies at Deadwood.—*Morrow photo. South Dakota State Historical Society.*

Stripped of their promised land, subdued and sometimes starving, the despairing Indians at last gave up and drifted into camps like this near Pine Ridge on the Great Sioux Reservation.'*By Grabill, 1891. National Archives.*

Indians were to "become self-supporting and acquire the arts of civilized'life," Washington ordered. But few could make the harsh adjustment and they clung instead to their ancestral ways, camping like this on Rosebud Creek.—*South Dakota State Historical Society.*

up their hunting rights on their vast "unceded Indian territory" between the Bighorns and the Black Hills. Now they could no longer hunt the buffalo and wild game and be independent of the white man for food and clothing. The harsh deed signaled the end of a once proud and powerful Sioux Nation.

Hounded and harassed, the worn-down, starving Sioux now began drifting into the agencies on the reservation and giving themselves up. Eluding the army all winter in Wyoming, the indomitable Crazy Horse led a thousand of his weary people into Camp Robinson, Nebraska, and peacefully surrendered during the spring of 1877. Shortly afterward, he was killed in a scuffle with soldiers who tried to arrest him. And later, in 1881, even the uncompromising Sitting Bull, with over 40 families, returned from Canada to surrender at Fort Buford. One after another, the starving, fugitive bands trekked into the reservation to lay down their arms and give up their ponies until nearly all had surrendered, and the red man's long and fierce resistance wholly collapsed.

Lamenting their cruel fate, thousands of defeated, dejected Sioux tried to settle down on the reservation.

They were to "become self-supporting and acquire the arts of civilized life," Washington officials ordered. "The reservation system was conceived to subjugate and assimilate the Indians," says historian Schell. "The Indian was to be made over in the image of the white man with little regard for his basic cultural traits and traditions. To hasten transition from the tribal or communal manner of living, the native culture was to be broken up as much as possible. Meanwhile, until the Indian could support himself, the government would provide rations of food and clothing. In this acculturation process the Christian missionaries joined their efforts with the schools and government agents."

But the process of subjugation and assimilation proved utterly unworkable. Few Indians could adjust to plowing a tiny strip of land with oxen and growing crops or learn to milk a cow. Instead, thousands were now compelled to lean on the Great White Father for daily subsistence. But there was widespread graft and corruption in the Indian agencies, and some unscrupulous white agents pocketed thousands of dollars a year from pilfering, stealing and by charging unwitting Indians for goods and supplies never

Now regimented, demoralized wards of the U.S. government, the hungry Sioux queue up in the bitter cold to await their beef rations at Pine Ridge Agency. But sometimes their handouts were unfit to eat and Indians were stricken and died.—*Western History Department, Denver Public Library.*

Sensing the end of the great Sioux Nation, Chief Spotted Tail endeavored to help his people adapt to subjugation, but to live in dignity. — *Western History Department, Denver Public Library.*

Forced to abandon their wild, free life on the plains and settle down to farming, a great many Sioux lived in crude log cabins with a brush stock shelter, such as shown here.—*South Dakota State Historical Society.*

delivered. On beef ration day, Sioux families traveled to the distant agencies to queue up in long lines and await meat distribution. But often there were short rations or spoiled meat that the Indians could not eat. Even worse were the freezing winters in shoddy housing, or none at all, and the terrible white man's epidemics of measles, smallpox and venereal disease bringing death. There was also the white man's rotgut whiskey, a curse even to this day.

And so there was much heartsickness and wailing among these aboriginal people who could not readily adjust to the culture clash and become "civilized" like the whites. To add to their plight, land-hungry whites now looked enviously on the rolling grasslands of the Great Sioux Reservation and began pressuring to acquire some of the territory expressly ceded to the Sioux under the Treaty of Laramie. For more than 10 years, however, the Sioux held out against the covetous land agents, boomers, railroads that wanted to cross the reservation to the Black Hills, town builders and cattle outfits who campaigned to take back a part of the Indian's rightful domain. In the end, political pressure triumphed and in 1889 the Sioux agreed to sell some nine million acres for 50 cents to $1.25 per acre. With further sizable reduction in the Great Sioux Reservation, land was opened up for the railroads, land buyers and homesteaders who flocked in to fence the open country with barbed wire.

These were the sorrowful last days of the great Sioux Nation. Stripped of their promised land, subdued and sometimes starving, the despairing red men prayed to the Great Spirit for deliverance. And then one day word spread across the reservation of a new Messiah. Out in the West, a Paiute prophet named Wovoka had been fired by a revelation that the white man would be destroyed, Indian country freed and the buffalo returned. Preaching non-violence, Wovoka introduced a ritualistic Ghost Dance, which he vowed would bring the end of the white man and restore happiness to the Indian. The religious craze spread like wildfire and joining in the frenzied dance, the tribesmen flaunted their ghost shirts which they believed protected them from the white man's bullets.

Fearing a serious uprising from this "Messiah Craze," the army promptly moved to round up the ringleaders. Up north on Standing Rock Reservation, in South Dakota, the great Sitting Bull was accidentally shot dead by two Indian police who had been ordered to arrest the "troublemaker." Now word was dispatched to seize Chief Big Foot, also suspected of fomenting trouble with the Ghost Dance. Camped with his people on the Cheyenne River north of the Badlands in December 1890, Big Foot was alerted to the army's order and slipped out of camp by night, eluding the soldiers. Although he now lay ill with pneumonia in his wagon, the intrepid chief led his band of about 340 men, women and children through the

dreadful Badlands, and in the dead of winter safely lowered wagons, horses, supplies and people over the precipitous Badlands Wall. After resting for a day or two in a hidden camp on White River, the Indians moved southward toward hoped-for protection by Chief Red Cloud already located on the Pine Ridge Reservation. But on December 28, troops of the 7th Cavalry intercepted the band at Porcupine Creek and Big Foot surrendered peacefully. Now the hemorrhaging chief was lifted into an army ambulance and hurried to a heated tent, while his people moved on to camp as directed at Wounded Knee Creek.

The rest is history. The next morning, December 29, 1890, as the army searched Big Foot's camp for concealed weapons, a crazed Indian named Black Coyote brandished his rifle which discharged. About the same time, an old medicine man, Yellow Bird, who had been haranguing the warriors, tossed a handful of dirt into the air. It was a signal to fight and five or six inflamed young men, who had hidden their rifles under their blankets, grabbed their guns and fired. Instantly, the troopers returned the fire and soldiers and Indians clashed in frightful hand-to-hand fighting. The army then opened up from a bluff with its Hotchkiss guns, cutting down fleeing women and children, in the last major clash between red men and white in North America. Big Foot was shot and killed. His grotesquely frozen body was found that winter day where he fell during the fight. Whether Indians or soldiers were mostly to blame for the bloodletting is still in bitter dispute today, more than 90 years later.

"A regrettable, tragic accident of war that neither side intended," historian Utley concludes in his book, *The Last Days of the Sioux Nation.*

With the coveted Black Hills firmly in possession of the whites, and vanquished Sioux confined to their dreary reservation, the promising region was now given over to the "thrift and enterprise of the hardy pioneer" that Annie D. Tallent had so eagerly hoped for. Gold and other mining ventures boomed; and on the sea of grass surrounding the Hills, the range cattle industry, that had begun by supplying beef to the hungry miners, soldiers, settlers and Indians, flourished as well. Thus the gold-and-grass frontier was opened, beckoning tens of thousands who would settle here and sink their roots in the sacred soil of the Sioux.

But the protracted struggle and bitter war had been enormously costly. Over the years, the U.S. government had spent untold millions trying to resettle this proud and fiercely independent people: feed them, provide schools, give them land, livestock and the tools and techniques to follow in the white man's footsteps. Only a comparative handful, however, ever succeeded and today the unhappy, demoralized Sioux are waging a futile campaign to regain their Black Hills.

Fighting for their lost cause, the Sioux tribes have been involved in costly litigation in the federal courts

Fearful of further troubles, Brig. Gen. Nelson A. Miles, accompanied by "Buffalo Bill" Cody, viewed the hostile Indian camp near Pine Ridge Agency on January 16, 1891.—*Grabill photo. National Archives.*

Once the proud, hard-riding horsemen of the plains, following the buffalo, now the defeated Sioux gathered in "hostile" camps like this under army surveillance after Wounded Knee.—*South Dakota State Historical Society.*

Near death with pneumonia, Chief Big Foot was shot and killed during the tragic encounter. His grotesquely frozen body was found like this on the snow-covered battlefield at Wounded Knee—a name forever symbolizing Indian defeat and despair.—*National Archives.*

On bitter cold New Year's Day, 1891, an army burial detail began loading probably 300 frozen bodies of Indian dead—men, women and children—scattered over the battlefield at Wounded Knee.—*South Dakota State Historical Society.*

As army troopers looked on, the Indian bodies were stacked like cordwood in a mass grave at Wounded Knee. "A regrettable, tragic accident of war that neither side intended," one historian observes.—*South Dakota State Historical Society.*

Leaving behind the dead and wounded, following the last major clash between red men and white in America, the U.S. Cavalry marches from the battlefield at Wounded Knee.—*South Dakota State Historical Society.*

ever since 1923, and only recently achieved a belated victory. More than a century after the Indians had won a memorable battle but lost the war for their holy ground, the U. S. Supreme Court on June 30, 1980, agreed that the United States had illegally seized the 7.3-million-acre Black Hills from the Sioux Nation. Voting eight to one the court awarded the Sioux $122.5 million as compensation. That breaks down to $17.5 million that the land was estimated to have been worth in 1877, plus $105 million interest at five percent. (The three lawyers who won the land claims case were allowed $10.6 million in attorneys' fees.)

The long overdue settlement is a pittance and divided equally among the 60,000 members of the Sioux tribes (after paying the attorneys' fees) would amount to less than $2,500 apiece. Rejecting this "ludicrous and grossly inadequate sum," the Indians are now pressing in Congress to regain their land and for years they have been engaged in sit-ins and demonstrations. Using the Rushmore National Memorial to dramatize their cause, a band of 21 American Indians—men and women—climbed the nearly 6,000-foot mountain to demonstrate in defiance of National Park Service regulations. After winning nationwide publicity, the demonstrators were arrested and brought down without violence or bloodshed. A Sioux council has declared that "our sacred Black Hills will never be for sale," and even if they were, some Indian leaders insist that the Black Hills today are worth $60 billion!

So the struggle for the sacred Paha-Sapa, goes on; and will go on, the determined Sioux swear, "as long as the grass shall grow, as long as the rivers shall run."

PART TWO

Whites Settle the Sacred Soil of the Sioux

Risking Indian attacks, fording flooded rivers, keeping constantly on the lookout for stampedes, hell-for-leather cowboys herded their bawling Texas Longhorns up the long, lonesome trail to the Black Hills.—*L. A. Huffman photo. Coffrin's Old West Gallery, Miles City, Montana.*

Overleaf. Where once the hard-riding Plains Indians hunted the buffalo for food, clothing and shelter, now the hardy breed of homesteader or "Honyocker" broke the virgin sod to lay claim to 160 acres and achieve his American Dream. — *Photo by pioneer photographer L.A. Huffman. Coffrin's Old West Gallery, Miles City, Montana.*

Texas Trail herds feed roaring Deadwood

With discovery of gold, the remote, little known Black Hills quickly attracted thousands of hopefuls from all over the country, and the immediate need was to feed them. By early 1876, probably 10,000 frenzied gold-seekers (some sources say thousands more) were crowding into primitive Deadwood Gulch and mushrooming mining camps nearby. Life was raw and rugged, and the army of miners, merchants and adventurers thronging the Hills lived chiefly on wild game, "sowbelly" and beans, supplemented with an occasional piece of meat from tough old oxen no longer serviceable in the bull-trains.

The hungry hordes were starved for good beef; and to feed them, hell-for-leather cowboys pointed their bawling herds of Texas Longhorns north up the long, lonesome trails to roaring Deadwood. Risking Indian attacks that killed their men and ran off their cattle, the dauntless trail-driving bosses undertook a hazardous but highly profitable venture. Buying Texas steers for $15 to $25 per head, they trailed the "critters" a thousand miles or more across the grassy plains to the Black Hills, where they were butchered and sold for as much as $125 apiece.

Lured by this lucrative market, an enterprising stockman, Martin Van Buren Boughton, brought probably the first beef herd to the Black Hills in the summer of 1876. Boughton, who had been mayor of the booming frontier town, Cheyenne, and was one of the biggest cattle and sheep ranchers in Wyoming Territory, owned some 700 head of Texas Longhorns. Recognizing the tremendous opportunity to supply beef to the gold rush, Boughton trailed about 200 head of his footsore cattle 300 miles across Wyoming to the Black Hills, where he pastured them on Lower False Bottom Creek, about 20 miles north of Deadwood, likely in the vicinity of lush St. Onge Valley. Leaving his Longhorns with a herder, Boughton rode into Deadwood to sell his beef to the town's first butcher shop. But his hopeful venture proved disastrous. For sweeping down on his livestock, marauding Indians killed the herder and stampeded the steers. Most were never recovered, and the few scattered head remaining perished or were killed by wolves the following winter. Practically broke and disillusioned, Boughton started a sawmill in Deadwood Gulch to recover his losses.

But the beef-starved multitude must somehow be fed, and the Black Hills were not only a profitable market but the region was promising cattle country as well. Custer had reported on his 1874 expedition that,

after marching upwards of 600 miles, "my beef herd is in better condition than when it started." The next year, 1875, a scout with Professor Walter Jenney's Black Hills survey party observed, "There's gold from the grass roots down, but there's more gold from the grass roots *up*." Favored with abundant nutritious range, ample water and winter shelter, this "short grass country," as it became known, was ideally suited for grazing and stock raising. The sturdy, drouth-resistant grasses cured before frost and could be grazed all winter. An old-timer summed it up, "The Black Hills, in fact, is the best damn cattle country that lays out of doors!"

Under the Treaty of Laramie, however, the whites had ceded this great cattle country to the Sioux Nation, and it was permanently sealed off from white occupation or settlement. But then came the Black Hills gold rush, violating the treaty and launching a beef bonanza! Braving Indian attacks and the daily hazards of trail-driving, fearless entrepreneurs delivered several droves of beef cattle to the Black Hills during the summer of '76. Cattle were trailed to the Hills from Wyoming, Colorado, Kansas, Nebraska and frequently as far away as Texas. Trail drivers had first begun bringing fresh beef to the army posts and Indian agencies following the Treaty of Laramie. Now, with the gold rush, drovers skirted the eastern edge of the Black Hills and turned westward to grazing grounds in the valleys nearest Deadwood.

Trail driving was one of the roughest but most romantic eras in our history, and cowboys used to sing a song heard up and down a thousand miles of trail from Texas to the Dakotas:

> I've finished the drive
> and drawn my money
> Goin' into town
> to see my honey.

To be sure, the bone-weary Texas cowboys were ready to celebrate after their thousand-mile drive across the unbroken prairies to the Black Hills. Normally, the drive required about 90 days and employed a dozen or more cowboys working as many as 65 horses. A 2,500-head trail herd traveled only 12 to 15 miles a day, and it was a long, dirty, monotonous grind both for men and cattle crossing the high plains, fording swollen rivers and keeping on the move, sometimes in blinding sandstorms and often in drenching rain or pelting hail. The Texas Longhorn

The Texas Longhorns were lanky, dun-colored brutes with a nervous, fighting disposition and wicked branching horns measuring six feet or more, tip to tip.—*Painting from Union Pacific Collection. American Heritage Center, University of Wyoming.*

alone was an ordeal. The lanky, dun-colored brute had a nervous, fighting disposition and wicked, branching horns measuring three to six feet, tip to tip. The lean, leggy animal rarely weighed more than a thousand pounds and was as fleet-footed as an elk. Altogether, the untamed Longhorn was a mean "critter" to trail across the plains, but provided sufficient water and grass, the hardy breed exhibited amazing endurance, traveling mile after mile, day after day. The cowboys' constant worry was the stampede. The mournful howl of a coyote, a sudden flash of lightning or crash of thunder, a stumbling horse, any little sharp noise could turn a quiet night herd into a bellowing, milling mass of horns and hooves that might blindly race 10 to 20 miles without stopping. "On night guard, we always sang to the cattle so they wouldn't notice any sudden noise and take off quick," an old cowboy recalled.

For enduring all this—dust, danger, monotony, isolation—and working from early daylight until the first night guard went on duty at dark, the hard-riding young cowboys earned from $30 to $45 per month, plus food—invariably bacon, beans, baking powder biscuits, jam, canned goods and plenty of Arbuckle's stout coffee. The typical cowhand supplied his own saddle, bridle, chaps, spurs, hat and breeches which probably cost him $60 to $75, and he slept in a bedroll under the stars. Such was the sweat, toil and trouble necessary to feed the thousands of fortune hunters pouring into the Black Hills during the great gold rush. But attracted by quick profits, more and more trail

drivers "pointed 'em north." One of the earliest, Milton C. Connors, trailed some 3,000 head of Longhorns from Texas and pastured them on the upper Belle Fourche River. In 1876–77, three brothers, Dan, John and Erasmus Deffenbach, trailed highly profitable herds from Colorado to the Hills, where they pastured them under guard on Redwater and Spearfish creeks. The Deffenbachs supplied Deadwood butchers with a choice grade of beef in place of the "sowbelly"-and-beans diet of the hungry miners.

Finding that the Black Hills was ideal cattle country, the Deffenbachs located a ranch in Spearfish Valley and, later, another in the Bear Lodge country of northeast Wyoming. But running cattle in the desecrated land of the Sioux was dangerous business. Raiding his Bear Lodge ranch, vengeful Indians killed John Deffenbach and stampeded his beef herd ready for marketing in Deadwood. Down on Lower False Bottom Creek, there was further trouble. A freighter, Capt. Oliver Dotson, arrived in the Black Hills with about 100 head of oxen which he put out to pasture where Boughton had met his disaster. Again, the Indians swooped down to kill and stampede his entire herd. Haymaking with scythes and cradles (as yet no mowers) those early days in the Hills was hazardous, too, and lookouts were stationed with field glasses to watch for the attacking red men. A stone marker on the ranch where I was born in St. Onge Valley, is erected to the memory of a fearless scout, Jimmy Iron, who was shot and killed on a hilltop as he watched over a haying

Dividing the vast open range country into districts or zones, the big cattle outfits rounded up their great herds each spring and fall. Here pioneer photographer L. A. Huffman pictures a typical roundup crew with cavvy of saddle horses in the 1880s.—*Coffrin's Old West Gallery, Miles City, Montana.*

The Spanish brought the branding iron to America where the first individual and unique brands appeared on the western range, Here in this early-day Huffman photo, cowboys wait for the irons to heat.—*Coffrin's Old West Gallery, Miles City, Montana.*

While a cowhand ropes and drags one bawling calf to the fire, a branding crew slaps the hot irons on another during roundup in 1888.—*Grabill photo. South Dakota State Historical Society.*

"The country north and east of Belle Fourche is rapidly being filled up with herds of cattle," a Black Hills newspaper reported in 1878. About this time, pioneer photographer Grabill of Sturgis induced this hearty roundup crew to pose for pictures.—*Grabill photo. South Dakota State Historical Society.*

crew in the meadow below during the summer of '76. A bullet had struck his cartridge belt and exploded. Jimmy's mutilated body was found soon after and taken to Deadwood for burial.

With soaring demand, the cattle outfits continued their risky trail drives, and by 1878 an estimated 100,000 head of cattle, many of which had been trailed over a thousand miles from Texas, were reported on grass in the Black Hills. Confirming that there was indeed "more gold from the grass roots up," many cattlemen, like the Deffenbachs, stayed on to locate ranches on the grasslands surrounding the Black Hills. In February 1878, the *Black Hills Daily Times* reported: "The country north and east of Belle Fourche is rapidly being filled up with herds of cattle many of which have been driven from Texas and Oregon. They are rolling fat and we are assured that they will need neither hay nor shelter during the coming winter."

It was a beef bonanza, all right, and with the abject surrender of the Black Hills by the Sioux in 1877 and their cession of the once "unceded Indian territory," the big cattle outfits moved in to run their herds on the gold-and-grass frontier. The English and Scotch were heavy investors, and in the early '80s, John Clay, rising young buyer for the thriving VVV outfit, reported enthusiastically to his Scotch bosses: "We spent the next three or four days riding over the range. My mouth waters when I think of the feed in that region. The bottom lands of the Belle Fourche had grass three feet high, although it was November. It lay in great swaths amid the gigantic groves of cottonwoods, cured, as well as the best hay in a stack. The divides were an ocean of surging grass, cropped only by a few cattle and countless numbers of antelope."

As a youth, I was fascinated by the handful of old trail drivers living out their sunset years in my hometown, Belle Fourche. There was rollicking, weather-beaten G. E. (Ed) Lemmon for colorful example. Setting out to be a cowhand at age 13, Ed trailed the great herds of restless Longhorns all the way from Texas to the Black Hills to feed the miners, settlers, soldiers and Indians, and thus he helped to establish the cattle industry on the northern Great Plains.

"Why I can remember back in the '80s," Ed recalled, "when from a single hilltop I saw eleven great trail herds of some 3,000 head each majestically moving down the Little Missouri." At the peak, Ed estimated, probably a million head of cattle pushed up the northern trails to the Black Hills and open range country. One of the best-known big spreads was the Turkey Track with 45,000 head. Another famed brand was the Hash Knife, which safely trailed some 68,000 Longhorns from Texas to the northern plains. The Sheidley Brothers ran 30,000 cattle; Sturgis and Goodell, 45,000; Franklin Cattle Co., 25,000; Anglo-American Cattle Co., 20,000; Clark and Plumb, 20,000; and Driskill Brothers, 5,000, to name a few.

Free to exploit the illimitable grasslands, the big outfits managed to run hundreds of thousands of cattle by an amazing system of organization: the roundup. Each year, the different outfits divided the vast range country into districts, or zones, with "reps" or representatives in charge, who proceeded to "work" the great herds on a set schedule of about six weeks. Early each spring, the cattlemen dispatched their cowboys and "reps" to round up the drifting herds, assess winter losses and brand the calves. In the fall or beef roundup, the cattle were again gathered, calves weaned, steers and old cows sorted out and trailed to the closest shipping point. The veteran "rep" Ed Lemmon recalled that in just three days one year, 300 cowboys, riding from 15 chuckwagons, rounded up and "worked" 45,000 head of cattle. Those were the epochal days of the open range. "I don't remember on roundup seeing a fence between Bismarck and the Black Hills," Lemmon used to remark.

Coining money, running their cattle loose on free range, the cattle barons were doing handsomely until the disastrous winter of 1886–87. Following a hot, dry summer, the winter churned up a series of blizzards that were among the worst ever recorded on the northern Great Plains. Blinded by driving snow, thousands of bewildered animals drifted to their deaths in the succession of storms. An old-timer, who had come up the Texas Trail, vividly described the plight of a herd of 3,000 Longhorns caught in the blizzards. "It was pitiful to see them steers, unused to snow and bitter cold, wandering around with their ribs sticking out looking for shelter," he recalled. "If you pulled one out of a snowdrift, he would try to hook you with his long horns. Only about 300 out of the 3,000 survived." During these howling storms, some of the big cattle outfits lost up to 90 percent of their herds and never recovered. About this time, the homesteaders and small farmers commenced to invade the domain of the cattlemen, string their barbed wire, fence in the waterholes, and the romantic era of the open range and the colorful cowboy began to draw to a close. Looking back on those days, Dave Evans, a pioneer rancher near Belle Fourche, once told me of that dramatic period in an interview for a Denver newspaper.

"One by one the big outfits—the Hash Knife, Turkey Track, VVV Cattle Co., among many—were crowded off the range," Dave reminisced. "In a few years, where previously 20,000 head had been run, now only a few hundred grazed on a ranch. Fences replaced watersheds for boundaries, towns sprang up where only sagebrush had held a lonely vigil, and the old range slipped into history."

Still there was a host of cowmen remaining around the Black Hills, many of whom like Ed Lemmon had

Finding "gold from the grass roots up," cattlemen established flourishing ranches in and around the Black Hills. At roundup time this family and hands proudly pose with their fine herd.—*Carper-Tscharner photo. Rapid City Journal.*

come up the Texas Trail in their youth, and these able, experienced men of the range now became the progressive leaders of the growing western South Dakota cattle industry. They improved their bloodlines with British breeds—Herefords on Longhorns—developed fine ranch spreads, fought cattle rustlers, secured tighter brand registration laws and organized the ruggedly independent cattlemen into an aggressive livestock association. It successfully lobbied Congress to reopen the Great Sioux Reservation in 1889 and make available for homesteading or sale nine million acres of choice grazing land.

Immediately, the cattlemen moved onto the reservation to buy or lease the reopened lands. This occured shortly before the tragic bloodletting at Wounded Knee and tensions were then extremely high between white man and red. As expected, many Indians bitterly resented opening the Great Sioux Reservation lands to whites and a band of several hundred young Sioux, hungry and defiant of the government, holed up on the Stronghold in the Badlands. This is a towering, grassy mesa accessible only from a narrow neck of land; and swooping down from this bastion, the vengeful Sioux burned ranchers' corrals, stole saddle horses and cattle and killed whites. The cattlemen were up in arms and, in retaliation, hotheaded cowboys lay in wait one day outside the Stronghold and ambushed a group of "renegade" Indians. They killed a score or more, so

pioneer cattleman pistol-packing Pete Lemley used to recall. Starving and still defiant, the remaining young braves held out on the Stronghold until January 16, 1891 (after Wounded Knee), when Chief Red Cloud persuaded them to surrender.

These were exciting years in South Dakota, and the cattle business that had begun in the Black Hills with feeding beef-hungry miners, settlers, soldiers and Indians grew into a giant industry. Drawing on a vast range country within a radius of about 100 miles, Belle Fourche became a flourishing "cow capital" (with a fancy pink-stone bank building costing $4,000) and for many years was the greatest cattle shipping point in the world. My old friend and veteran cattleman, Mert Fowler, vividly recalled shipping season. He said that frequently there was a continuous sea of cattle, one herd bunched up right after the other, spread out about one and a half to three miles wide along Middle Creek, waiting in line to enter the stockyards just outside Belle Fourche. In the banner year, 1902, alone, more than 5,500 carloads (110,000 head of steers) worth some $6 million, were shipped out of the cow town to eastern markets.

So it happened that where Red Cloud, Crazy Horse, Sitting Bull, Big Foot and their people had once freely hunted the buffalo and looked up in awe to the lofty Black Hills, now cowboys and cattlemen came to ride the range, and a new breed settled the sacred soil of the Sioux.

Cracking their 20-foot bullwhips, freighters parade their plodding oxen in early-day Deadwood. They tied up Main Street!—*Centennial Archives, Deadwood Public Library.*

Their bull-trains tie up Main Street

Visiting historic old Deadwood, I marvel at the bold breed that first drove their crawling ox-teams into the rugged Black Hills, bringing supplies and the necessities of life to the roaring mining camp. Today the motorist drops down into the scenic city on paved highways, but in 1876 it was hazardous travel descending the steep cliffs into Deadwood Gulch. Freighters had to rope their axles, take a half-hitch around a tree and pay out the rope slowly to let down their heavy wagons with three-ton loads. Then cracking their 20-foot bullwhips over their plodding oxen, the sweating, cursing bullwhackers slowly moved their trains up the crowded gulch to deliver their goods to pioneer merchants doing business in tents, log and false-fronted stores. Unloading while the panting, fagged out oxen slumped in the dust to rest, these bull-trains frequently tied up Deadwood's jostling Main Street for hours on end.

Following old buffalo and Indian trails, the bullwhackers usually took 30 to 40 days to make the rough journey from Cheyenne to the Black Hills, for example. Trudging beside their lumbering wagons in scorching heat and choking dust, in bitter cold and blowing snow, they guided their bull-teams with the simple commands "Gee" to turn left and "Haw" to go right. The sharp, staccato crack of their bullwhips in the air was enough to keep the cattle moving, and a good bullwhacker never drew blood from the oxen.

In this fashion, the first freighters delivered their goods to the Black Hills gold rush camps at rates of 3½ to 6 cents per pound. Passengers, who also walked, were charged $10. Fearing Indian attacks, some bull outfits posted outriders or scouts ahead and at the rear. Traveling only 12 to 15 miles a day, the freighters battled mudholes and mountains, forded flooded streams and lived on fat bacon, beans, prunes, black coffee and hardtack for $50 a month pay. They freighted from the frontier towns of Cheyenne, Wyoming Territory; Sidney, Nebraska and Bismarck, Dakota Territory; ferried across the wide Missouri at Fort Pierre, and their creaking wagons were piled high with flour, sugar, coffee, picks, shovels, gold pans, guns, medicines, boots and clothing, together with enough whiskey to stock Deadwood's dozens of shady saloons.

When they completed their arduous journey, the bullwhackers had to corral, water and feed their weary, footsore cattle (often Texas steers) or trail them 8 to 10 miles out to Centennial Prairie on the northern rim of the Hills, where they grazed under guard from marauding Indians. Frequently, the herders were killed. To forestall these stealthy attacks, Deadwood built two log stock corrals just off Main Street where the animals were guarded at night. Before long, the first rough trails and toll roads were being hacked out of the mountainsides, and freighting to the Black Hills became lucrative big business. Twenty outfits, using over 400 wagons, hauled out of Cheyenne alone; and one major firm, the Fred Evans Company, employed from 1,000 to 1,500 men and worked from 2,000 to 3,000 oxen and mules. "Fast Freight" was usually provided by mule teams. That colorful character, and lady wildcat, "Calamity Jane" was a muleskinner, making frequent trips between Cheyenne and Deadwood. She could crack a bullwhip and cuss out a mule team along with any man. Another woman, a Madame Canutson, freighted in the Black Hills.

The day of the overland freighter was an important era in our history, and Charley Zabel, one of the last of the old bullwhackers who traveled the Ft. Pierre–Deadwood trail in the '70s and '80s, left us a graphic picture in an article he authored for *Outdoor Life* in August 1933. Charley describes a typical bull "outfit" of which there were scores:

Three wagons were coupled together and 10 yoke of oxen pulled them. The first was the *lead* wagon and carried about a 7,000-pound load; the *swing* wagon was next with a 5,000-pound load, and the *trail* wagon last with 3,000 pounds. This was called a team, and there were usually ten teams to a train.

On the trail we spread out so that each team had fresh ground to roll on. Even then the 4½ inch tires cut in hub deep in wet weather. From Ft. Pierre to the Cheyenne River all was "gumbo" and when mixed with long grass this stuck to the wheels in wads, until cleaned off to lighten the load.

We made 12 to 15 miles a day in good weather, and sometimes 5 miles in bad going, but we always got through. At times we had to uncouple and take one wagon through a bad stretch, or put on more oxen. We forded all the streams from Ft. Pierre to Deadwood after crossing the Missouri by ferry. The Cheyenne was the widest but not deep enough to bother us.

At night we camped at some water holes or streams. The wagons were corraled in a circle and the cattle driven out to graze. My job was to keep

It was a bold breed that drove the first crawling ox-teams into the rugged Black Hills, and Madame Canutson could hold her own with any man as a bullwhacker. So could Calamity Jane.—*South Dakota State Historical Society.*

As the Black Hills boomed, freighting became big business with bullwhackers and muleskinners bringing supplies and the necessities of life to the needy mining camps.—*Centennial Archives, Deadwood Public Library.*

These freighting outfits coming into Deadwood had to rope their axles, take a half-hitch around a tree and pay out the rope slowly to let down their heavy wagons in steep Deadwood Gulch.—*Centennial Archives, Deadwood Public Library.*

them from getting lost, or killed by wolves, or stampeding and to watch things generally. I always had about 200 oxen to watch all night. Just before dawn I roused them so they could graze some before we started, as they worked better on a full stomach. Then I rode to camp and would sing out "Roll out, r-o-ll out, bulls in the corral," which would bring the boys out of their blankets. The cattle were driven in then and yoked up, and the drivers cracked their long whips as we pulled out of the corral, one by one, forming a long line stretching across the prairie.

We drove until it started to get hot, then we stopped for breakfast, and stayed in camp until towards night when it got cooler, as the oxen could not stand the heat very well. The night drive lasted until almost dark, and sometimes we drove by moonlight, but after I crawled out of the wagon where I slept I went to work. . . . The old freighting trail went straight west from Ft. Pierre, and (at last) I had my first glimpse of the Black Hills. The spruce and pine that cover them give a black color to the summits, resembling a thunderstorm hanging low in the West.

Just as the bull-trains carried vital supplies, they also brought many of the first business and professional men to the Black Hills. There was enterprising young Peter Gushurst of Denver, for striking example. Hearing about the gold rush in the spring of '76, he journeyed to Fort Laramie and joined a freighting outfit of about 80 men—the second to enter the Hills. Well-armed scouts, carrying field glasses, rode ahead of the party looking for Indians; and at night the wagons were drawn up in a circle and rifle pits dug on the perimeter where the men stood guard duty. Thus protected, young Gushurst safely reached Deadwood, where he found many broke and disillusioned gold-seekers already eager to sell their supplies and leave the Hills. He bought them out and opened for business in a tent on Main Street. Then for $75 and a Winchester rifle, he purchased a lot and put up a building which became the thriving Big Horn Store. Gushurst went on to develop one of the most successful mercantile enterprises in the region. Similarly, George V. Ayres walked beside a bull-train from Cheyenne to Deadwood, where he became a leading pioneer merchant.

Thus the bullwhackers brought brisk business to the Black Hills. They hauled an amazing variety of goods and equipment, including heavy mining machinery, sawmills, hand printing presses, tools, furniture, store fixtures, medicines, caskets and even tombstones to supply the aggressive pioneer merchants. From rail's end at Sidney, Nebraska, ox-teams hauled the Homestake's first locomotive and an 80-stamp mill over 250 miles through the mountains to Lead in deep snows. Dozens of animals died from exposure and starvation. The freight bill: $33,000. But the strangest shipment of all to the Black Hills was a consignment of cats! Some enterprising genius back East conceived the idea of selling cats to brighten the domestic lives of the homesick miners; and a wagon, divided into compartments one above the other, arrived with every conceivable breed and color of felines. Miners crowded around the curiosity on Main Street, and sure enough the entire shipment was speedily sold out, the favorite Maltese bringing up to $10 in gold dust.

Amply supplied by the bull-trains, Deadwood's false-fronted Main Street emerged from the Dakota wilderness, complete with bakers, barbers, blacksmith shops and bath houses. By the summer of '76, the mining camp boasted "the first completely equipped grocery store," two-story frame hotels with crude bunks or floor space for blankets if the occupant chose, livery stables, a newspaper, undertaker, dance halls, theater and "sporting houses." There was regular mail service to and from Cheyenne. The crowning achievement was the telegraph, opened on December 1, 1876. The railroad would not reach Deadwood until 1890.

As the big freighting outfits prospered, so did Deadwood, which was becoming the "greatest little city on earth." Reported the *Black Hills Daily Times*: "There are five hotels, numerous restaurants, chop houses and lunch rooms. There are about 75 saloons in North and South Deadwood, besides many billiards and card halls. Two brass bands enliven the monotony of mining life, from the principal balconies, and scores of lesser musicians toot the horns and rasp the viol in the halls of chance, the concert salon, and in the public thoroughfares. Gardens loom up around the hills. . . . The three banking companies (handling over $100,000 a day) ornament their windows with bullion, bar, retort gold, dust and coin in careless quantities."

Writing in her rare book, *The Black Hills* or *Last Hunting Grounds of the Dakotahs*, Annie D. Tallent gives us a vivid picture of Deadwood's original Main Street crowded with bull-trains:

Conjure up in your minds one long, narrow street, which was practically all there was of Deadwood in the summer of 1876, deeply lined on both sides from one extreme to the other with a dense, dark mass of surging, pushing, struggling, male humanity, every business place open and traffic in full blast. Imagine the arrival upon the scene of several bull-trains, heavily laden with merchandise, and the bustle and confusion of unloading the same at the doors of the many hustling dealers along the crowded street. Imagine you hear the oaths of the pitiless drivers accompanied by the sharp crack of their long, cruel lashes, the plaintive mooing of the tired, panting cattle, and the loud resonant braying of many mules, and above all the

Street View of Lead City, ills, D. T., the centre of the Gold District.

Ox-teams like these slumped wearily in Lead's Main Street, hauled the Homestake Mining Company's first locomotive and huge stamp mill 250 miles from the railroad at Sidney, Nebraska. — *Centennial Archives, Deadwood Public Library.*

This was bull-train traffic in Rapid City before the railroad came in 1886. Freighting outfits like these played an important role in supplying Black Hills towns.—*South Dakota State Historical Society.*

Business boomed with the rape and plunder of the Black Hills and profiting handsomely were the dozens of saloons, gambling joints and raucous dives like the Gem Variety Theater and dance hall.—*Centennial Archives, Deadwood Public Library.*

incessant rasping of numerous saws and the resounding blows of many hammers, and you have a faint mental reproduction of Sunday in Deadwood during the pioneer days.

Sunday, in fact, was "the maddest business day of all," Mrs. Tallent recounts.

That was the day on which hundreds of miners and prospectors in the surrounding camps and gulches threw down their picks and shovels and came to Deadwood to replenish their stores of supplies, get their mail, have a jolly good time, and spend their week's earnings. Naturally, the businessmen, not having braved the dangers of a journey to the Black Hills for their health, were nothing loath to exchange their goods and merchandise and otherwise cater to their pleasures for gold dust. Hence Deadwood on Sunday was a scene of extraordinary business activity and excitement, and one not easily forgotten.

So Deadwood, the metropolis of the Black Hills, boomed beyond imagination and three years later the *Daily Times* reported on January 14, 1879:

[The town] contained 6,000 inhabitants, 500 business firms, churches, schools and numerous secret organizations. The assessed valuation of the three counties composing this region has increased from $300,000 two years ago to over $3,000,000 today, without taking the mines into consideration. The Black Hills settlements number about 30 and are scattered over a region 6,000 miles square lying between the south and north forks of the Cheyenne River. There were 15,000 passengers carried to and from the Hills during the past year by the stage lines and the mail which arrives at Deadwood, amounts to 500 pounds daily. These stage lines employ 200 experienced men, 1,000 animals, and fifty fine Concord coaches and have a capital of about $500,000 invested.

It was a euphoric report the *Daily Times* had given in January 1879, all right, but when Deadwood's placer diggings presently gave out, its halcyon days of glitter and glory were largely over. With introduction of the revolutionary cyanide process for extracting gold from the ore, Deadwood benefited from employment in its Homestake cyanide plant. The once roaring mining camp settled down to the mundane business of serving as the Lawrence County seat and as a railroad center. But it maintained its lively night life and bawdy houses, thus preserving its reputation as wide-open, wicked old Deadwood.

Meanwhile, the rugged freighters had played an important role in the development of other Hills towns: principally, Custer, Sturgis, Lead and Rapid City. Nearly depopulated in 1875 when gold was discovered in Deadwood Gulch, Custer staged a comeback as a stable mining community. Up north, Sturgis boomed as bullwhackers freighted mountains of supplies to the military post, Fort Meade. Founded in July 1876, soon after discovery of the fabulously rich Homestake Ledge or "*leed*," this mining camp grew from a rutted Main Street, likewise tied up with bull-trains, to a prosperous, mile-high city whose citizens quickly became accustomed to the continuous roar of the Homestake's great stamp mills, crushing gold ore day and night.

Disheartened with hunting gold, a handful of prospectors gathered around a campfire near Rapid Creek on February 23, 1876, and decided this was a good spot for a trading center to serve the state west of the Missouri River. Thanks to their vision, Rapid City was born, and soon it was thronged with bull-trains like Deadwood and Lead. Building a blockhouse for protection against the warring Sioux, the citizens platted the present townsite and went on to develop a thriving Main Street and to secure the School of Mines. On July 4, 1886, a steam locomotive, pulling five gaily decorated passenger coaches, puffed into Rapid City from Gordon, Nebraska, the first train to link the Black Hills with the outside world—and the days of the bold breed, the bullwhacker, were doomed.

Soon railroads served the entire Black Hills, and the last crawling bull-train vanished into the sunset along with the buffalo and warring Sioux. But sometimes as I roam the gold-and-grass country, I fancy I can hear the crack of the bullwhip and the raucous cry of the grizzled old bullwhackers echoing again through the storied Black Hills.

This mile long awesome gash, now known as the Open Cut, was a solid mountain when three prospectors, the Manuel brothers and Hank Harney, found a rich outcrop of gold ore here on April 9, 1876. They had located the Homestake, America's greatest gold mine.—*Homestake Mining Company.*

Rich Homestake yields endless treasure

When venturesome Fred and Moses Manuel left Helena, Montana, for the Black Hills in the fall of 1875, they hoped to strike it rich, but doubtless they scarcely dreamed they would discover America's greatest gold mine that would be producing more than a century later.

Reaching Custer City, the Manuel brothers were disappointed with their gold grubbing in that vicinity and they worked north, prospecting as they went. They located placer claims in the northern Black Hills, but they were searching for "quartz" mines. Late in 1875, they arrived in Deadwood Gulch, but finding it overcrowded by miners and with too little "free" gold, they tramped three miles up the hills to a side ravine called Bobtail Gulch. Here, with their two partners, Hank Harney and Alexander Engh, they looked for "float"—pieces of quartz with bits of gold broken off from an outcrop that might indicate the presence of a vein of ore or lode nearby. During the next year, 1876, the prospectors found what they were searching for. In a graphic account published years later, Moses Manuel tells the story of their amazing discovery:

Toward spring, in the latter part of March or April, four of us found some rich float quartz. We looked for the lode but the snow was deep and could not find it. When the snow began to melt I wanted to go back and hunt it up again but my three partners wouldn't look for it as they did not think it was worth anything. I kept looking every day for nearly a week, and finally the snow melted on the hill and water ran through the draw which crossed the lead and I saw some quartz in the bottom and water running over it. I took a pick and tried to get some out and found it very solid; but I got some out and took it to the camp and pounded it up and panned it and found it very rich. Next day Hank Harney consented to come and located what we called the Homestake, the 9th of April, 1876.

"Homestake" was a prospector's term, meaning a man had struck it sufficiently rich to return home with a fancy stake. But the Manuels did vastly better. As Moses indicated in his story: "We started to dig a discovery shaft on the side of this little draw and the first chunk of quartz weighed about 200 pounds and was the richest ever taken out. We came over the next day and ran an open cut and found we had a large deposit of rich grade ore. We ran a big open cut and

saved the best quartz by itself. Afterwards we built a road to Whitewood Gulch [Pluma] and bought an ox-team and wagon, built an arrastra [a crude stone mill to crush the rock] and hauled the ore over. We ran the arrastra the following winter and took out $5,000."

On that lucky day in April 1976, the Manuels staked out a single claim, about 150 feet wide and 1,340 feet long, comprising nearly five acres. But finding rich ore, they hurriedly staked out a second claim of about nine acres nearby. Before long, news of the strike had reached "civilization" and in June 1877, an expert practical miner, L. D. Kellog, representing a group of California mining men, came to the Black Hills to investigate. He visited and reported favorably on the Manuel properties which, subsequently, the California group bought for $115,000—equivalent to about $1 million at today's inflated prices.

The California mining interests were three San Francisco capitalists: James Ben Ali Haggin, land speculator; Lloyd Tevis, president of the Wells Fargo Express and Banking Company; and George Hearst, who had just made his fortune on the famed Comstock Lode in Virginia City, Nevada. A bold, enterprising mining magnate, Hearst immediately journeyed to the Black Hills where he began to corner nearly every major claim located near the original lode. Thus he laid the foundation for the 8,000 acres of patented mineral claims the Homestake owns today. At the same time, Hearst set out to acquire a monopoly of vital water rights, which were eventually to make the Homestake the single largest water owner in the Black Hills. Understandably, these aggressive moves engendered bitter enmity among local mining interests, there were court battles, and the new Homestake owners were vigorously assailed for their monopolistic greed. However, the Black Hills *Daily Times* came to Hearst's defense.

"What difference does it make," the newspaper editorialized, "whose money puts in such great enterprise—whether it is Geo. Hearst's or the Angel Gabriel's—only so we get the big mills and the wealth of our country is developed? . . . Instead of speaking of that 'd----d old Hearst,' he should be honored, and every courtesy extended to him by everyone expecting to live and prosper in the Hills."

Quick to consolidate their growing holdings, the three partners incorporated as the Homestake Mining Company in California on November 5, 1877—12 years before South Dakota became a state. The newly

Fred Manuel, one of the three prospectors who discovered the fabulous Homestake. The lucky partners took out $5,000 worth of gold the first year and sold their claim for $115,000. — *Homestake Mining Company.*

organized company purchased an 80-stamp mill in San Francisco and shipped it by Union Pacific Railroad to Sidney, Nebraska. From rail's end, it was then hauled 250 miles in deep snows to Lead City by ox-teams. The company also shipped a small locomotive to pull its ore and timber trains—the first railroad *in* the Black Hills. The mill was completed and the thunderous stamps began pounding the first ore on July 12, 1878. A month later, Homestake sent its first shipments of gold bullion, valued at about $57,000, to the United States Mint in Philadelphia. By August 1879, the Homestake was pounding nearly $2 million a year in gold and would soon double that yield, paying handsome dividends. The whole amazing development, executed in record time in a remote, rugged region still stalked by hostile Indians, was ranked as one of the greatest mining achievements in American history.

The "open cut," or good-sized ditch, that the Manuels dug to assay their outcrop of ore was scarcely a scar on the side of the mountain in the spring of '76. But with the Homestake mining operations, a huge, cavernous open cut began to develop, laying bare rocks probably two *billion* years old. These extremely ancient rocks—silts, iron-bearing muds and sands—had been deposited on the bottom of a great salt sea which covered the Black Hills. Geologists label these rocks

pre-Cambrian, meaning they were formed long before fossils appeared. Indeed, they may have been laid down before the beginning of life on earth. Over eons of time, fantastic pressures folded, contorted, altered and changed these simple sediments into a complex series of rocks known as slates, schists and quartzites in which Homestake ore is found. Then sometime between 30 and 60 million years ago, these molten igneous rocks deep beneath the Black Hills were extruded upward in a massive upheaval that lifted them above the great salt sea.

Out of this fascinating sequence of geologic events was formed Homestake gold, and today the deposit occurs in an intricately folded layer, or bed of rock, known as the Homestake Formation. It consists of a succession of large, pod-shaped ore bodies plunging generally southeast at a 35-degree or steeper angle. The exceedingly hard, tough ore—possibly more resistant than Mount Rushmore's granite—lies in a deposit 50 to 250 feet wide, between two roughly defined vertical walls, and the gold is scattered in minute particles throughout the ore. Only rarely does the gold occur in specks large enough to be seen by the naked eye, and the highly efficient Homestake must mine and process a ton of ore in order to glean a bit of gold the size of a pea!

During the very early days, the Homestake was worked as an open-pit mine, with horses hauling out the ore in one-ton cars. But soon it was discovered the ore body plunged so deep that underground mining was necessary. A shaft was sunk near the Manuels' original claims, and horizontal "drifts" or tunnels were driven through the mountain to mine the ore-bearing rock. In time, as the large "stopes" or openings were mined out without backfill, the overlying rock caved in to form the great Open Cut now seen in Lead. It grew to become an awesome gash 500 feet deep, 1,300 feet wide and today extends nearly a mile through the mountains into the old mining camp of Terraville. By 1945, when the last ore was taken out of the Open Cut, the once solid mountain had yielded nearly 50 million tons of rock, 15 percent of which was gold-bearing ore.

During its first century of operation—almost unheard of for any mine—the Homestake yielded over $*1 billion* in gold at prices far below the current markets. The mine also produced substantial silver. Prophetically, the Indians had said that God Almighty placed great wealth in these Hills for their use, but they feared the gold would make the white man rich. The fabulous Homestake had done just that.

It took a bold breed to accomplish all this, and foremost were the hard-rock men of many nationalities —Cornish, Finns, Germans, Irish, Italians, Slavonians —who first drilled and blasted and mucked out the rich ores of the Homestake mine. Tunneling into the formidable mountain in the early days, the immigrant

During the early days at the Homestake, miners worked 10-hour, six-day shifts, labored by candlelight under hazardous conditions and hauled out ore in these horsedrawn cars.—*Homestake Mining Compay.*

Transported over 250 miles in winter by ox-team from Sidney, Nebraska to Lead City, this was the first locomotive in the Black Hills. It was named for J. B. Haggin, one of the California capitalists who bought the gold mine.—*Homestake Mining Company.*

Where the Manuel brothers had first discovered the Homestake ledge, miners drove "drifts" or tunnels into the mountain and here in the early 1880s the locomotive, J. B. Haggin, began hauling ore from the bottom of the Open Cut.—*Homestake Mining Company.*

Progress at the Homestake about 1900: At left, drilling by the old-fashioned "double jacking" method while at right a miner uses the new-fangled, faster pneumatic drill.—*Homestake Mining Company.*

A polyglot crew—Cornish, Finns, Irish, Italians, Slavonians—these miners pose to be photographed beside gold-bearing rocks two billion years old at the bottom of the Open Cut.—*Homestake Mining Company.*

Waiting to descend by "man-cage" into the steamy depths of the Homestake gold mine about 1900, these men worked when mining was vastly more hazardous than it is today.—*Homestake Mining Company.*

miners labored by candlelight. Shoveling the ore-bearing rock, they loaded it into cars which were either pushed by hand or pulled by horses and mules. The unventilated mines were hot, humid, dust-choked, and the miners lived in constant danger and threat of death. The Homestake in 1879 opened a four-room, log cabin hospital with one untrained male attendant. He did the best he could, until the company improved its medical facilities with a large frame hospital in 1886, staffed with doctors. But the crumbling tombstones in Lead and Deadwood cemeteries bear mute witness to the miners' shortened lives.

Working by candlelight in two-man teams, the hard-rock men first had to drill holes in the ore body by *hand*. While one miner held and rotated a heavy steel drill, his partner swung an eight-pound sledge, with which he drove the drill, inch by inch, into the granitic rock. This was called "double-jacking" and an expert miner could make 50 strokes a minute. But it was hazardous work, for if he missed striking the drill head, he might break his partner's arm or smash his hand.

Next, the miners placed black powder charges in the drill holes, attached a short fuse and ran for cover. The fuses were set to burn together, and with a deafening roar the blast brought down tons of loose and shattered rock, which the miners would later "muck out" and load into cars. But sometimes a fuse would burn too slowly, creating a delayed blast after the miners had returned to work. There were other serious hazards. With each blasting, the miners choked in acrid fumes and black powder smoke. The early mines were not properly ventilated as they are today and miners died young of "miner's consumption" (Silicosis) as they called it. There was constant danger from drilling, falling rock, cave-ins, fire and even more spectacular accidents. Descending hundreds or thousands of feet into the earth, miners ride in a steel "cage", which is lowered and hoisted like an elevator, and operated by a hoisting engineer on the surface. But occasionally in the old days the bell signals between miners and the surface were misunderstood, or the hoisting cable failed, plummeting the men to the bottom of the shaft or hurtling them right through the roof of the headframe. Such accidents were rare, but they happened. Today, the cage tender talks directly to the hoist engineer by radio telephone.

The worst disaster that can occur in underground mining is fire, and luckily the Homestake escaped a major blaze until one began in a timbered "drift" or tunnel at the 500-foot level on the evening of March 25, 1907. According to Homestake's *Centennial History:*

By midnight the fire had raged completely out of control. For three weeks, Superintendent Thomas J. Grier and his men fought the blaze with every means at hand. Water was pumped through compressed-airlines and sprayed directly on the fire by men wearing leather gas masks and working in 15-minute shifts, but a massive cave-in soon cut off their access. Openings in the caved rock were sealed with clay and steam forced into the fire area. It didn't work. Under a constant spray of water, men attempted to cut through the rock, which was incandescent with heat, but the working conditions were impossible.

"Man, after today," one of the miners said, *"I've been to hell. I don't need to go back."* Water was allowed to seep into the 500-foot level from the level above; that, too, failed. Finally, Grier ordered every man and animal out of the mine and did the only thing left to do—he flooded it. Every minute of every day for 40 days, 2,196 cubic feet of water was poured into the mine until it was submerged in an estimated 80 million cubic feet of water, and the fire finally died.

Although the upper levels of the mine were ready for working by July, it was October before the last water was drained from the flooded Homestake. The fire cost an estimated half million dollars in lost production alone. The Homestake suffered another major underground fire in 1919 at the 800-foot level. After 20 days of futile fire-fighting, the mine was again flooded, and production was halted for weeks as powerful pumps and huge bail-buckets lifted the water out of the mine. The damage this time was so great the Homestake was unable to pay dividends for a year. There was another underground fire in 1945, when the mine was temporarily closed during World War II, but eventually it was controlled. On July 10, 1930, the Ellison headframe or hoisting room burned in a spectacular fire. Caught on a cage, two miners were killed when 2,000 feet of oil-covered cable burned and fell on them, sending their cage crashing to the bottom of the 2,300-foot shaft.

Like any great corporation, the Homestake faced labor problems, but it escaped the bitter union activity and bloody strikes that frequently plagued most of the other mining camps in the West. The Homestake was an unusually stable operation; it paid well for the times ($2.50 a day on the surface and up to $3.50 underground); and the company provided fringe benefits: virtually free hospitalization for miner and family; interest-free home loans, credit at the Hearst department or "Brick Store"; and company-supported free public library, kindergarten, schools and community events. Since 1880, the miners had also had their own union, which was originally a charitable and benevolent organization.

So labor peace prevailed in the Homestake until 1909, when the American Federation of Labor sent organizers to the Hills. Within a few weeks, the local

Sitting on top of America's greatest gold mine, Lead was a booming city as evidenced by this early-day traffic: ore train at top, busy railroads below.—*Homestake Mining Company.*

Armed and alert, these Wells Fargo Express Company guards transport $250,000 in gold bullion from the great Homestake mine.—*Grabill photo, 1890. South Dakota State Historical Society.*

Handling gold bullion is serious business. A turn-of-the-century guard stands watch over Homestake's shipment to a U.S. mint.—*Homestake Mining Company.*

Beneath this sprawling complex of shaft hoistroom and headframe, mechanical shops, mill and treatment plants at the Homestake in Lead, miners continue to find gold-bearing ore today at the 6,800-foot level.—*Homestake Mining Company.*

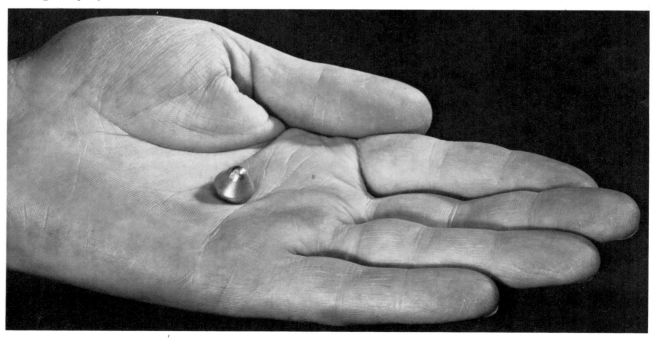

Unbelievably, the Homestake mine has to produce one ton of ore to yield this tiny bit of gold—nearly four-tenths of a Troy ounce.—*Homestake Mining Company.*

miners' union had signed up more than 2,000 members and boldly announced its intention to make Homestake a closed shop. The paternalistic company promptly retaliated, declaring it would employ only nonunion men after January 1, 1910. The union voted to strike, whereupon the Homestake completely shut down the mine and mills and put them under Pinkerton guard.

The Hills were plunged into a period of divisive labor strife, but in the end the lockout was successful. For a time, Homestake hired 500 strikebreakers to start up the mines, the union floundered and miners returned. Within six months the great mine was in full operation again. The Homestake had no more serious labor troubles until the 1950s and '60s. After repeated attempts to organize the miners and win an election, the United Steel Workers in 1966 signed the first union contract in Homestake's 90-year history.

While the rest of the country suffered during the Great Depression of the thirties, times in the mile-high city of Lead were never better. Reasons: After the catastrophic stock market crash of 1929, investors turned to gold instead of securities; and in 1934 Congress raised the price of gold from $20.67 an ounce to $35. So jobs were plentiful at the Homestake, which during this period continued to modernize its complex operations: to sink new and deeper main shafts, expand mechanization, drive millions of cubic feet of air per minute into the mine to insure proper ventilation, train miners for underground and provide ever-safer working conditions.

Meanwhile, both the Homestake and the city of Lead had begun to share a mounting concern. After more than 50 years of continuous mining, ground slippage around the Open Cut and caving within the cavernous mine, as timbers rotted away, began to endanger the company's mills, shops, hoists and the city itself. Streets buckled and sank as much as 27 feet, power poles leaned, water mains burst, and business buildings and homes alike, had to be condemned. Homestake faced a colossal and costly task, but over a period of 20 years, from about 1919 to 1939, it moved a good part of the town uphill and out of danger. Today, Homestake backfills its drifts, stopes and tunnels with wet sand to forestall further subsidence.

As the Homestake was being mined over a half century, and geologists blocked out new ore-bearing strata, there was always the question: How long will the old mine last? The Homestake is basically a low-grade ore mine, with infrequent rich deposits. Gold mines, moreover, are short-lived and there was the perpetual fear that someday the Homestake would finally play out. That fear appeared to be confirmed in 1919. After consulting the mine's chief geologist and appraising all the studies and rock samples, Homestake officials concluded there was only about 10 years' ore left in sight for the humming mills. The great mine, at last, was "pinching out" and appeared doomed!

It might have been, but for a timely government study showing that the ore-bearing rock of the Homestake was *not* pinching out and instead might well extend thousands of feet deeper into the great folds of the pre-Cambrian schist. About this time, the company hired an able young consulting geologist, Donald H. McLaughlin, who, after extensive study, became convinced that the Homestake Lode indeed dipped deeper and deeper and the old mine still had a future after all.

Geologist McLaughlin was right; and today, miners, working in oppressive heat and humidity, are driving development drifts below the 6,800-foot level, where they continue to find the same gold-bearing ore. As Homestake general manager, Allen Winters, told me optimistically: "Provided that gold prices make it economic to operate, we intend to keep on mining. We have utmost faith that the Homestake ore bodies will continue. This is one of the greatest mining deposits in the world, and there's nothing to suggest that it will end."

The sacred soil of the Sioux seems destined to yield everlasting treasure.

They're nearly all gone now, the hardy breed of homesteaders symbolized by this old-timer of Pennington County who was photographed during the "Dirty 30s."—*South Dakota State Historical Society.*

The "Honyockers" flock to free land

Even today in the short grass country around the Black Hills, you can occasionally spot a homesteader's tumbledown claim shack. Its tar-paper siding has long since weathered away, the battered door bangs in the gusty wind and gaping windows look out forlornly on the high, dry lonesome land.

Too bad that the old claim shanty, now fallen on evil days, can't talk, for it stands as a solitary monument to one of the epic periods in American history. Here on these prairies once lived hardworking, venturesome men and women who endured drouth and dust storms, hail and hoppers, privation and isolation in a valiant struggle to settle the land of the Sioux and achieve their American Dream. Confidently, they carried on—always with the hope and trust that another season would be better. They were incurably "next-year" people and they used to sing a ditty:

> Way out west in South Dakota,
> In my homestead on the plains;
> In my shack upon the prairie
> Where they say it never rains.

They're all gone now, this hardy breed of homesteaders, or "honyockers," as we used to call them in western South Dakota (the origin of the name is unclear). But like the cowboy, freighter, miner and all of the other true pioneers, they played a tremendous role in settling the West. Stringing their newly invented barbed wire across the plains, they fenced out the big cattle outfits and ended the day of the great roundups on the open range. Those who survived became successful farmers and ranchers—the backbone of their prideful communities.

This epic era in American history began officially on May 20, 1862, when Congress, after bitter debate, passed the Homestead law allowing every U.S. citizen, 21 or over, to file a claim to "one-quarter section," or 160 acres. The homesteader would be required to live and work on the land for five years, after which he could "prove up" and acquire deed. President Lincoln enthusiastically signed the measure, and promptly at midnight on January 1, 1863, a furloughed Union soldier became the first homesteader in the United States.

Learning of choice lands out West, Daniel Freeman of Ohio journeyed to the frontier town of Brownville, Nebraska Territory, to look around during his holiday leave. He found the town already thronged with hungry land-seekers and good sites going fast. The soldier borrowed a horse and rode 70 miles westward in an icy wind to stake out 160 acres of rich bottomland on Cub Creek, then galloped back to town. There the crowd of land-seekers good-naturedly agreed the furloughed soldier should be allowed to make the first homestead filing, and the U.S. land agent obliged by stepping out of a New Year's Eve dance and opening the land office for a few minutes after midnight. Daniel Freeman made history and hurried back to his regiment. After the Civil War he brought his bride and settled on the homestead for life. Today the Freeman farm, located four miles northwest of Beatrice, Nebraska, is officially considered Homestead Entry No. 1 in the United States and is a national monument.

As the rich, subhumid areas of the Midwest, like the Freeman farm, were settled, land-hungry Americans moved on to the semiarid Great Plains and mountains—the West that nobody wanted! Homesteaders by the thousands poured into the empty land before the turn of the century. The story of Ole Christensen of the Black Hills is told in the Lawrence County history issued during the Dakota Territory Centennial: "Ole carried his plow on his back from Deadwood to his homestead southeast of Spearfish because oxen would have taken two days whereas he made it in one day. Christensen [soon after the gold rush] was the first to plow a furrow in that section. A breaking plow with two oxen was used, the grain was sown by hand. A harrow was made of oak branches and pulled by oxen. A cradle or scythe was used to harvest the grain, then it was tied and shocked in bundles. A flail, which looked like a long whip, was used to get the grain out of the head."

This early period of homesteading, however, was not its heyday. Surprisingly, about two-thirds of all land successfully homesteaded in the United States—over 270 million acres in 100 years—were "proved up" in the twentieth century. This occurred between 1900 and 1930. More than a quarter of this total acreage was homesteaded in the 10-year period alone during and after World War I, when wheat sold for an unprecedented two dollars per bushel.

The stage was set for South Dakota's last big land rush with reopening of the Great Sioux Reservation (originally everything west of the Missouri River) in the treaty negotiated during the summer of 1889 and effective on February 10, 1890. Under this treaty, the last with the Sioux Nation, the Indians relinquished all the lands between the White and Cheyenne rivers, all of what is now Perkins and Harding counties and the

Locating a choice 160 acres, east of the Black Hills, Danish immigrant Louis Jensen walked 50 miles to the U.S. Land Office in Rapid City to file on his claim. Then building this frame house, he proudly brought his family to the lonely, wind-swept homestead.—*Leonel M. Jensen.*

Sitting forlornly outside her treeless claim shanty, this courageous pioneer was one of the many women who tackled homesteading alone. Fortunately, her isolation and loneliness is relieved by a neighbor living just up the hill. — *South Dakota State Historical Society.*

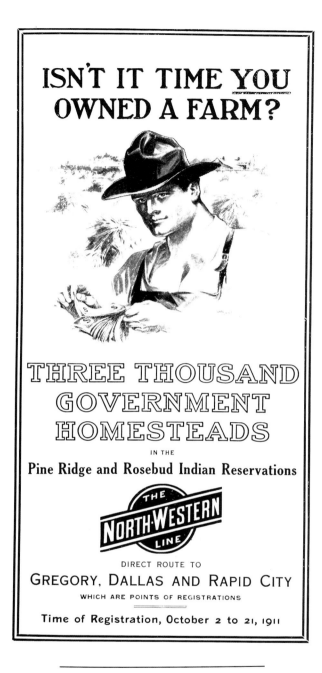
portions of Meade and Butte counties north of the Belle Fourche River. A part of these nine million acres was opened to purchase by railroads and land buyers and the remainder to homesteading.

Sam Bober, an enterprising Russian immigrant living in St. Louis, was one of thousands who joined the homesteaders' rush for this last free government land. Sam "filed" on 160 acres five miles outside the windswept town of Newell. He put up a tar-paper shack and dug a well. It took money to build fences and improve the land, so the young immigrant hired out to the U.S. experiment farm at Newell. By 1916 he had saved enough to journey to St. Louis to marry Rose

Stolar. For she and her Russian refugee family had followed the Bobers to America.

Sam and his bride jolted across the South Dakota prairies in his new buggy, and finally pulled up in front of the tar-paper shack. "We're here!" he said jubilantly. "We're where?" groaned Rose. There wasn't another house or human being to be seen for miles.

But next morning Rose awoke to hear a girl outside singing. A thoughtful neighbor had ridden over to greet the bride. A little later another neighbor arrived with some meat. "We just butchered," he explained.

The first winter was unforgettable. The mercury skidded to 30 below zero, almost freezing Sam and Rose in their tar-paper shack. Then one day Sam rode home from town with an important, legal-looking envelope. "Rose, look!" he exclaimed. "A deed signed by President Woodrow Wilson!"

It was the patent for his 160 acres. "Now I feel," Sam said, "that I have been elected a stockholder in the most wonderful corporation on earth."

The honyockers came from all walks of life—bakers, barbers, carpenters, clerks, salesmen, schoolmarms—and most seem to have arrived dead broke. They used to joke that "the government bet you 160 acres against your $18 filing fee you would starve out and give up before five years." Countless hopefuls did. The honyockers endured both privation and isolation. Lucy Peterson, a rancher's wife in the Slim Buttes country, north of the Black Hills, relates her experience in the Butte County history, *Pioneer Footprints*. Mrs. Peterson said it was a week's trip to trade in Belle Fourche: three days driving in the wagon to town, one day shopping and three days more driving home. Stricken with serious illness, honyockers often had to ride a day and night to summon a doctor, who traveled just as far and hard reaching his patient.

Life in a 12-by-14 foot cramped, dreary claim shack, papered with newspapers and scantily furnished with bed, wood stove, table, cupboards and few amenities, was extremely rugged. During bitter, sub-zero winters the honyockers sometimes took their potatoes to bed with them so they wouldn't be frozen solid by morning. During the sweltering summers, the flimsy claim shanty, standing in the pitiless sun on the treeless plains, was often suffocating. Families also had to keep a sharp watch for rattlesnakes that crawled out of their dens in the heat and lay coiled in the dooryard—if not inside the shanty itself.

The lot of a honyocker's wife was unbearably hard and lonely. Sometimes she rarely saw another woman to talk to for days, even weeks on end, and the vast emptiness of the prairie, the wailing winds, the mournful cries of the coyotes at night made her heartsick. The housewife lugged drinking water from a

Enjoying better furnishings than most Honyockers, this family gathers around the all-purpose kitchen stove where they cooked, warmed their cold feet, dried wet socks and heated water to bathe on Saturday night. — *South Dakota State Historical Society.*

Weary from the day's labors, this honyocker sits down to cook his supper on his new wood-burning stove complete with hot water tank. Likely, he's wearing his high-buttoned shoes for company. — *South Dakota State Historical Society.*

Hell on women! Surprised by a photographer as she scrubbed clothes on her washboard, this woman reflects in her toil-worn face and hands all of the labor, sweat and stress of a homesteader's wife. — *South Dakota State Historical Society.*

On a bitter cold but sunshiny day, a bachelor hangs out his wash to dry, but alas, it is soon frozen stiff in the South Dakota winter. — *South Dakota State Historical Society.*

well, or with the help of her husband, hauled it in wooden barrels from the nearest neighbor or closest stream. Often, water was so scarce that settlers' wives washed their chapped and sunburned faces with milk. They saw the garden they planted so hopefully in the spring wither and die in the hot, dry summer winds. Drouthed out every few years, the honyockers often went hungry and were derisively called "wrinkled bellies."

Homesteading in western South Dakota took a lot of grit and guts, but there were also the good years of hope and pride and belated reward; when the rains came, the pastures greened and the young wheat plants stooled out, their sturdy shoots growing into a beautiful, waving field of grain. The honyockers experienced both success and failure, and the stories of two other families I knew well typify this era. One pioneered out in Harding County north of Belle Fourche and the other settled east of the Black Hills in Pennington County. First, the Claude Olsons.

An amiable, black-hatted honyocker, who rolled his own cigarets from a Bull Durham sack in his shirt pocket, Claude Olson was born in a woodchopper's cabin at the foot of the now famed Mount Rushmore National Memorial. One of 14 children, he was the son of a Swedish immigrant who had walked to the Black Hills goldfields from eastern South Dakota. Unable to strike it rich, the immigrant went to work for wages and with amazing ambition and frugality managed to accumulate a few head of cattle. The elder Olson was just getting launched in ranching when his grazing land was designated as Black Hills National Forest, and in 1900 the family moved to Harding County to file on land withdrawn from the Great Sioux Reservation.

The Olsons located in a stretch of picturesque but isolated grass country 20 miles from the nearest neighbor, 50 miles from the mail and over 80 miles from the principal trading center, Belle Fourche. Their first home was a dismal dugout in the side of hill, with a smoke hole through the dirt roof supported by poles. It was both warmer in winter and cooler in summer than the customary tar-paper shack. And here the hardworking, courageous family survived the bitter winters, scorching summers, hailstorms, grasshoppers and bad times that caused hundreds of settlers to curse their bad luck and give up—a few of the latter departed, leaving unpaid grocery bills.

"The trouble was that we'd have maybe two or three good years, and people would go plumb crazy," Claude recalled those erratic times. "The honyockers plowed up more land and figured they had it made. Then we'd hit another dry spell and not a damn thing would come up."

But the Olsons were rugged "next-year" people, and they doggedly hung on. In 1924, Claude married the daughter of another pioneer ranch family and the young couple homesteaded on adjacent land. But he and his bride Inez worked on the neighboring Bar-H Ranch for $25 a month in order to make ends meet. Claude acquired a small cattle herd of his own, and with this start built the K/O Ranches, one of the most successful livestock outfits in the West. As long as I knew him, Claude Olson was a vigorous champion of free enterprise and proud that he had never accepted a government subsidy check.

"The Homestead law was a terrible mistake," Claude always insisted. "People just couldn't make it on 160 acres of dry land in South Dakota." Recognizing this reality, Congress increased the homestead grant to 320 acres and eventually to a "stock-raising" homestead of 640 acres. But even this acreage was insufficient, and as the homesteaders failed and fled the country, their lands were bought up and consolidated with ever larger ranches.

About the time the Olsons were pioneering north of the Black Hills, a Danish immigrant, Louis Jensen, was seeking a fresh start in America. Hearing of newly opened lands on the Great Sioux Reservation, he reached the Cheyenne River country where he tramped over the Badlands and surrounding unsettled prairie looking for a choice piece of land. At length, he located 160 acres of fine, level benchland and then walked on 50 miles to the U.S. land office in Rapid City to file on his claim. That was in 1906, and that fall he built a stout claim shack with dirt floor and dug a brackish well on his homestead claim. He then returned to eastern South Dakota to gather his possessions for the journey west. The railroad had just come in, and in April 1907, Jensen rode west in an "immigrant car," tending milk cows, a team of horses, two cats, some farm implements, a well rig and household goods. His railroad fare: $40.

At last, the new home in the West was ready, and in May 1907, the family arrived on one of the first passenger trains. Meeting them at the end of the line, Jensen bundled his wife and three small children into a lumber wagon and drove about six miles to the lonely, wind swept homestead. They plowed through sticky clay (gumbo) that balled up on the wagonwheels until the horses could scarcely move. Hopeful and prideful, the 34-year-old Dane broke the prairie sod and planted his first crops. They yielded well, and America looked good to Louis Jensen until the disastrous year of 1911 when searing drouth and a cloud of grasshoppers, so thick they darkened the skies, devastated the entire countryside. "The potatoes we planted in the spring didn't have enough moisture to sprout until it rained in September," Leonel Jensen, the immigrant's stalwart son, who farms the benchland today, vividly recalls. "There was no feed for the cattle except thistles that had to be mowed green and put up for hay. Of the 21 homesteads then located on our benchland, only seven

The life of a homesteader was lonesome, unbearably hard and any visitors were warmly welcomed. From this snapshot, it appears someone took pictures of the visitors from town to mark the occasion.—*South Dakota State Historical Society.*

"Sodbusters" was the name for homesteaders, who built their "soddies" out of tough, closely matted buffalo grass—warmer in winter, cooler in summer.—*Western History Department, Denver Public Library.*

Homesteading during the "Dirty 30s," absolutely the worst years in South Dakota's history, this Pennington county farmer momentarily puts aside his cares to fiddle for his youngster outside of their dust-choked dugout. — *South Dakota State Historical Society.*

Arriving in wagons, on horseback and even in an early automobile, settlers gather to visit and trade during Honyockers Sales Day at Fairpoint (then Pop. 6) in Meade County. — *South Dakota State Historical Society.*

families survived. That terrible year wiped out most of the honyockers on the land that Uncle Sam had taken away from the Sioux."

Today the original 21 homesteads and adjacent lands are consolidated into a single 6,000-acre, big-time farming operation. Here where the Danish immigrant first turned the prairie sod with his one-man steel plow, his son and grandson now farm with a pair of air-conditioned tractors worth $100,000, and using costly plowing and planting equipment, they produce abundantly to help feed America and a hungry world. Standing in his knee-high, beautiful waving wheat, Leonel told me with feeling, "I am proud of all this and what my father pioneered."

By the late 1920s, the homesteaders had virtually conquered that part of the "Great American Desert" lying in western South Dakota, and the supply of desirable land, even for stock raising, was running out. The disastrous drouth and black blizzards of the "Dirty Thirties" bankrupted a host of honyockers who up to then had managed to hang on. Broken in spirit, the impoverished families loaded up their belongings and departed the country. Sometimes they left a grass-grown mound protected by a sagging fence. Crossing the prairies one day to visit a deserted homestead, I was moved to find a solitary fenced-in grave. As I knelt to read the weather-beaten wooden marker, the silence was eerie and profound in the empty land, broken only by the song of the western meadowlark and the yip-yip-yip of the alarmed prairie dogs scurrying to the safety of their mounds. And here, in this desolate, demanding land some starry-eyed homesteaders had staked everything and stuck it out until the day-to-day struggle and the death of a loved one had proved too much.

During the prolonged drought of the thirties, some of the burned out farmers stopped at our ranch on the rim of the Black Hills to water and feed their ganted up, tired horses. It was sad to see the ruined, disillusioned honyockers flocking back East with their scanty belongings, sometimes loaded on a hayrack together with their hungry shabby children. The day of the homesteader was finished.

So gone are these plucky people, who braved blizzards, drouth, floods, twisters, prairie fires, isolation; and, as one recalls, put up "a hard fight with a short stick" to lay claim to 160 acres. Perhaps the prairie statesman, William Jennings Bryan, paid them their finest tribute, "They were men and women who gave the world more than they took from it." And they paid a high price indeed to settle the free land once roamed by the nomadic Sioux.

PART THREE
Out of the Mud and Into High Gear

A pioneer family's struggle.

The automobile would never go anywhere because there were no roads to drive on, a leading farm magazine once predicted, as indeed this early car being pulled out of sticky gumbo illustrated. But in time, with mechanization, farmers and ranchers did get out of the mud, shifted into high gear and helped to prosper and feed the growing nation. — *South Dakota State Historical Society.*

Rising in the Black Hills, False Bottom Creek meanders through lovely St. Onge Valley; now flowing swiftly, now lying in limpid pools, then briefly disappearing altogether, hence its name. Fed by heavy snows or spring rains, it becomes a raging torrent. Ice-sheathed, a bit of winter wonderland. — *Photo by author.*

Father settles on False Bottom Creek

About the time of tragic Wounded Knee and the last fateful days of the Sioux Nation, two plucky people pioneered in the rough and rugged Black Hills. Eventually, they met, married and settled in the fertile St. Onge Valley, where, in 1876 marauding Indians had stampeded and destroyed the first herd of Texas Longhorns trailed to the Black Hills. This proud, ambitious couple were my parents and their story typifies the early settlers' struggle to wrest a living from the "Land of the Dakotahs," as our State was named after the Sioux.

Pioneering in the Black Hills, our family spanned a fantastic period of progress and change: from the horse-and-buggy era around the turn of the century to the automobile, truck, tractor and big-time power farming; from the coal-oil lamp, flatirons, wood stove and ceaseless drudgery to electricity, convenience and liberation; from the primitive one-room country school, isolation and mail-order catalog to the telephone, good roads, better schools, rural free delivery, radio, movies and the modern age. Happily, we were not yet distracted by television. It was a good time to be alive—an America now vanished—of which I cherish fond memories.

At 17, my father, William Paul Friggens, sailed to America, from the remote seaside village of Gulval, in Cornwall, England, with scarcely more than the clothes on his back—and small wonder. Recently, visiting the humble stone cottage and postage-stamp size farm where my father was born, I discovered that the rocky, timeworn land has been owned by the same gentry, or upper-class family, for over 200 years. Father had no future there. So cooped up in smelly bunks below decks, and eating mouldy bread, he traveled "steerage" like millions of other immigrants to reach the United States and he was tearful at his first glimpse of the Statue of Liberty in New York harbor.

Father was to find America good!

Working across the country, he dug ditches in the then malarial South; labored as a farmhand in Blue Island, today a teeming industrial suburb of Chicago; and then headed West in 1889 to the booming Black Hills. He arrived in the unsightly log-and-shanty mining camp, Central City, wedged in a narrow gulch between mines and mills that cluttered the pitted, terraced hillsides, and became an ordinary miner. He earned the unheard-of wage of 35 cents per hour for a 10-hour day, seven days a week. No Sunday layoffs in those times.

Working conditions in the early-day gold mines of the Black Hills were appalling. Climbing out of the steamy depths of the DeSmet and Caledonia mines (later acquired by the Homestake) after a back-breaking 10-hour shift of blasting and "barring down" the ore-bearing rock, Father was compelled to trudge home to his boarding house in his sweat-soaked "digging" clothes. On bitter winter days, his clothes froze stiff on his body and in the time before antibiotics, he miraculously survived double pneumonia. His younger brother, James, whom he later helped to immigrate to this country, died of diptheria. But here in the Black Hills, Father worked in the mines, and also prospected until he had saved enough money to start farming and ranching.

Youngest daughter of an English-born mining foreman, John Hosken, my handsome high-spirited mother, Caroline Clemens Hosken, was born in Nevada City, California. When some of the gold mines there petered out, the 12-year-old journeyed with her mother, two older sisters and younger brother to join her father already in the Hills. Mother arrived in a snowstorm on September 6, 1889, the same year that South Dakota became a state. "It was the first passenger train into Lead, and we were greeted by a big crowd and a band at the depot," Mother recalled. "Then we rode back in a hack to a small frame house that Father had rented in what we then apologetically called Slavonia town—among Slav miners." Throughout America, those days, there was bitter ethnic feeling and racial tension among the new foreign immigrants.

That evening after her father had gone to work on the night shift in the mines, Mother's family was frightened by a terrible din and shooting outside. "We had been told," Mother recalled, "that Sitting Bull and the Sioux were on the warpath with their Ghost Dance and we feared an Indian attack. We all got out of bed, dressed in the dark and barricaded the front door with our heavy dresser. The scare turned out to be Slavonians celebrating a wedding across the street."

Having made a modest stake in mining, Father took up ranching in partnership with his younger brother, Tom, on the rolling Centennial Prairie near Spearfish. But fate, and a vivacious 16-year-old girl he had seen fleetingly in Lead and never forgotten, were forever to change Father's life. The girl was my mother. A gifted, imaginative young woman, she yearned to be a writer and already had composed reams of romantic fiction on cheap foolscap paper. I'm sure that had she been given an education and the opportunities that women rightfully enjoy today, Mother would have been a successful author or editor.

But she had only a grade school education and impetuously was married in her teens to a young Cornish miner. She was widowed and left with an infant son when her husband was killed in the mines. Now thrown onto her own meager resources, Mother worked 10-hour days sewing in a Deadwood basement "sweatshop" to care for herself and baby. Becoming a highly skilled seamstress, she was invited out to Centennial Prairie to make a wedding dress for my Father's sister, Mary, who kept house for her two bachelor brothers.

Thus Father, at age 40, met again the striking young woman with the wavy dark hair, flashing brown eyes and spirited temperament, he had first seen when she was 16 and never forgotten. Love flowered, Mother was happy to have a home for her little boy, Earl; and in September, 1907, my parents were married in the Methodist-Episcopal church in Lead. Father rented a small farm and introduced his bride to rural life on cottonwood-fringed Lower False Bottom Creek (appropriately named because the stream abruptly disappeared underground in many places) in picturesque St. Onge Valley. This was the homesteading era and hopefuls like my parents were now settling the choice lands, once the sacred soil of the Sioux, all around the Black Hills.

It was at once a toilsome and often painful experience for my mother. Born and raised in a rough-and-ready California mining camp, emigrating to the Hills when she was only 12, she had no farm or ranch experience whatsoever; and the sudden plunge into country life with all the loneliness, privation and drab dawn-to-dusk drudgery was incredibly harsh. But Mother was never one to shirk responsibility. She pitched in, cooked, washed and patched work clothes for the family and hired men. She learned to milk a cow, raised chickens, planted and tended a big garden, canned fruit, made soap from bacon grease and saved scraps from her sewing to make quilts. A so-called "city" girl, Mother courageously adjusted to the rigors of ranch life, was a good neighbor and soon made friends with just about everybody in St. Onge Valley.

Settled in 1881 by Michael St. Onge and some French Canadians, St. Onge was a typical frontier farming community. The tree-shaded, pastoral village consisted of a rudimentary school through the eighth grade, small frame Catholic and Protestant churches, a lodge hall, saloon or two, cafe, bank, railroad depot with its wondrous clickety-clack telegraph key keeping in touch with the outside world, livery stable and grain elevator, together with a combined general store and cubbyhole post office. On one side, the general store smelled of vinegar, coal oil, chewing tobacco and new harness, mingled with the pleasant aroma of freshly ground coffee. The other side of the store smelled of drygoods, bolts of gingham and calico cloth, along with leather gloves, rubber boots, work shoes and bib overalls fresh from the factory.

Here my folks made their weekly trip to town in a light spring wagon to sell the eggs and cream that helped pay for their groceries. They traded; picked up the mail and local newspaper, the St. Onge Quiet Tip; chatted about crops, prices, politics; and put down their roots in the pioneer community. Father and Mother were warmly welcomed, and our family couldn't have been treated with greater religious tolerance and genuine friendship. St. Onge was dominantly Catholic and our family was Protestant. But our best friend was Catholic storekeeper Charley Furois—a saint in overalls—who used to let my father run up a big bill all year for groceries, hardware and farm machinery until harvest time in the fall. And if the harvest was poor, Charley carried Father on his books—without interest. Charley Furois, as was the custom in those days, expected every man to be as good as his word—and he was rarely disappointed. Eventually, Father paid every cent. That was the West at its best, in the days before credit cards and computers were to dehumanize business affairs and customer relations.

Such was the stout breed that settled the Black Hills, and indeed the West. They had no guaranteed security, there was no one to bail them out in tough times, no welfare or disaster relief. People didn't run to government—nor did government encourage them— every time they got into trouble. Above all, the pioneers and immigrants, like my father, were eternally grateful for the independence and bounties our country had given them. My father rode his favorite saddle horse, "Queen," ramrod straight, like one of the Queen's Household Cavalry today at Buckingham Palace, and he was infinitely proud. For coming to America he had escaped Old World feudalism, and he was now monarch of all he surveyed.

Thus I started life with a goodly heritage. I was born on the dining room table in a lonely ranchhouse located in the very same hay meadow that pioneer scout Jimmy Iron was guarding when he was killed by Indians the summer of 1876. A young horse-and-buggy doctor delivered me by the flickering light of a coal-oil lamp while my father lugged in buckets of well water to heat over the wood-burning kitchen range. So much hot water wasn't necessary, but in those days country doctors used it as a diversion to give nervous fathers something to do besides pace the floor.

Father had plenty to worry about. Fearful that my mother might not survive childbirth, he had galloped to nearby St. Onge, where he used the only telephone to summon a doctor from the thriving new cow town, Belle Fourche. Childbirth on an isolated western ranch around the turn of the century was a risky ordeal; and frequently the doctor, who may have had to drive a team or ride horseback anywhere from 10 to 100 miles, arrived too late. Moreover, childbirth was often followed by the dread childbed fever and other complications, with high mortality. As for prenatal care, it was virtually unheard of in the rural areas of the West.

So now, the good doctor was seeing my mother for the first time. Equipped with the pioneer physician's usual implements (black instrument bag, medicine case, lantern, hammer, shovel, Colt revolver and a wire cutters to cut the fence and take off across country where there were no roads) and driving a fast team, he made the 15-mile trip in good weather to our ranch in about two hours. He arrived that balmy October 4, 1909, just in time to hurriedly chloroform my mother and deliver me—battered, bawling and "branded" for life by the crude forceps with which he brought me into the world. Quite possibly today, my mother would have had a Caesarian, but miraculously she pulled through. Like many a country doctor in those days, "Doc" Rathbun was likely to sew you up and stick the needle back in his coat lapel.

Ecstatic, like most fathers over birth of a son, Father hoisted a hot toddy with the weary doctor, and then inquired, "Well, Doc, what do I owe you?" It was around $35 for that horse-and-buggy house call, but Doc, who knew farmers and ranchers were suffering searing drouth, poor crops and worse prices, said right off he'd wait. He knew that my father was "good" to pay up—some time. As a sign of the times, a gold-framed motto, "In God We Trust," decorated our frontier home, and indeed in Him people trusted, somehow, to pull them through. There was nowhere else to turn for support in the days of rugged individualism before Franklin D. Roosevelt's New Deal introduced farm price supports, drouth relief, government handouts; and our country made an historic turn away from free enterprise and independence to the beginnings of the welfare state.

Life was comparatively simple in the United States when I arrived in the first decade of this century. America was at peace, the U.S. Treasury had a sizable surplus, there was no income tax, no inflation and the nation was just commencing to gear up as the superpower it was to become. For spectacular world news that wasn't bounced off a satellite in space, as is routine today, people excitedly read in the newspapers about Admiral Robert E. Peary's dog-team expedition that year to discover the North Pole.

The United States was then dominantly rural with some 11 million farm families eking out a living. The average city dweller earned about $13 for a six-day, 60-hour workweek, and prices were unbelievably low. Imagine an era when the current Sears & Roebuck catalog advertised coffee at 19 cents per pound, a washing machine for $5.62, a four-piece oak hand-carved bedroom set for $24.95 and a fine three-piece man's suit for $5.83. The telephone was still a novelty for most country folks, automobiles were primitive, just coming into use and Henry Ford advertised, "Any customer can have a car painted any color that he wants so long as it's black." There wasn't a bus, truck or electric refrigerator in the land, and no computers to foul up your magazine subscription or bank balance. Most folks didn't have a bank balance! People had other, more fundamental things to worry about, such as making ends meet and avoiding the dread diseases of tuberculosis, diptheria, smallpox, typhoid, and even the common cold, which quickly turned into pneumonia and killed untold thousands.

Even so, it was a good time to be alive, and I grew up in a rugged country with rugged, prideful people. (We had a few ne'er-do-wells and scoundrels, too!). It was the exciting gold-and-grass frontier of the miner, cattleman, cowboy, homesteader, pioneer, railroader, town builder, gambler and some captivating characters. It was a good time to be alive for another reason: We saw the West at its pristine best—long before the population pressures and pollution that we lament today—and Badger Clark, South Dakota's beloved cowboy poet, could autograph his book of poems for me with the aphorism, "I love my fellowman the best when he is scattered some." It was a time of different and more fundamental values, too. A time to be more neighborly and to share our concern for others; a time to unabashedly show pride in work and love of country; and above all, an epic time in our history when fiercely independent men and women pushed back the frontier, tamed mountains and prairies and wrested a living from one of the most bountiful but toughest pieces of real estate on earth.

Since the Plains Indians had now been defeated and driven off their sacred lands, there were no more Indian uprisings or scares during my childhood. Yet it was still easy to evoke the recent dramatic past. There was scout Jimmy Iron's grave on the ranch where I was born. Later on, our family—my parents and older half brother, Earl—moved to 320 acres of homesteaded and deeded land a few miles down the valley on Lower False Bottom Creek, and there as a child I was fascinated by the trapdoor that led to a secret hiding place directly beneath our living room floor. Here, the original homesteader, old Dan Powers, had hurriedly secreted himself during the Indian scares. When my mother wasn't around, I watched my chance to lift the trapdoor and disappear into the dark hideout, where I played I had narrowly escaped being scalped.

Until I walked three miles to country school at age six, I lived in my own obscure but wonderful world, where I played alone and entertained myself by the hour. I had no television, transistor radio or electronic games such as amuse and divert children today. Thankfully, as I grew up, I found it was a pretty good thing to be self-sufficient: to be able to dream and discover and entertain one's self; to live with excitement and wonder and to think interesting thoughts.

Altogether, it was a priceless experience growing up on the gold-and-grass frontier. Puddling in False Bottom Creek on a hot summer's day, I made dams, dredged out rivers and harbors and set sail with my paper boats for ports afar. Fishing with my old bamboo pole and worms, I hooked my first sucker and later learned the thrill of landing a fighting trout. My constant companion was my big shaggy Collie, Shep, who once dragged me out of the water when I fell off the foot-plank crossing the flooded creek. Whenever I disobeyed or got into trouble, I ran to old Shep for protection. He bared his teeth and with a deep throaty growl, held everyone at bay.

Unhappily, Shep began chasing alongside the passenger trains which ran through our ranch, and one day he was caught between the train and a pile of railroad ties stacked beside the tracks. He was mangled and died. It was my first brush with death and I cried unconsolably. I was beginning to sense dimly what George Graham Vest has expressed so well in his *Euology on the Dog*, "The one absolutely unselfish friend that a man can have in this selfish world, the one that never deserts him, the one that never proves ungrateful or treacherous is his dog."

This was the enthralling world of my boyhood, and I grew up with an exhilarating feeling of freedom and inquiry and adventure; of wonder about the sun, the moon and the stars; about the seasons and birth and death. As for sexuality, I learned it from our ranch animals in breeding season. We weren't overstimulated in my day by porno movies, drugs and hard rock.

Like all of our neighbors, our family experienced good times and bad. We knew both plenty and privation, and I learned to deal with disappointment and denial and be grateful for what I had. As a family, we reaped rich rewards. We gloried in the clean, earthy smell of freshly turned sod, the beauty of growing grain, the benediction of grass, the thrill of seeing a newborn calf struggle shakily to its feet and begin to suckle. And as a youth I had time to dream and build air castles about the boundless future and what it might hold for me beyond the hills and horizon.

Looking back now, I realize that growing up at this time in the storied Black Hills, I enjoyed the best of all boyhoods.

A Salute to All Pioneers
Plucky people! William Paul Friggens, English immigrant, and his California-born bride, Caroline Clemens Hosken, when they were married and homesteaded in the Black Hills. Like their neighbors, they waged a valiant struggle to settle a bit of the sacred soil of the Sioux, and their story is essentially the saga of all those who pioneered this bountiful land.

"It don't take long to sleep here!"

It is five o'clock on a beautiful summer morning, and already the sun is streaming through my window. I feel a big, rough hand gently shaking my shoulder. It's Father. "Time to get movin', old chap," he orders, and then joshes: "Today's Monday, tomorrow's Tuesday, next day's Wednesday. Half the week's gone and nothing done yet."

Father exemplified the work ethic so often scorned today. He was a hard-driving, hefty man, just under six feet, who walked with his head held high and shoulders erect. Handsome, with steady blue eyes, a high forehead and finely chiseled features set off by a carefully trimmed moustache, he had the military bearing of a British general. Although a cordial and friendly man, he was instinctively reserved and neighbors seldom called him Paul, but addressed him instead as "Mr. Friggens."

Now father was rousing me out of a sound sleep, and like any kid, I hated to get up. But jumping out of bed, I pulled on my overalls, blue work shirt, socks and shoes and hurried out to our lean-to kitchen. Mother, who was openly more affectionate and loving than my Father, greeted me with a big hug, and cheerily remarked, "Morning, Son. God's in His Heaven—All's right with the world," her favorite bit of verse from Browning. Mother was already preparing breakfast and the aroma of sage from the homemade sausage in the warming oven was mouth-watering. She handed me a pail of potato peelings and table scraps to feed the chickens, and I stepped out into the glorious morning—sparkling with dew on the cool, velvety grass and radiant with the rising sun. Feeding the chickens, I followed my father to the barn, where we pitched into almost an hour's chores before breakfast.

Thus began a typical 10- to 12-hour day on the ranch in our busiest season. Father, who customarily wore the big, wide-brimmed Stetson popular with ranchers of the time, and his work pants tucked into his high boots, looked first thing to his horses. He loved horses, possibly a trait he had inherited from England, where you were a lord if you owned a horse.

We kept three breeds of draft or workhorses on the ranch: the Clydesdale of Scotland, the French Percheron and the Belgian—all great heavy draft horses, standing 16 to 17 "hands" high (just under six feet), and weighing around 2,000 pounds. First, father curried his eight sleek workhorses, then fed them hay and grain, after which he threw on the heavy harness. When I was about 9 or 10, I was enlisted to help, and climbing up on the manger, I struggled to bridle old Prince, a big, handsome Clydesdale. But tossing his head high, Prince repeatedly foiled my attempts until I lost my balance and tumbled into the manger.

Before long, however, I had managed to bridle old Prince and the other high-spirited, beautiful animals, but little did I realize they were linked with romance and history. Much later, I was fascinated to learn that these prancing, plodding draft horses were direct descendants of the great war-horses that heavily armored knights of the Middle Ages rode into battle. The medieval hero, King Arthur, who held court with his wife, the lovely Guinevere, likely rode around Camelot on one of these spirited steeds; and his gallant knights Lancelot and Galahad mounted these fine equines to ride off in search of the Holy Grail. Now pulling my father's gang plow to break the virgin prairie, these slow-footed but powerful offspring provided a tremendous source of energy and indeed they put power into farming. American farmers owned about 20 million horses in 1910, worth from $200 to $300 a team. Significantly today, with the energy shortage, these great draft horses are no longer relegated to a bygone era, but are now selling for $3,000 a team to do small tractor work on some farms.

Having tended the horses, our next chore was milking. Squatting on spindly stools, we milked our five or six Holstein and Jersey dairy animals, while trying to dodge their lashing tails as they flicked the flies off their backs. But milking demands constant attention. Abruptly, a touchy cow with sore teats would slap me in the face with her wet, smelly tail, and then raising a hind leg, knock me off my stool and spill my pail of milk. However, as a kid, I found that milking also had its diversions, and whenever Father wasn't looking, I had an amusing time aiming a teat straight at our row of hungry barn cats and squirting the warm milk directly into their mouths. I derived another dividend from learning to milk: Mother said that the exercise would limber up my fingers to play the piano. For a time, I took music lessons from a long-suffering neighbor lady, but the milking never helped.

Lugging the morning's milk to the house in a five-gallon cream can (they've become collector's items today) we "separated" on our revolutionary new DeLaval cream separator. I was intrigued by this mechanical wonder. You poured the milk in at the top, turned the crank and skim milk came out of the bottom spout while the cream, being lighter, flowed from the

Four-horse teams, like these beautiful draft animals used here in discing, put real power into farming and by 1910 American farmers owned about 20 million "oatburners." — *South Dakota State Historical Society.*

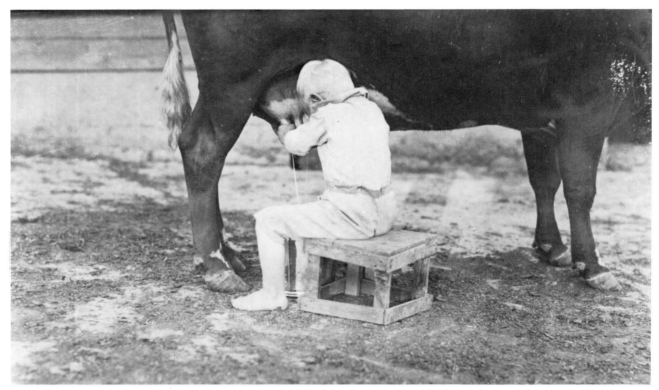

One of a farm kid's first jobs used to be milking. It looks easy here, but abruptly a touchy cow with sore teats might slap you in the face with her wet, smelly tail, kick you and then step in the milk pail. — *South Dakota State Historical Society.*

top spout. After separating, we finished the remaining chores: "slopping" the few hogs, cleaning the barns and oiling and readying our mowing machines before going into the field.

By now, I was starved, as only a kid with a bottomless pit in his stomach can be, and racing to the house, I hurriedly washed in the granite basin to join the family at the breakfast table. I dived into a bowl of oatmeal, followed by Mother's homemade sausage, fried eggs and newly baked bread with chokecherry jelly. Though times were tough and farm prices poor, we never missed a meal on the ranch. Probably, we ate too much meat, judging by today's nutritional requirements, but we worked it off. "Eat up!" Mother encouraged the hired hands. "Would you believe it, fresh eggs are only a dime a dozen at the St. Onge store," which prompted one of the men to observe: "Ma'am, at that price, it hain't worth the wear and tear on an old hen's rear end to lay eggs these days."

Blushing a bit, Mother remarked, "You're quite right, Mr. Howell," and passed off the earthy comment. But the family all had a hearty laugh when we were alone. We liked to laugh. Father relished a good joke, although I seldom saw him shake with a real belly laugh. Mother, on the other hand, literally laughed until she cried and my older brother Earl who was easygoing and good dispositioned, was easily convulsed, too. Thus, we had jolly meals and neighbors dropping in for a visit, relaxed and laughed with us. I think that being able to laugh at herself, throughout life, helped my mother to live to be nearly 90.

Mother sent us away from the breakfast table well-fed for the morning, after which I stuffed my pockets with oatmeal cookies and ran to join the menfolks before seven o'clock in the hayfields. One of my first jobs at about age 12 was mowing Father's purple-blossomed, rippling fields of alfalfa with a two-horse team; a far cry indeed from today's fancy farming in which the operator rides in the glass-enclosed, air-conditioned cab of a complicated behemoth that mows and windrows, bales or chops the hay in a single, speedy operation.

But I enjoyed no such comfort and efficiency. Instead, my job was downright dangerous! I drove a team and sat on a mowing machine geared to a five-foot sickle bar equipped with sharp, serrated teeth that whizzed back and forth, cutting the hay in wide swaths. But unexpectedly hitting a prairie dog hole or bumping over an irrigation ditch, you could be thrown from your seat and pitched in front of the flashing sickle bar. Also, you had to be careful to throw the mower out of gear before oiling or touching the sickle or you might lose a few fingers. Another danger was skittish horses. Suddenly a bee or horsefly might sting one of your animals, the team would bolt, sending the whizzing sickle bar into a shrill hum or scream, and you were in

danger of having a runaway. It happened to me, but hanging on to the reins for dear life and yelling "Whoa Pete, whoa Bess," I finally halted the team and avoided a disaster. Aside from these dangers, mowing was a pleasant enough job, making round after round on a summer day and breathing the sweet aroma of the new mown hay. Riding out to check my progress, Father sometimes praised me and I grew up with a feeling of new-found importance.

Our haying operation was equally antiquated and inefficient by today's highly mechanized standards. We mowed, raked into windrows and then bunched the hay, after which we bucked it into the stacker with our two-horse sweep. The stacker was an ancient affair by means of which we lifted the hay on elevated tracks or rails and dumped it to the sweating men on the stack. The stacker was powered by old Pete, a draft horse, hitched to a long cable on a pulley. Pete elevated the hay by rails to the stack. One of my first jobs, as stacker boy, was to lead old Pete up and back as we dumped each load and then lowered the clumsy stacker contraption.

Now three hours' labor in the hot hayfields, with the mercury hovering above 90 degrees, is dirty, exhausting work and about mid-morning Father usually signalled for the men to come down off the stack and for everybody to "take five." Trudging a mile or more across the alfalfa stubble, Mother arrived with a refreshing gallon can of ice-cold lemonade and a plate of cookies to tide us over until the noon hour. Thus fortified, we resumed stacking, the menfolk taking turns at the stifling hot job and watching out for any rattlesnakes dumped with the hay. I remember my brother, Earl, forking into a pile of hay that had nearly buried him, and shouting, "There's a rattler up here that just slid down my back!" He wasn't bitten.

Promptly at noon, we unhooked, fed and watered our horses and then hurried to the house for *dinner*— no light lunch! Following Father's usual practice, I pumped ice-cold well water on my sweaty hands and arms and felt a delightful cooling sensation. Then we sat down to a hearty meal of roast beef, roasting ears and apple pie. Afterward, we stretched out for a half hour under the huge elm tree by our house to snooze or listen to the hired men spin tall tales. Farm labor was easy to come by in those rugged days before food stamps and welfare. "Riding the rods" of the slow freights through our ranch, a drifter would hop off and go to work for a dollar a day and board. They were young men and old, educated and illiterate, some good workers but more loafers, while occasionally I suspect we hired a fugitive from the law. Whoever they were, these widely traveled, likable "bums," as we called them, brought the flavor of the outside world to our door, and I listened entranced to their often funny and even weird yarns. There was, for example, our two-fisted eater, Bud Pea, who packed away tremendous meals and was still lean as a hound dog. Bud got to talking about an Arkansas tornado. "Yes, sir," he regaled us, "after the storm passed we heard a rooster crowing up in the hayloft. Well, we climbed up there to look and the crowing seemed to come from a demijohn (gallon jug) that was blown up by the tornado. Sure enough, the old rooster was trapped inside. We had to smash the demijohn to get him out. He wasn't hurt none, but he didn't have a feather left on him!" After the noon meal and a few such stories we returned to the hayfield.

Meanwhile, back at the ranch house, Mother was putting in a prodigious day of her own. After breakfast, she cleared the table and washed the dishes, then painstakingly washed and scalded the cream separator with its score of different sharpened discs, so that our cream would not sour. Next, she tackled a monstrous Monday washing, which she sorted into three piles—the white things, colored things, overalls and rags. By 10 o'clock, she had turned out four machinefuls on her hand-powered washer with old-fashioned wringer and hung them out to dry. Now she hurried to catch a couple of her big Rhode Island Red chickens to prepare for the evening meal.

To begin with, Mother had watchfully hatched these spring chickens in a kerosene-heated incubator. Now, since the menfolk were not handy, she ran down the fleet-footed fryers in the barnyard, snaring them with a noose on the end of a stout wire. Next, she whacked off the birds' heads on the chopping block, after which she scalded the chickens, plucked the feathers, removed the entrails, cut up and washed the chicken parts before cooking. I wonder how many city women would be able to kill and dress a chicken today!

Now in the peace and quiet of the afternoon, Mother washed dishes again, brought in the dry clothes and sprinkled them, trimmed the wicks, washed the glass chimneys and filled the kerosene lamps. Another chore was to hang cloth strips above the kitchen screen to ward off hordes of flies, a constant bane of existence in a farm home. Next, she proceeded out to weed the garden and gather fresh vegetables. On the way back, she picked up the eggs, and returning to the house she set about preparing the third big meal of the day: her fried chicken for supper. Come what may, we always ate three big meals a day on the ranch. "Nice for the husbands but death to the wives," an early woman columnist lamented in *Farm Journal* magazine. "Nobody but a farmer's wife knows what a cavernous region there is under a farmer's vest; nobody knows so well as she how much stuff it takes to keep him from caving in. The farmer's wife has really no time to call her own. Her position smacks of serfdom."

I am sure that my father, like most men in those days, took all this for granted with little or no thought of the woman's labor involved. Take the occasion of my parents' wedding anniversary. Beaming that morning, my mother asked, "Paul, do you know what day this is?" Characteristically, he didn't remember the occasion.

"Well, it's our anniversary," Mother reminded ruefully.

"So it is, my dear," said Father. "Why don't you catch a couple of chickens for dinner and we'll celebrate."

Like Mother, the haying crew labored late this summer day. We plodded homeward about seven o'clock—sweaty horses and tired men. The sun was just beginning to set, a great red fireball in the West, and would soon leave the world, as the poet penned, "to darkness and to me." While the menfolks unharnessed, watered and fed the horses I rode bareback on my pony, High Moon, to fetch the milk cows from the back pasture. Then we milked again and finished the evening chores. My last job was to shut the chicken coop to keep out marauding weasels. We used to laugh about the story of the farmer who forgot to shut the hen house. During the night he heard a commotion among the chickens, and still in his nightshirt, he grabbed his shotgun and hurried to investigate. As he peered in the door, his old dog cold-nosed him. The farmer jumped, blasted away, and killed a dozen of his wife's fat hens!

At last, about eight o'clock, we sat down to a hearty meal of fried chicken, freshly baked bread, mashed potatoes with chicken gravy, and lettuce from the garden served with sour cream, sugar and vinegar. We topped it all off with delicious coconut cream pie. At this point, Father, contently patting his stomach, pushed back his plate to announce: "We're going to ship some steers in the morning and I want to move 'em to Redwater Siding before it gets too hot. So better turn in early. We'll roll our tails about four o'clock."

"Hell," grumbled the new hired man as he left the table, "it sure don't take long to sleep here," which is how it was working for Father.

The Winter It Snowed "Five Foot Wide"

The sun that brief December day
Rose cheerless over hills of gray
And, darkly circled, gave at noon
A sadder light than waning moon.

Snugly bundled up to trudge three miles cross-country to our one-room school, I stepped that morning into a wintry world reminiscent of the poet Whittier's immortal *Snowbound*. The hard snow crunched underfoot, the sullen gray sky was ominous and by noon it had begun to snow again; first, a few flurries, which then turned into a wild, gusty storm; seemingly blowing from everywhere with the shifting winds. At noon, we huddled around the big potbellied stove in the schoolhouse to eat our cold lunches, while our teacher paced the floor watching the weather.

"Children," she announced as we returned to our desks, "I think it's storming too bad for you to go home alone, and so we'll hold school until your folks come to get you." There was no telephone, no way to quickly communicate with the dozen or more widely scattered families in Todd School District, and of course, no radio or television storm watch such as we have to warn people today. But, intuitively, ranch folks learn to keep an eye on the fickle weather, and in due time wary parents commenced arriving in buggies, sleighs and on horseback to take their children home early. It was the beginning of the kind of howling blizzard that even to this day blocks country roads and highways, maroons farms and ranches and takes a devastating toll of unsheltered livestock.

But huddled under a great buffalo robe, and skimming swiftly over the snowy fields in Father's homemade sleigh or "pung"—a crude box on runners—I reveled in the mounting storm and powdery snow the horses kicked up in our faces. Safely back home at the ranch, we stabled the horses and set about doing the evening chores. I had two daily tasks: lug in firewood for our two stoves and fill the reservoir (hot water tank) on the kitchen stove. Meanwhile, Father and my brother Earl milked in a cold, drafty barn, bedded down the cows and horses on fresh straw and carried the evening's milk to the house to run through our cream separator.

The storm howled all through the night and Father, getting up every hour or two, kept a roaring fire with wood gathered on the ranch, together with a few big chunks of coal, while the mercury plunged below zero. By morning, our homesteader's abode, **really a** flimsy four-room shack with a lean-to kitchen, was so cold that the windows had frozen over solid, ice stood in the wash basin and frost glistened on the outside bedroom walls. If we had owned a thermostat, it would have run out of degrees. That was an energy crunch to remember!

The poets rhapsodize over the wonders of winter—"Oh! the snow, the beautiful snow, filling the sky and the earth below"—and indeed it is beautiful to behold. Consider the marvel of the snowflake, which always appears as a tiny, six-sided shimmering ice crystal. But no two crystals are exactly alike. And there is the breathless beauty of the bubbling brook, now delicately filigreed with arabesque borders etched in blue-white ice. But you should have to slog through the ice and snow on a frigid winter morning to reach the outdoor privy! It's 20 degrees below zero, and dusting a small drift off the icy seat, you gingerly reach for a few pages from the Sears & Roebuck catalog and get it over with. Like James Whitcomb Riley in his celebrated ode to the outhouse, "We tarried not, nor lingered long . . . "

The storm temporarily abated, and the scene the next morning, as novelist Rose Wilder Lane wrote about another South Dakota blizzard, was overpowering, "Air and sun and snow were the whole visible world." But the gritty pioneers, unaccustomed to the insulated houses, warmer winter clothing and storm warnings that protect us today, stolidly faced the perils and discomforts of a prairie blizzard. As old Joe, a French Canadian bullwhacker in St. Onge, scoffed: "Paul, this is *no* storm at all. I remember Can-a-da. Up there, she snow five *foot wide!*"

Shoveling out next morning, it appeared we had matched Canada. A huge drift blocked our kitchen door. The woodpile was transformed into a shapeless white mound and the fence was covered with three- to five-foot drifts. Breaking a path to the barn, we fed the horses and milked, filled a dish of warm milk for the scrambling cats, chopped holes in the ice-bound creek so the animals could drink, and we carried fresh water and feed to the chickens and hogs. Then braving the bone-chilling wind, we hurried back to the house to warm ourselves around the kitchen range before breakfast.

Mother was inordinately proud of her nickel-plated, ornamented kitchen range, designed to burn either wood or coal and equipped with a warming oven and a 28-quart reservoir to store hot water: price, $21.50 from Sears & Roebuck Co., Chicago. Keeping a box of corn cobs handy, she quickly started a fire, but it fell to me to keep the big, yawning woodbox full. Standing at our ice-sheathed, ancient pump, I drew well water to fill the kitchen range reservoir as well. Looking back now, it seems that a good part of our lives turned around the all-purpose kitchen range. Mother cooked, baked and heated water for everyday use. Hurrying in from the cold, we sat around the open oven to warm our feet, and to dry our wet mittens and soggy socks. Filling a tub with warm water, we bathed in front of the kitchen range on Saturday nights. Now, sitting so as to warm our backs by the hot stove, we tackled a memorable breakfast of pancakes and pork chops.

Unlike the average American family shopping two or three times a week at the supermarket, we laid in most of our staples for the winter. Each fall with the coming of frost, it was butchering time when we slaughtered a beef or two and two or three hogs for winter eating. Dispatching a young beef with a .22 rifle, we quickly bled, skinned and dressed the animal, after which we left the carcass hanging all night to cool thoroughly. To butcher a 200-pound hog, we heated a huge cast-iron kettle over a blazing fire, where we scalded the animal to remove the hair and scrape the hide. Then we dressed it and pulled it high by block and tackle to cool. Hauling the carcass down, Father expertly quartered the meat, carved out hams and bacon, and trimmed off the excess fat, while Mother made sausage, head cheese, pickled pig's feet and rendered the lard. Some difference from the self-serve, prepackaged costly meat you buy now. But then Americans were infinitely more independent, frugal and resourceful than we are today.

Since all roads were blocked by the storm and there was no school, I eagerly climbed on the hayrack with Father and Earl to feed some 150 head of Hereford or "white-face" cattle that Father had wintered along sheltered Lower False Bottom Creek. Though the snow had stopped, the temperature hovered around zero, and with the icy, biting wind, the chill factor was probably 30-below zero. While I drove our faithful team, Prince and Bess, Father and Earl pitched off the still green, leafy alfalfa hay to the cattle. "Come boss, come old boss," Father used to call in his stentorian voice and the brawling, hungry animals came running to feed. The older cows looked all ganted up in the bitter cold, and I noticed they always stood with their backs arched to the raw wind. At length, we

finished feeding, and then driving to one of the haystacks we had put up the previous summer, we loaded up in the bitter wind for the next day's feeding. Back at the corrals, Father was greatly concerned to find a young heifer, that had unfortunately been bred too early, was now dropping her calf. He quickly saw that without help she would lose it in the bitter cold, so hurrying with some gunnysacks, he rubbed the spindly, shivering newborn until it was dry, then tried to help it to its feet to suckle.

"No use," Father shook his head after repeated attempts. "We've got to drench it," and wrapping the calf in gunnysacks like a blanket, he hurried to the house. Mother quickly filled a quart bottle with warm milk, added a touch of ginger and Father forced the feeding down the calf's throat or "drenched" it. He then placed the animal in front of the open oven to revive. By nightfall it appeared the calf would live and Mother put it to bed in a big wooden box behind the stove. Next morning the calf was standing up and Father returned it to the heifer. She sniffed suspiciously and then accepted it. I remember my Father keeping vigil all night in the big cattle shed to save both cows and calves, or bringing a litter of baby pigs to be warmed back to life by our kitchen range. No labor, no effort was too great for my pioneer parents to save every animal, and harvest every bit of crop in order to survive. In God they trusted, but as my father used to say, "The Lord helps those who help themselves, and we've been pretty damn busy down here on our own."

At nightfall, I hurried to fill the empty woodbox again, pumped from the well to replenish the stove reservoir and at last sat down to eat supper with usual relish. Then hurrying from the table, I helped with the supper dishes, for now I looked forward to the most exciting time of the day—the family fun and entertainment. My biggest thrill was playing our wondrous new talking machine, Mr. Edison's phonograph, that the inventor didn't think would amount to much. Our machine, advertised in the Sears & Roebuck catalog as a "graphophone" at $14.95, was a small, oblong, highly-polished brown box, fitted with a huge, brass-rimmed "flower horn" and hand-wound spring that played a scratchy, cylindrical wax record. It always opened with the nasal announcement, "Edison Record." You could hear the wind-up motor humming above the sound of the music, and if you didn't wind the machine frequently, it would run down in the middle of a song.

But keeping the motor tightly wound, I played such popular band selections as John Philip Sousa's "Stars and Stripes Forever" march, for which, incidentally, he sold the rights for $90. For laughs, we split our sides listening to "Uncle Josh and the Lightning Rod Agent" and the witty sallies of the

Wintering cattle in blizzards and sub-zero weather is part of the struggle of ranching and losses can run high. The prudent rancher here is rounding up his herd and heading for shelter before the howling storm strikes in full fury. — *South Dakota State Historical Society.*

"Arkansas Traveler"; and for only 18 cents a record we greatly enjoyed the then current hits: "Bill Bailey," Hello Central! Give Me Heaven," "Hot Time in the Old Town Tonight," and "Meet Me in St. Louis, Louis." By the time I was listening to the phonograph, it was recording both popular and classical music for millions isolated as we were on the farms and ranches of America.

At length, the winter storms stretched into Christmas, with no rural mail delivery, while the passenger and freight trains used snowplows to clear the tracks through our ranch. But unhindered by snow, Santa Claus was certain to arrive, and a little boy waited with starry-eyed expectancy. Father had cut a pine tree up in the hills, and we strung popcorn, cookies and homemade ornaments. But the big thrill was lighting the tree on Christmas eve. Mother and Dad touched a match to the wax candles and then stood by to guard against fire. The candles glowed for only a few minutes, but golly, what a spectacle!

And then in the early morning, I was awakened to welcome Santa Claus—the first time I had ever seen the *real* Santa. He wore a great buffalo-hide coat, said little and carried three presents: a gleaming red train engine, a pair of boy's lined leather mittens and a rare treat—an orange. Strange, but it was years before I realized that Santa's buffalo-hide coat was exactly like my brother Earl's.

Digging out at last from the deep snows after

Christmas, father drove six miles to St. Onge in our big sled to stock up on staples and another load of coal. While he chatted with storekeeper, Charley Furois, I helped myself to a stack of free folders in a rack advertising the exciting new farm equipment. There was the mechanical manure spreader, so you didn't have to pitch it off, yourself. While Father fertilized his irrigated lower fields to grow more alfalfa and corn and potatoes, spreading the manure was still one of the hardest jobs on the ranch, and I thought how wonderful it would be to run a machine that did your work while you just sat there and drove the team.

Then my eye caught two really big wonders: pictures of the first lumbering tractors that they claimed would do about the same work as two men with four-horse teams; and a sensational new motor "buggy," built for country roads, that foreshadowed the automobile down on the farm.

That would be my futuristic world, and I wondered whether someday I would be running some of these wondrous machines and maybe seeing the faraway factories, pictured on the folders, where they were built. Riding back home with Father on the sled, I talked about this, and later I dreamed about it. "Nothing happens unless first a dream," the poet Carl Sandburg wrote, and I've always been grateful for the chance to dream and to grow during those long winter evenings when it snowed "five *foot wide*" on the ranch.

One-room country school in South Dakota was a crude experience, and "schoolmarms" had one of the loneliest, hardest jobs on earth with next-to-nothing pay. But all honor to these long-suffering teachers who started the fires, swept the floors and taught us all they could, forever touching our lives. — *South Dakota State Historical Society.*

School opens my window on the world

You could tell by the smoke curling from the leaning brick chimney on a frigid winter morning that the teacher, Miss Wilson, was there, had built a roaring fire and would be holding classes today in our one-room country school. Rural school teachers on the Black Hills frontier were expected to arrive early, start a fire, sweep the floor, tidy up the place and have the drafty, dreary schoolroom reasonably comfortable by the time the children arrived afoot and on horseback.

A country "schoolmarm," as they were called in those days, had one of the loneliest, hardest jobs on earth with next-to-nothing pay—usually about $30 a month. Customarily, she boarded and roomed with a ranch family and walked to school. Todd school was sequestered just off a dirt road in a cow pasture—"A ragged beggar sleeping"—and in the days when South Dakota was still upgrading its rural school system, attending Todd was a primitive experience indeed. The original school was a ramshackle frame building with cracked plaster walls, through which the wind whistled, while snow drifted in through the woodpecker holes. "Why aren't you doing you work, Paul?" Miss Wilson confronted me one day while I was drawing a horse. "I can't," I said. "It's snowing on my paper." The room was lighted by four fly-specked windows with well-worn shades, and the floor was rough boards full of slivers.

It was a conventional schoolroom such as was seen on the frontier 75 years ago. At the front stood the teacher's desk with her school bell, a globe, Webster's big unabridged dictionary and the blackboard. Seating for some 15 to 25 children, depending on the season, was graduated from primary to adult-size desks. Up front, the little tykes sat at their small desks, and the older children occupied larger desks at the rear. These were deeply pitted by the rowdy older boys, who delighted in carving their jack-knifed initials on everything and in bullying the teacher. To protect her legs from the knee-deep snows, one teacher wore a heavy pair of bloomers under her dress. Taking them off before school commenced, she hung them up to dry by the stove. Came St. Patrick's Day and the rowdies ran the green bloomers up the flagpole to billow in the wind.

Our schoolroom was heated by a large potbellied stove, around which we gathered to eat lunch on the coldest winter days. We lined up our tin lunch buckets along the wall behind the stove, and my lunch usually consisted of a roast beef or pork sandwich, a sweet pickle, an apple and some cookies or cake. But kids used to steal some of my "fancy" lunch, while others came to school with little or no lunch at all. One bedraggled girl used to bring a boiled goose egg: "More to 'em," she explained.

Sanitation was no big worry. We had a water pail with one long-handled dipper from which all the kids drank. Thus we democratically shared every germ from coughs and colds to measles and chicken pox. And here in this solitary room, the young, inexperienced teacher (often little older than some of the lanky 16- and 18-year-old pupils who came to school only after working in the fall harvest) was expected to teach all eight grades and start us on the high road to life.

It was a perpetual Babel and nearly impossible task. First thing in the morning, we lined up at the front of the room and, accompanied by our teacher on a wheezy, foot-pedal organ, we sang such stirring songs as "Columbia, the Gem of the Ocean," "Carry Me Back to Old Virginny," and "Massa's in the Cold, Cold Ground." That was before integration. Next, we returned to our seats for individual instruction and recitation, and I was enthralled as the older children stood up to recite such favorites as Longfellow's *Village Blacksmith*. There was one earnest but struggling boy who never got things right. One verse reads, as I recall:

> And children coming home from school
> Look in at the open door;
> They love to see the flaming forge,
> And hear its bellows roar.

Raymond started out all right, but apparently he had not understood all the words. So now, standing up to recite, he panicked and blurted out:

> The children love to look
> in at the open door
> And hear his bowels roar.

I used to panic for a different reason—I stammered. Mother said I began to stammer after a crazy old sheepherder on a neighboring ranch, wearing a sheep's pelt over his head and brandishing a club, chased me on my way home from school. It gave me nightmares. Or maybe I stammered because I was just a serious-minded, high-strung youngster. In any event, I tensed up when I was summoned to recite and fighting to utter a single syllable, I became the laughingstock of the school. It got so that kids even laughed as soon as I stood up to recite. But when they mimicked me out on the playground, I got fighting mad, waded into them—and talked without difficulty. Years later, a sympathetic speech teacher would coach me in debate and oratory, and like the orator Demosthenes, who overcame his handicap by shouting above the roar of the ocean waves with his mouth full of pebbles, I orated to the horses while I cultivated corn. Catching me unawares one day, Father overheard me and was furious because I had let the horses wander and plowed out several hills of good corn plants.

Despite my anxiety and even anguish over stammering, I profited by my one-room school experience. I was determined to overcome my affliction, and I think I was actually motivated to read better and to learn my multiplication tables faster by listening to the other children recite. But also, I owe a lot to the poorly-paid, but long-suffering teachers, who could rarely stick it out more than a year or two at Todd school. They helped the little ones on with their overshoes, joined in the games and our snowball fights and endeavored to teach us all they could under the most trying conditions.

I'm also grateful for the sheer, carefree joy we had in country school: idling through the fields; listening to the meadowlarks' song; and splashing, barefooted in the creek on our way home; romping with the other children and playing the popular games, Blind Man's Bluff and Pump, Pump Pullaway. A painfully shy sixth-grader, I was sweet on a pert, freckle-nosed girl, but I could scarcely summon the courage to speak or even look at her.

The high point of the year was the Christmas play, for which we all practiced several weeks. Came the thrilling night when everybody gathered at the schoolhouse to see their young ones perform. (Father thoughtfully blanketed our horses standing outside in the bitter cold.) Earlier, we had drawn names and now, after the play, we exchanged homemade presents, while Santa Claus arrived with his heaping bag of goodies to hand out stick candy and nuts. I treasure other memories of school picnics and the long, lazy fall and spring days when we raced out at recess time to play games, pick wild flowers, walk in the woods or hunt gophers.

Gopher hunting! Now there was a thrilling pastime. Gopher holes abounded around the schoolgrounds, and organizing a daily hunt, the older boys enlisted us little fellows to fetch the water from the creek in tin pails. The game was to pour water down the hole, drown out the gopher and force it up on top, whereupon the boys descended with sticks, baseball bats or anything handy. How the wildlife conservationists would frown on this mayhem today!

Dutifully working up from lowly water boy to big-game hunter, I followed one of the older boys one day on a gopher safari. Suddenly, I heard him shout: "Here's where one's been duggin!" We drowned out a big one and that kid never lived down the nickname. He's affectionately known by his friends as 'Duggin'" to this day—no tribute to our grammar teaching to be sure, but a delightful reminiscence.

At length, the school board abandoned the old Todd school and erected a spanking one-room building on a new site, complete with furnace, sanitary drinking facility, separate toilets for boys and girls and a horsebarn to shelter our animals. By now, South Dakota's school officials had vastly upgraded the curriculum and teacher training, and I was making commendable progress when I became seriously ill and was rushed home with the dread influenza or "flu" that killed tens of thousands during the 1918–19 epidemic. Worldwide, about 20 million persons died—more than lost their lives during World War I. Unable to get a doctor, Mother plastered my chest with a poultice of raw onions, fed me plenty of liquids and fruit, and after a 10-day delirium, I slowly recovered. Graduating from the eighth grade, I rode horseback six miles each way to attend ninth grade at the St. Onge school. I completed high school in the rip-roarin' old cow town, Belle Fourche, once the greatest livestock shipping point in the world.

I have had many teachers through the years, but very few who genuinely motivated and inspired me, and only one who enchanted me with the lure of faraway places, instilled love of language and taught me lights to live by. A sweet-faced, brown-eyed woman, usually wearing a dark, ankle-length dress with a businesslike yellow pencil thrust through her luxuriant hair, Laura Rhodes McCutchen was a homesteader's daughter who taught high school English and foreign languages in Belle Fourche. In a day when almost no one from our country town had the time or money to travel, Mrs. McCutchen, or "Lady Mac" as we called her, hoarded her modest earnings and over the years managed to travel to every state, Europe, the Orient and around the world. She was something of a hometown sensation, enjoying wide respect, support of school board and parents. She was rare even in her day.

In her sunny classroom, in our small-town high school, the English teacher had hung imposing photos of the Acropolis in Athens and the Colosseum in Rome; and standing tall and straight, for she was a demanding disciplinarian who abhorred slouchy posture as she did sloppy minds, she captivated us with her world travels. "And someday," she would close, "who knows, but you will travel to Greece and Rome and faraway places, too, and you must be prepared to know what you are seeing." She taught us the old Spanish proverb, "He who would bring home the wealth of the Indies, must carry the wealth of the Indies with him." And so Lady Mac took us to the fabled Aegean Sea as we studied Homer's *Iliad* and the *Odyssey*, and we walked hand-in-hand with her through the Holy Land when we studied the Bible as literature. She taught us reverence for the Twenty-third Psalm and introduced us to one of the most beautiful passages in the Bible, Isaiah 40:31—"They that wait upon the Lord shall renew their strength; they shall mount up with wings as eagles; they shall run and not be weary; they shall walk and not faint."

But Lady Mac's most lasting contribution, I think, was her unique Literary Alphabet. This was a selection of famous quotations and classical allusions, one for each letter of the alphabet, which we were required to memorize and be ready to recite on a moment's notice. "Paul, give me the verse for A," she might request as I entered her classroom, whereupon I would respond, "Abstain from all appearance of evil—*Bible, First Thessalonians*, by Paul."

Or she might greet you with a demand to recite the verse and author for H, which was a stanza from William Cullen Bryant's beautiful poem, *To a Waterfowl*:

> He who from zone to zone
> Guides through the boundless sky
> Thy certain flight,
> In the long way that I must tread alone
> Will lead my steps aright.

Throughout the years, I have found these gems inspiriting to recall. Often I repeat Emerson, "Every day is the best day of the year;" and in my dealings with people, I am greatly mindful of the wisdom in verse R, "Remember that when you are right, you can afford to keep your temper, and when you are wrong, you can't afford to lose it." That's Plato.

And so I treasure Lady Mac's priceless Literary Alphabet, and these days when I jet across the continent, I find it good mental exercise and freshly inspiring to run through all 26 quotations from A to Z. I realize that today's educators scoff at such memorization as mechanical rote and old hat, but I wish that every high school in the country would require something like it before sloppy teaching and television cause us to lose our love of literature and command of the English language altogether. As Lady Mac so aptly quoted Bacon, "Reading maketh a full man."

Driving down the street on a visit to Belle Fourche, I last glimpsed my old teacher on a bitter winter morning as she trudged through the snow to tutor Spanish and French classes at the local high school. Head bowed, braving the wintry blast, she appeared old, feeble and weary. She was 76. Just two months later, she passed away, and I thought of her lasting gifts to me and how she had opened my window on the world. I suppose, as author John Steinbeck said of his own inspiring mentor, "that to a large extent I am the unsigned manuscript of that teacher. What deathless power lies in the hands of such a person."

HARNESS DEPARTMENT.

WE INVITE ATTENTION to our very complete Harness and Saddlery Department. On this line of goods we undersell the retail dealer by a big margin, as in most cases our prices to you are less than the prices at which manufacturers and jobbers sell to the ordinary retail dealer. It is no exaggeration for us to say that WE CAN SAVE YOU FROM 35 TO 50 PER CENT on these goods, besides giving you a LARGER assortment and a BETTER grade of merchandise than is found in the regular harness stores in other towns.

WE HANDLE THE VERY BEST OF HARNESS that is possible to be made. Our harness is made of the very best of **high grade leather with fine trimmings.** Our single and double buggy harness is of the **very latest styles** and the trimmings the very best nickel composition or **Davis rubber trimmings. Our Farm, Team and Concord Harness is of the very best that can be made, and we invite the closest comparison of quality and price.**

OUR ONLY TERMS ARE CASH WITH THE ORDER. **We have discontinued C. O. D. shipments purely in the interest of our customers in order to do away with an expense, which saving permits us to make lower prices than ever, as fully explained on page 1 of this catalogue. Our Harness and Saddlery Goods are fully guaranteed by us.** We know they are reliable and just as we describe them. If you order anything from this department and it does not prove entirely satisfactory in every particular, simply return it to us and we will return your money pleasantly, together with what you paid for transportation. Our motto is: **"Entire satisfaction or your money back."**

NOTICE. **WE WILL MAKE ANY CHANGE** you want in any of our team harness you may order from our catalogue, and only charge you what it costs us to make such changes, except where we say no changes made.

ALWAYS STATE the parts you want in place of the ones which are listed with the harness. **ALWAYS STATE** the size of collar wanted when ordering the harness with collars or in ordering sweat pads; if you want a harness without the collar always state the size of hames it will require to fit your collar. **ALWAYS STATE** the kind of checks wanted, whether overchecks or side checks. **IF YOU DO NOT STATE** the kind of check wanted, we will send you overcheck. **ALWAYS STATE** the style of the harness you want, whether single or double, also the kind of trimmings, whether XC, nickel or imitation rubber. **ALWAYS STATE** the weight of your horse. Give us the measurement of your horse around girth where saddle or pad work, and from gig saddle to horse's tail. The size of bridle from bit ring to bit ring over the head, and state style of horse, if long ranged or short chunky horse.

HARNESS DEALERS, LIVERY MEN, **everyone interested in these goods, is invited to compare our prices with what they have been paying for equal goods.** Many goods we list dealers can buy from us at less money than they have been paying jobbers and wholesalers. Look carefully over our very complete line of **blankets, fly nets, dusters, robes, etc. Nowhere will you find as complete an assortment, nowhere will you be able to match our low prices.**

NOTE. **EXTRAS: Russet Hand Parts** on any harness over $8.00, **25 cents** extra. **Extra for Buckles on Crupper on Single Harness, 15 cents; Double Harness, 30 cents.**

WE MAKE NO CHARGE FOR BOXING, CRATING, PACKING OR CARTAGE, BUT DELIVER ALL GOODS AT ANY EXPRESS OFFICE OR FREIGHT DEPOT IN CHICAGO FREE OF CHARGE.

Single Breast Collar Buggy Harness.

WE MAKE NO CHANGES IN THIS HARNESS.

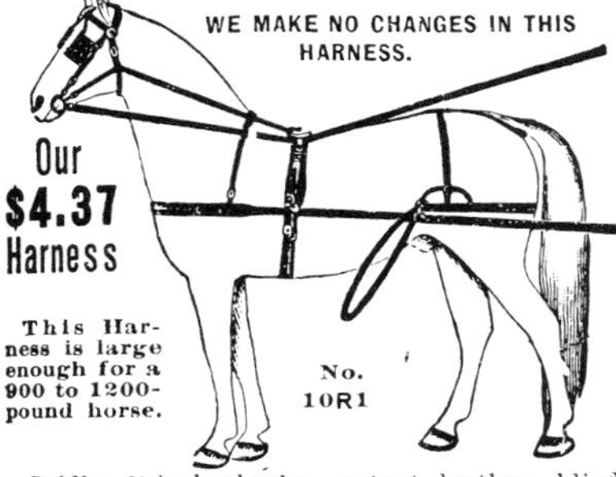

Our $4.37 Harness

This Harness is large enough for a 900 to 1200-pound horse.

No. 10R1

Bridle, 5/8-inch checks, patent leather blinds, flat winker brace and check reins, ring bit, fancy front and rosettes, overcheck or side reins, as desired; **lines,** 3/4-inch flat, all black, to loop in bit; **breast collar,** folded and stitched; **saddle,** 2½-inch, enameled cloth bottom, doubled and stitched bearers; **shaft tugs,** 1-inch with 7/8-inch buckles and 3/4-inch bellyband billets; **bellyband,** 7/8-inch flat; **breeching,** folded and stitched, 5/8-inch flat hip strap, 3/4-inch turn back, lapped and stitched to crupper pieces, folded crupper, docks sewed on breeching straps, 3/4-inch; **traces,** 1-inch doubled and stitched to breast collar. This single buggy harness comes in full XC trimmings, imitation hand sewed. **Shipping weight, 12 pounds.**

No. 10R1 Price....................**$4.37**

Our Texas Single Harness, $4.90.

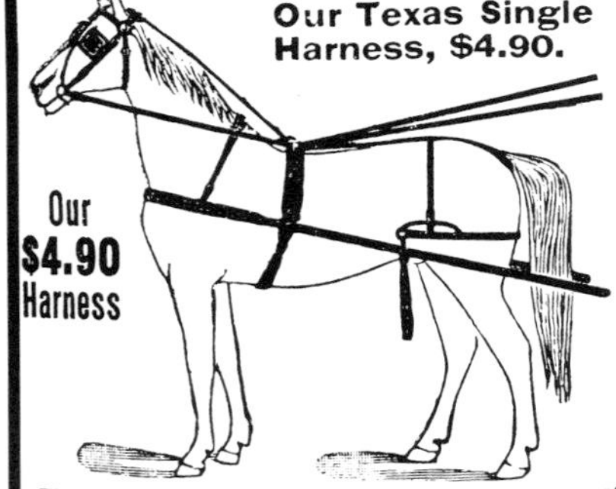

Our $4.90 Harness

This harness is full size; a cheaper harness must be made smaller size. This harness will be large enough for a 900 to 1200-pound horse. Don't buy a cheaper single harness than this one. We don't make any changes in this harness.

Bridle, 5/8-inch checks, patent leather blinds, flat winker brace and check reins, ring bit, fancy front and rosettes; overcheck or side reins, as desired; **lines,** 3/4-inch flat, all black, to loop in bit; **breast collar,** folded and stitched; **gig saddle,** 2½-inch, enameled cloth bottom, doubled and stitched bearers; **shaft tugs,** 1-inch with 7/8-inch buckles and 3/4-inch bellyband billets; **bellyband,** 7/8-inch flat; **breeching,** folded and stitched, 5/8-inch flat hip strap, 3/4-inch turn back, lapped and stitched to crupper pieces, folded crupper, docks sewed on breeching straps, 3/4-inch; **traces,** 1-inch doubled and stitched to breast collar. This single buggy harness comes in full XC trimmings, imitation hand sewed.

No. 10R5 Price (**Weight, about 12 lbs.**)....**$4.90**

No. 10R10 Same as the description of No. 10R5 with the exception of collar and hames in place of breast collar, kip collar, any size, traces attached to hames. Price **$6.25**

State size of collar wanted. **Weight, about 18 lbs.**

Our Georgia Single Harness, $7.69.

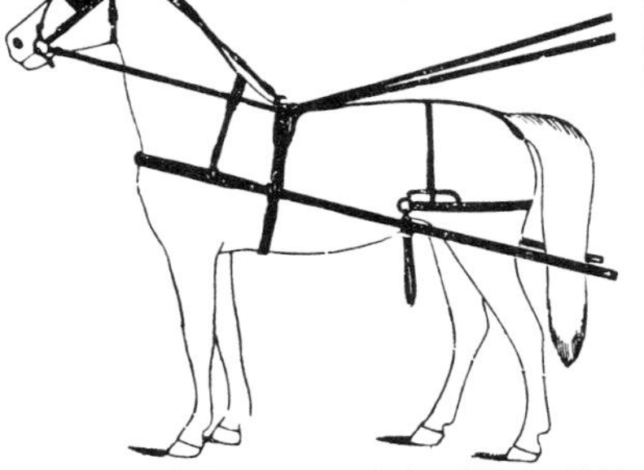

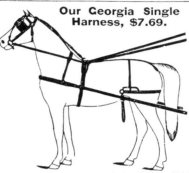

This harness is large enough for 900 to 1200-pound horse.

Bridle, 5/8-inch overcheck, box loops, round winker stay, initial letter rosette; **breast collar,** folded with wide layer and box loops; **traces,** 1-inch, double and stitched, round edge; **breeching,** folded with wide layer; **side straps,** 3/4-inch; **hip strap,** 5/8-inch; **turn back,** 3/4-inch, round crupper; **saddle,** 2½-inch, single strap, all leather skirts and bottom, patent leather jockey; **bellyband,** Griffith style; **lines,** 7/8x1-inch, all black loop in bit; XC trimmings throughout. This harness will fit 900 to 1200-pound horse.

No. 10R15 Price....................**$7.69**

No. 10R20 Same as the description of No. 10R15 with the exception of collar and hames in place of breast collar, 3½-pound iron hames, box loop, hame tugs, kip collars, 1-inch trace, double and stitched with round edge. Price....................**$8.69**

Weight, about 22 pounds.

Our Vicksburg Single Harness.

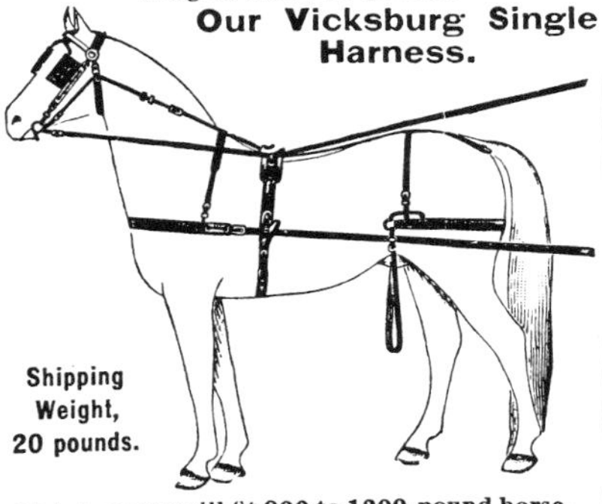

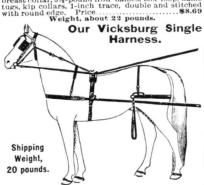

Shipping Weight, 20 pounds.

This harness will fit 900 to 1200-pound horse.

Bridle, 5/8-inch overcheck, box loops, round winker stay or side rim; **breast collar,** folded, with layer, box loops; **traces,** 1⅛-inch, doubled and stitched; **breeching,** folded with layer, side straps 7/8-inch, hip strap 5/8-inch, turnback 3/4-inch, round crupper sewed on; **saddle,** 3-inch, iron jockey, harness leather skirts, leather bottom, double and stitched shaft rig; **bellyband,** Griffith style only; **lines,** 7/8-inch, all black, to loop bit. Trimming XC or japanned. This harness made for 900 to 1200-pound horses.

No. 10R25 Our special price....................**$7.92**

Will furnish this harness extra large for 1400-pound horses add, extra....................**$1.00**

Add extra for buckle on crupper....................**15c**

No. 10R30 Same style harness as No. 10R25, only made in nickel trimming with **Patent Leather Jockey** saddle, selected quality leather, and smooth hames throughout, always sent with overcheck (unless ordered flat side rein).

Price, for nickel trimmed harness....................**$8.75**

Our Ashby Single Harness with Collar and Hames, $8.97.

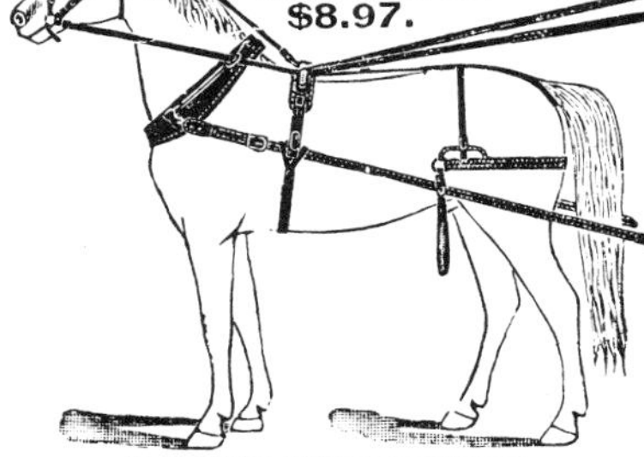

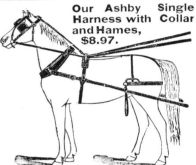

For 900 to 1200-pound horse.

Bridle, 5/8-inch box loop check, patent leather blinds, round winker brace, overcheck or side rein; **lines,** 7/8-inch, all black, to loop in bit; **traces,** 1⅛-inch doubled and stitched, round edge finish, 3½-pound hames, iron hame, full japanned on japanned harness and full XC plate on XC harness; **hame tug** with box loop; **breeching** folded with layer, 5/8-inch single hip strap, 7/8-inch side strap and 3/4-inch back strap, with crupper sewed on; **gig saddle,** 2½-inch single strap skirt, leather bottom with iron jockey; **bellyband flat,** Griffith style only; **collar,** full kip. We do not make any changes in this harness, only furnish it as described above. This harness made in one size only for 900 to 1200-pound horse.

No. 10R35 Our special price with collar....**$8.97**

Weight, boxed, about 35 pounds.

Our Iowa Single Harness.

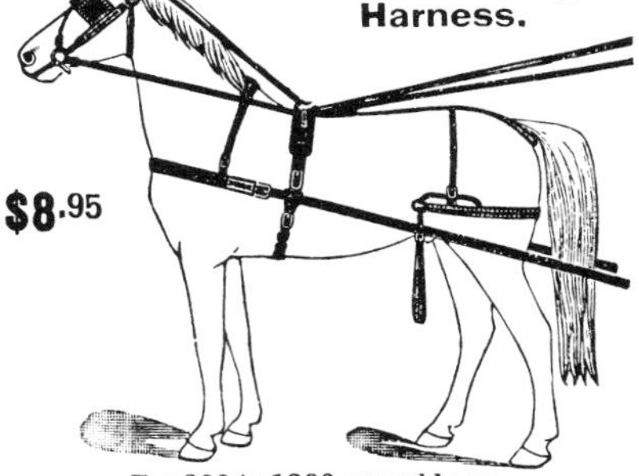

$8.95

For 900 to 1200-pound horse.
Weight, boxed, 23 pounds.

Lines, a very important point about this harness is 1-inch black line, loop in bit; **extra good stock; gig saddle,** extra good single strap, harness leather skirt, with heavy bearer and shaft tug; **bellyband** folds Griffith style, 5/8-inch hip strap, 7/8-inch side strap, 3/4-inch turnback scalloped, with round crupper sewed on; **breast collar,** folded with heavy straight layer and box loops; **breeching,** folded with heavy straight layer double and stitched breeching brace; **traces,** the most important part of this harness, are 1⅛ inches by 6 feet long, extra good stock, well made, smooth round edge to buckle in breast collar; **bridle,** 5/8-inch box loops, round winker brace, patent leather blind, overcheck or side rein, fancy front and **initial letter rosette; trimmings, fine nickel or Davis imitation rubber.**

No. 10R40 Price, as illustrated....................**$8.95**

Add extra for russet hand parts.................... **.25**

Add extra for buckle on crupper.................... **.15**

Will make this harness extra large for 1400 to 1600-pound horse add, extra....................**$2.00**

To the harness section by June

They called it "The Cheapest Supply House on Earth." That was the slogan of the early Sears & Roebuck mail-order catalog, and there was an equally indispensable "Monkey-Ward" (Montgomery Ward) catalog that touched our everyday lives as well. Recognizing that the poorly paid American farmers had little choice but to pay dearly for goods to wear and things to use, these mail-order houses determined to change all this. Buying the world's wares direct from the manufacturers and selling them direct at only a small profit, they brought the markets to the farmers by mail, and profoundly affected rural life in America.

Those wondrous free catalogs relieved our isolation, and enabled us to shop economically for countless necessities, together with a few luxuries that we couldn't buy at home. They kept us abreast of the outside world of progress and invention, fashion and entertainment, to say nothing of sex education. Young males—and the hired man—got their titillation in my day by poring over the women's long underwear and corset sections in the exciting catalogs; and in place of the soft, sissified toilet tissue we are pressured to buy today, farm and ranch folks used to make the 1500 or more pages of the discarded old catalogs last all year. We figured to get to the harness section—about half way—by June.

As a wide-eyed country kid, leafing through the Sears and "Monkey-Ward" catalogs, scanning everything from sleds to saddles to shotguns, I never dreamed that we were helping to start the great mail-order houses of today, creating tremendous business and industry, spawning fortunes and building America. Farmers created the boundless wealth to build most of our towns and cities. Says well-known farm chronicler Wheeler McMillen, "Most of our great railroads, hauling products to and from the farm, our great mail-order houses, the huge implement companies, the buggy, wagon and harness factories, and even the automobile industry owed a great deal to the American farmer." In 1908, Sears sold its first automobiles— really horseless carriages or buggies propelled by 14-horse power motors—at prices ranging from $395 to $495, depending on such extras as acetylene headlights and generator in place of oil lamps, a $25 speedometer and a $35 magneto. "Any lady or child can start or run it," Sears advertised.

Thus American farmers and ranchers were given their first opportunity to escape isolation, but as a leading farm magazine pointed out, the automobile would never go anywhere because there were no roads to drive on. Abruptly dismissing the whole subject, the editor of *Farm Journal* magazine sagely concluded, "The auto is a fad just now, this is certain."

Having only sticky "gumbo" dirt roads to drive on, and no money to indulge in an automobile during those years, our family shopped in Sears for bare necessities: everything from harness to hardware, curry combs to corsets. Sears did a large volume business in farm supplies and advertised its best set of harness for $24.75. Likewise, we shopped in the catalog for horse collars, horseshoes, buggy whips, wagons, axle grease and veterinary supplies. Sears was among the first to offer the sensational new Pasteur's Black Leg vaccine for cattle that saved my father and countless cattlemen from disaster. A devastating disease, Black Leg killed young calves by the thousands, leaving a telltale leg, turned black with shriveled, crackly hide. Until my father was able to obtain the new vaccine, he suffered frequent calf loss, and he hurried to bury the dead animals to keep the dread disease from spreading.

We shopped in the catalogs for other necessities. My older brother and I ordered .22 rifle shells and traps to catch muskrats and skunks so that we could earn a few extra dollars during the winter season. Trapping a skunk, we shot it with the .22 rifle; then changing our outer clothes, we skinned the animal, after which we dressed again so as not to carry the pungent smell home. For the household, we ordered soda crackers that we could buy fresher and cheaper than at home; boxes of codfish that my English-born father, reared near the sea, greatly relished; strawberry preserves—a treat for the whole family— and such everyday necessities as gloves, mittens, stockings, and long underwear. We called the underwear "union suits," and by Saturday night bath time in front of the kitchen range, we were glad to shed our union suits. But a sheep herder I once knew boasted that he never took off his union suit all winter. "You could smell him all the way to town," the neighbors complained. The big trouble with long, heavy, woolen underwear was that it itched like the very devil just as soon as you got inside by the stove. Also, I hated my longies because they bulged beneath my long, black stockings, causing the girls to giggle at school.

A skilled seamstress, Mother scanned the catalogs for yard goods, shirtwaists, hobble skirts and the latest fashions. Noting the way dresses were trimmed, she then altered her own. Being pleasantly plump, she also

STEREOSCOPES

STEREOSCOPES AND VIEWS NEVER WERE MORE POPULAR THAN AT THE PRESENT TIME.
With the large assortment of views which we list, there is an endless amount of entertainment to be obtained from an outfit of this kind, at a very small expense. We do not list the cheapest line of stereoscopes made, for we cannot conscientiously recommend them to our customers.
YOU CAN MAKE BIG MONEY SELLING THESE STEREOSCOPES AND VIEWS.
Our 36-cent views readily bring $1.00 per dozen. Our colored views, for which we ask you only 54 cents, will sell easily for $1.50, and our best grade views should never be sold at retail for less than $3.00 per dozen. Our 24-cent stereoscopes sell like hot cakes at from 75 cents to $1.00 each.

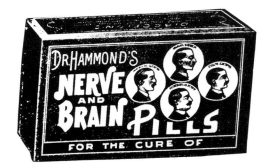

studied the "stylish stouts" that Sears advertised to "make you look slimmer than you ever thought." Importing great bales of hair from Europe, the mail-order houses did a thriving business in switches and wigs. Promoting cosmetics, hair bleach, toilet water and bust developers, Sears urged: *"Women, be beautiful. It is simple when you use the best beauty products."*

Back in the so-called "good old days," women never had legs. They were called "limbs." But sometime before World War I, my lady's limbs came out of hiding. Sears sold the first silk stockings and shortly the catalog progressed from cotton drawers to silk panties.

Despite Lydia Pinkham's famous vegetable compound that first opened the door to the flood of remedies specifically designed for "female" trouble, the catalog people in our time were reluctant to get into this delicate business. No doubt they never dreamed of today's vastly lucrative trade in feminine hygiene, ranging from tampons to "the pill." Sears did offer women "Dr. Worden's Female Pills" for 38 cents per box, with this sympathetic message, "Every woman will understand, far better than pen or word can tell, the suffering her sex must undergo by what is known as female trouble; suffering which is usually borne in silence, because only a woman can be confided in."

116

Mother did buy a big popular book, Professor Fowles *Science in Life*, which I surreptitiously scanned every time I got the chance, seeking some clues to my adolescent growth and approaching puberty. But I was sorely disappointed. It was certainly no substitute for *Playboy*. It was just as unexciting as advertised in Sears: "This work treats of Sexual Science, which is simply that great code of natural laws by which the Almighty requires the sexes to be governed in their natural relations. It is pure, elevating in tone, eloquent in its denunciation of vice."

Depending on our present state of prosperity, the family looked over such luxuries and entertainment as the catalogs offered. Sears advertised pianos for $165—on 30-day trial—and we could have bought "The Handsomest Organ We Have To Offer" for $51.95. Moreover, Sears would throw in low-cost, easy-to-learn music lessons so that Mother might, on a Sunday afternoon in the parlor, proudly play "Silver Threads Among the Gold"—for less than 10 cents per lesson!

We were tempted by other status symbols of the time: one a genuine Black Forest Cuckoo clock ("A clock you will be proud to own") for only $9.48. But Father settled for a hunting-case watch instead, engraved with a noble stag, antlers belligerently raised as if it were the rutting season. The gold-filled chain was $3. No doubt the heartrending catalog appeal of 1915 was enough to sell anyone. Said Sears, "As the years go by, you will conceive a genuine affection for your watch, until it comes to seem more a thing alive than an affair of wheels and springs; its loss or disability the cause of very real grief; its possession a constant stimulation to effort."

In those days when we lived far from town and saw a doctor only in dire emergencies, farmers and ranchers relied heavily on the catalogs for laxatives, linaments, digestive, stomach and rheumatism remedies and there was a whole array of sure-cure patent medicines. They ranged from "Wonderful Little Liver Pills" to "Reliable Worm Cakes." But the miraculous panacea, a favorite with hired men, was Dr. Hammond's Nerve and Brain Pills. You could buy six boxes for three dollars. "Positively guaranteed to cure any disease." Leafing through an enchanting old Sears catalog— today a collector's item—I found Dr. Hammond's intriguing advertising for his Nerve and Brain Pills. Promised Dr. Hammond in Sears, "This will cure you if you feel generally miserable or suffer with a thousand and one indescribable bad feelings, both mental and physical, among these low spirits, nervousness, weariness, lifelessness, weakness, dizzyness, feeling of fullness like bloating after eating, or sense of goneness or emptiness of stomach in the morning; flesh soft and lacking firmness, headache, blurring of eyesight, specks floating before the eyes, nervous irritability, poor

memory, chilliness, alternating with hot flushes."

Incredibly, the list of ills these pills would cure was endless: "Lassitude, throbbing, gurgling or rumbling sensations in bowels; with heat and nipping pains occasionally; palpitation of heart, short breath on exertion, slow circulation of blood, cold feet, pain and oppression in chest and back, pain around the loins, aching and weariness of the lower limbs, drowsiness after meals but nervous wakefulness at night, languor in the morning, and a constant feeling of dread as if something awful was going to happen."

Supposedly, for consumer protection in those days—long before the FDA—Dr. Hammond's ad closed with this warning, "Beware of quack doctors who advertise to scare you into paying money for remedies which have no merit."

Altogether, rural America ordered just about everything it needed from the great mail-order houses: from teething rings to tombstones. But then in the years up to and following World War I, life in the country was dramatically changed and vastly improved. By the 1920s, most of the country was on wheels and farmers and ranchers enjoyed their first gravel roads to get out of the mud and isolation. The smalltown stores were now more abundant, better stocked, offered better buys, and country folks commenced flocking to town to trade. The result was that Sears & Roebuck and Montgomery Ward were compelled to make drastic changes in their pioneering mail-order business and to open their own retail stores.

But our family was everlastingly grateful for the priceless old catalogs. They not only served our everyday needs and saved us money, but they gave us some fun and entertainment; nurtured our culture and got us through the harness section by June!

Roundup and branding was another exciting time as ranchers traded help, and the cowhands went to work roping, branding, dehorning, earmarking, and vaccinating the new calf crop, while castrating the bull calves. — *South Dakota State Historical Society.*

Hot Irons and Hearty Threshers

Like any country boy of my day, I jumped with joy over two big exciting events of the year: the roundup and threshing. First was the spring cattle roundup, at which I gloried in the cowhands who were roping, wrestling and branding Father's new calf crop. I delighted in the dirt and smoke, the bawling cows and calves and as I grew up I took my turn with the hot irons. I have been intrigued ever since with the whole absorbing saga of cattle: from the days of "cattle upon a thousand hills," as we read in Psalms, to the rugged, proudly independent cowboys and cattlemen of America, who helped to make this country great.

Men and cattle have been closely associated in history for thousands of years. Archaeologists have found prehistoric drawings of cattle on the walls of caves in France and in Spain. Sacred bulls were worshipped in ancient Egypt, where cattle were so reverenced that cows were never killed. Cattle worship abounds in India today. The first cattle were used as work animals as well as for producing milk and meat; and it was the domesticated, plodding oxen, yoked in bull-trains, that transported the gold-seekers and early settlers to the Black Hills.

Our modern cattle breeds descended from two species: the humped cattle of Asia and the wild cattle of Europe. Most U.S. breeds descended from European cattle, chiefly the large, longhorned cattle known as the *auroch* or giant ox. The bison or buffalo of our western plains belong to the ox family, and they might now be as extinct as the auroch were it not for the efforts of men like Scotty Phillip, who preserved a small herd in South Dakota. Ruthless hunters, as we know, killed thousands of buffalo on the Great Plains for their meat and hides in a single year.

How did my father's cattle get started in the United States?

Certainly, Christopher Columbus brought longhorn cattle to the New World from Spain on his second voyage in 1493, and descendants of these cattle were ancestors of the famous Texas Longhorns that first supplied beef to the Black Hills. The Plymouth Colony also brought cattle to New England in 1624 and cattle raising spread westward. Appropriately, my British-born father preferred British breeds of cattle, but with good reason since the British Isles led the world in development of the principal beef breeds. Father raised Herefords, big, beautiful cattle with red bodies and white faces—we called them "whitefaces" —developed in Hereford County, England. The famous southern statesman, Henry Clay ("I'd rather be right than be President!") imported the first Hereford cattle to his Kentucky farm in 1817; and because they were good grazing animals that got out and rustled for their feed, the Herefords became the most popular beef breed in the United States.

So Father gloried in his Herefords, as I did in the spring roundup. That was one of the most thrilling times of the year when we worked the back pastures, rounding up the cows with their spring calves, and herding them into the home corrals. I rode a snaky little black cutting horse, High Moon, that whipped in and out of the bawling herd, nipping the cows and calves on their rumps to keep them moving. I would ride after a stubborn straying cow and my pony would stick right with her until she joined the herd again. In this fashion, we brought in the cattle while Father and two or three cowhands got ready for the branding.

Branding goes far back into history: to the early Egyptians, Greeks and Romans who fire-branded their prisoners and slaves. From the time of that great Biblical herdsman, Jacob, and the ancient Chinese with their ideographs, man has been branding livestock. Bringing the first cattle and horses to the New World, the Spanish introduced the branding iron to America. In time, as the first individual and unique brands appeared on the open range with the big cattle outfits— the Hashknife, VVV, Turkey Track, to name a few— followed by the brands of thousands of western cattlemen, America developed a kind of heraldry of the range, and a man's brand became his protective and distinctive trademark.

Father's trademark was a big, old brand which he designed himself. It was O R E, carried on the left side of his cattle. O R E—for ore— was reminiscent of Father's mining days in the Black Hills, but the distinctive brand in three big letters had a special value. No cattle rustlers could possibly work over this unalterable combination.

While we were rounding up the cows and calves, Father had built a blazing fire in one corner of the corrals, hauled out his big O R E branding irons, sharpened his knife and now was ready to commence operations. Our cowhands went to work wrestling the whitefaces. "Heeling," or roping the scrambling calves by their heels, they hustled them to the fire. Now "flanking" the 400-pound spring calves and throwing them on their right sides, two cowhands held them down while others branded, dehorned, earmarked and also vaccinated for hemorrhagic septicemia, a disease fatal to cattle. The calves would bawl and bleat as the hot irons lightly touched their hides. Lastly, Father, with lightning speed and surgical skill, castrated the bull calves. The whole job was accomplished with an easy rhythm, relieved by some earthy jokes and stories and time out for the men to roll a cigaret or two from their tobacco sacks with drawstring and familiar Bull Durham tag.

"Altogether, this branding, castrating and calf wrestling is absolutely the cruelest, most uncivilized operation I have ever witnessed," one of my eastern friends exploded the first time he saw anyone work cattle as we did on the ranch. "This would never be permitted in Boston!"

Scrambling to their feet and shaking their heads after branding and earmarking, the hurting and confused calves were turned loose to rejoin the bawling mothers outside the corrals. Later, in the fall, we had another roundup when we cut out the spring calves from the herd and corraled them until they were weaned. It was a painful parting, and hanging around the corrals, the cows kept up an incessant din, crying for their young ones. At last, hungry and thirsty, they gave up and wandered back to pasture in utter resignation. Reflecting on these faithful cows, I wonder whether they weren't better mothers than a great many we see in human society today with all of our parental neglect, desertion and tragic child abuse.

While the roundup was an exciting time on the ranch, raising cattle was a demanding business 365 days a year, and Father looked after it well. His principal worries were having plenty of feed and water, securing big, hardy range bulls to sire a rugged calf crop and selling at a good price in order to pay off his notes and keep his credit at the bank. Like the typical western cattleman, Father took good years and bad in stride, paid his debts and was fiercely independent. Hail to the cattleman, who has served mankind throughout history.

Likewise, hail to the old steam-powered threshing rigs that once served the American farmer and the country so well. "Here come the threshers!" I used to shout as the lumbering old steam engine, belching smoke and sparks, pulling a long, silvery grain "separator" and trailed by a water wagon to keep up steam in the engine's boiler, arrived at our ranch each year. Following closely behind came the cooperative neighbors with their teams and wagons to help us thresh, while one or two neighbor women arrived to assist Mother with feeding an army of 25 to 30 ravenous men during the next two or three days. She would cook some of the best meals and fanciest desserts I ever ate. Altogether, there was an an allure and romance about threshing that would enchant me all through boyhood, and for a hungry, excited ranch kid it was better than having company.

In the days before early maturing varieties of grain were developed—crops that farmers now combine in mid-summer—our wheat was not ready to harvest until late July or early August. Then we had to wait for the only available threshing rig to make its rounds, but some years threshing was delayed by rains and mechanical breakdowns until September and even October. If we threshed late, the folks allowed me to stay home from school, and I hung around the threshing rig eagerly observing every step as the crew made its preparations. First thing, the six-foot-four, gangling Scandinavian engineer, "Ole" Hanson, positioned the separator just where Father wanted it so he would have a convenient strawpile. Next, he lined up the engine about 75 feet directly opposite the separator and the crew, unfolding the biggest, longest, heaviest belt I had ever seen, connected engine and threshing machine. Momentarily, the gigantic belt sagged and hung loose. Then Ole backed up his engine a few paces and the belt was taut.

Now Jim Kinghorn, the craggy-faced, genial separator man, wearing coveralls caked with grain dust and grease, got out his oilcan and went to work. Fascinated, I tagged after him as he clambered over the separator, poking the long, slender spout of his oilcan into every moving part of the wondrous threshing machine. "Here, kid, have a squirt on me," Jim joked, handing me the king-sized oilcan to lubricate a few places myself. I descended from the separator somehow feeling bigger and older.

At length, Jim signalled to "try 'er out," and I raced to the engine to see Ole start up the threshing rig. Already sooty-black from firing the huge boiler, Ole yanked open the door of the firebox to shovel in more coal. A scowling, taciturn man, the engineer grumbled, "Okay kid. You can sit up there on the coal bin if you behave yourself." It turned out to be a grandstand seat, where I could watch the whole absorbing operation. Pulling the whistlecord, Ole gave a short warning toot, he pushed the throttle forward, there was a little puff of smoke and the mammoth steam engine engaged the ponderous flywheel. Slowly, the fabulous 75-foot belt began to turn; then, slapping and swaying as it gained full speed, it delivered power to the separator. Standing just above the yawning throat of the threshing machine, Jim watched the flashing, serrated teeth that cut up and slashed the grain sheaves; then he signaled okay to the engineer and to shut down. But first Ole moved the engine slightly forward to leave the belt slack overnight. Now everything was ready for the threshing, that would begin in the morning, just as soon as the sun had burned the dew off the bundles and the grain was sufficiently dry to thresh. Having seen the threshing rig readied, I hurried to ride with loquacious Joe, the "water monkey," who was pumping from the creek to

With a four-horse team protected by cotton fly nets, farmers harvested with their revolutionary McCormick-Deering grain binder, which kicked out the neatly tied bundles. No fancy $75,000, glass-enclosed, air-conditioned combine cabs in our day! — *South Dakota State Historical Society.*

keep steam up in the big boiler. It was a job I thought I might like someday, myself.

But before we got around to threshing, I discovered as I grew up, there was the long, hot, backbreaking harvesting job. As Father's McCormick-Deering grain binder cut the wheat, barley and oats, it elevated the loose sheaves and tied them with one of the most ingenious devices ever invented—the twine knotter. Modeled after a bird's beak, the knotter was the idea of an 18-year-old Civil War soldier who whittled the original out of an apple bough and sold it for $35,000. Once tied by the knotter, the bundles were kicked out from the grain binder onto the field, where we gathered them in neat, nearly waterproof piles or "shocks." But tramping all day through the rutted wheat stubble and bending over hundreds of times to pick up the bundles, after which we carefully set them up in a "shock", was one of the most demanding jobs on the farm. Grabbing the bundles by the twine, you cut your gloves and got sore hands. Frequently, a bearded wheat or barley husk would work its way down my back or beneath my shirt front, adding to the itching and discomfort. Parched with thirst in the boiling sun, we drank tepid water from a gallon demijohn, and we had no place to rest in the shade. Sweat-soaked and weary, we trudged home at night eager to take a quick dip in the old swimming hole before supper. Some difference from today's sophisticated farmer, riding in the cab of a $75,000 glass-encased, air-conditioned combine that cuts, threshes and stores the wheat in a huge hopper until it can be unloaded.

At last, after cutting and shocking the grain, we were ready for threshing. It was a happy community affair and neighbors paraded into the fields with their teams and wagons to load bundles and help us. As a man drove his hayrack down the long rows of shocked grain, "spike" pitchers deftly tossed the bundles up to him. Fully loaded, he then joined the other wagons at the threshing rig. Pulling up on each side of the separator, the bundle wagons awaited their turn to unload, but sometimes a skittish team would balk and shy away from the roaring monster. Grabbing the horses by their bridles, threshers quickly quieted them down. Jim Kinghorn wouldn't tolerate the slightest lag or interruption in feeding his separator, and when it was each wagon's turn to pull into line, the sweating drivers pitched off their loads with dispatch. Catching the cascading bundles, the voracious separator chopped them into pieces and hungrily devoured them.

From my grandstand seat on Ole's steam engine, I watched the whole exciting scene, and I thrilled to the rhythmic slap-slap-slap of the big belt powering the separator. Clambering up and down on his roaring, jiggling threshing machine, amidst a cloud of dust and chaff, the separator man kept a sharp eye on everything. Jim made sure that a steady stream of clean, golden wheat was augured into the waiting grain wagons and little or no grain was blown into the strawstack. From the separator, the threshed grain was promptly hauled to the granary for storing. Just as soon as I was old enough, I surrendered my grandstand seat on Ole's steam engine and was impressed into one of the hottest, dirtiest jobs in threshing: shoveling the

121

"Here come the threshers!" boys used to shout as the big rigs arrived at harvesttime. To be allowed to sit up on the old steam engine, belching smoke and sparks, and to watch the "separator" spewing out a great strawstack, was one of the big thrills of the entire year. — *South Dakota State Historical Society.*

dusty, loose grain back in the granary bins as fast as it was unloaded. That was supposed to be a kid's work, but I could hardly wait to grow up and take my place with the men in the field as a spike pitcher.

Promptly at noon and again at six o'clock, Ole gave a long, shrill blast on his whistle, throttled his steam engine and the threshing rig was shut down, while everybody headed for the ranch house to eat. But it was no romance for Mother! She had worked incessantly, getting ready to feed this army: buying fresh beef and ham in town, frying chickens, baking bread, rolls, pies, cakes, making gallons of coffee and setting a table to feed the men in shifts. Short of chairs, she used benches to seat everybody. It was something like the famed Grant Wood painting portraying the threshing table.

Washing briefly in the tin basins out under our shade trees and drying with rough "roller" towels, the hungry threshers literally surged into the house, elbowing each other through the kitchen door. Grabbing seats at the long table, joking and laughing, they pitched into the bountiful meal; one man, I recall, spearing another's hand as he endeavored to fork a piece of bread across the table. Keeping on the run, Mother and a neighbor lady served up great plates of meat, potatoes and brown gravy; green corn, peas and beets fresh from the garden, and hot rolls. The hearty men finished with generous servings of pie or cake.

Just as soon as Mother had fed the first table of a dozen or so ravenous men, another line was waiting outside. It was customary to feed a big crew, whereupon Mother had to get organized to feed them again the following day and perhaps a third. Sometimes we got half way through threshing when abruptly it rained, or the separator would break down. If it was a lengthy delay, the neighbors would return home, but Mother still had to feed the threshing rig crew and any extra men my father had hired. It's a wonder that Mother didn't collapse after the ordeal. But happily, as I remember, she sat down with a great sigh of relief to eat with the family in the evening after all the threshers had gone. It was a jolly time and I helped myself to an extra slice of mouth-watering, three-tiered chocolate layer cake, garnished with walnuts nestled in the rich frosting!

Thus I write of my romance with threshing, but it was a laborious, costly, frustrating operation for farmers. Father looked to the day when he might buy his own small threshing machine and Mother was ready for liberation. Sure enough, before many years, farmers were using the first internal-combustion tractors, operating their own small threshing machines, and the era of steam-powered threshing was over. Today, you can find some of the historic steam engines preserved in rural museums. For me, they evoke enchanting memories. May those old steamers rest in peace!

The Fourth I Remember Best

We were hitching up our fastest team to the spring wagon when my father glanced at the sullen, frightening sky and shouted, "Unhook, son—it's hail!"

In the year that I was nine years old, Fourth of July had started out hot—boiling hot. I remember that after breakfast the hired hands stretched out under the big elm at the corner of our house, glad to have a day of rest from stacking hay. While they rested in the cool shade, I cranked the wobbly old ice-cream freezer, and Mother prepared a couple of her finest spring fryers for us to eat.

At noon we feasted on her tender fried chicken, fresh strawberries and homemade ice cream. After licking the freezer beater, I danced out behind my father to hook up the horses, a skittish bay team they were. We were going to drive eight miles to Belle Fourche to celebrate the glorious Fourth—next to Christmas, the most thrilling holiday of the year. We would see the Tri-State Roundup (rodeo) with some fancy bronc riding by the cowboys from nearby ranches in Montana, Wyoming and the Dakotas. We would even stay, my father promised, to see the fireworks and carnival downtown after dark.

And now, at midday, it was already growing dark.

Hastily, we unhooked the team and raced to the barn. I listened as a thunderous roar swept down the green and golden St. Onge Valley. I felt a blast of icy air on my cheek. Then it struck—HAIL.

We scarcely reached the safety of our lean-to kitchen when the terrible tattoo began on the roof. In a few seconds, it rose to a deafening roar. We had to shout to hear ourselves. I looked out the window. The big elm and cottonwoods were shedding their leaves as if stripped by an autumn gale.

No one who has not experienced heavy hail on his own acres can fully understand the agony of the moment. I can see my father now, pacing in front of the windows, his hands clenching and unclenching, his face white and grim. Mother stood by, trying not to cry.

The hail increased. By now the falling stones—some as big as hen's eggs—shut out everything except the blob of our bunkhouse some fifty feet away.

But my father saw *clearly.*

He must have seen a half-mile off—into the south forty—where his corn and wheat lay beaten into the earth. He saw his year's feed and seed and hard-earned cash—everything he'd worked and hoped for—wiped out in one single, disastrous blow. Nothing could survive this merciless hail.

Presently the pounding slowed, then ceased altogether. A gentle rain began to fall. The whole thing was over in ten minutes. Hail lay piled in the yard nearly a foot deep. My father was ruined.

I stood beside him, trying, at my age, to comprehend the frightful loss. Then I felt his big, rough hand squeeze in mine.

"Come on, old chap," he said, "we're going to celebrate anyhow. Take this and have a good time on the Fourth!" He pressed a 50-cent piece into my hand.

He waded out in the mud after the storm, hooked up the team again, cracked the whip, and the family started off to town almost as if nothing had happened. On the way, I remember, we stopped and my father got out and knelt in the soggy field to examine his shattered wheat. He sifted all that remained—the empty chaff—through his strong fingers. Then we drove on.

Father never whimpered. The English immigrant, who had worked his way to this country when he was 17, was accustomed to disappointment and reverses; and whatever his fate, he was fervently patriotic. His eyes used to fill with tears at the sight of the Stars and Stripes, and on the Fourth of July, I imagined, he used to wear his hat a bit jauntier than usual.

My father never asked anyone for help. Independence to him meant fighting his own battles—and winning them. While we tend to glorify the Indian fighters, gold-seekers, bullwhackers, cowboys and even the desperadoes, I think of the unsung pioneers like my father as the real heroes. They battled the forces of nature—and won—to produce an abundance of food for America and the world.

And so the Fourth of July never rolls around but what I reflect on my father, the hail, the shattered wheat, the 50-cent piece and the trip to celebrate in town. To Father, Americanism and Independence were the same thing. And since that summer, they've meant the same to me, too.

Pioneering in South Dakota, rural families spanned a fantastic period of progress and change. It was indeed a struggle, but once out of the mud, they truly shifted into high gear as symbolized by this woman who learned to drive a car and fix a flat! — *USDA Photo.*

Out of the mud and into high gear

At precisely the same time that gold-seekers were flocking to the Black Hills, and the Sioux Indians were wiping our "Yellow Hair" Custer's immediate command in just revenge, a significant event was occurring in Europe that was to profoundly affect American farmers and ranchers, our country and the world.

A German inventor, Nickolaus Otto, built a noisy contraption, the first internal-combustion engine. Ultimately, his invention would give the American farmer the automobile and tractor to help him get out of the mud, shift into high gear and so usher in a revolutionary new era in our nation's farming and ranching.

That revolution touched our family the day just before World War I, when Father reluctantly sold some of his best milk cows to buy our first car for $590. Eagerly, my plucky brother Earl, with only scant instruction, took the wheel of the shiny black Chevrolet touring car at the automobile dealer's showroom. "Climb in folks," he boldly invited. Father was aghast, but Earl drove us merrily home at about 30 miles per hour. Our "Chevy" was equipped with self-starter, acetylene headlights, a spare tire and semitransparent isinglass side curtains that promptly shattered with a blast of wind, or when hit by a rock. Also, our new car had one recurring costly defect—the rear pinion gear, which gave out with a hard pull. "Dammit, there we go again!" Earl used to swear. We had to keep two or three extra gears on hand, and my mechanically minded brother used to jack up the car and put in a new one frequently.

So we "got out and under," as we used to sing, but we still had no good roads to drive on, and the first time we got caught in a rain with our Chevy, the sticky gumbo soil balled up on the wheels and beneath the fenders and we were stuck in the mud. Poking the gumbo out from between the wheel spokes, and freeing the fenders, we managed to advance a few yards before we got stuck again. But eventually we made it to town and back, and in time we ventured on a bit of Sunday sight-seeing as well.

The toughest drive in our vicinity was to climb some 20 miles up in the mountains to Deadwood—a real challenge. The route was a tortuous, dusty road with sheer drop-offs that gave me the shivers, and so steep that it was customary to stop at a halfway house to add water and cool the engine. One summer day, a St. Onge farmer, who had never driven an automobile and was blissfully ignorant about engines, blithely headed for the hills. His car badly overheated and stopped dead just as he pulled up to the halfway house.

"I see you need water," said another motorist, whereupon he unscrewed the farmer's radiator cap and the thing just blew—like a small geyser in Yellowstone National Park.

"A-ha," exclaimed the astonished French Canadian farmer. "I see where the boiler be!"

But crude as were the first automobiles, we found them highly useful. We jacked up the old Chevy, strung a belt from a rear wheel to equipment around the ranch, started the engine and sawed wood or ground feed for the livestock. The early-day cars were simple to operate, economical to run and certainly more easily repaired than our fancy computerized new cars today. If a fender rattled, we just tied it up with bailing wire. We did have our troubles with winter driving. First, to get started, we had to fill the radiator with boiling water and put a blow torch to the block to heat it. Once the motor started running, we slipped a blanket over the radiator to keep it from freezing. With only side curtains to protect us and no heater, we were in danger of freezing, too! But with no good roads to drive on, we stayed home during most of the winter anyhow. Eventually, however, we did make progress—from dirt to gravel roads and, in a few places, even paving—and farmers and ranchers got out of the mud and went to town. On Saturday nights their "Tin Lizzies" were parked the full length of Main Street. By the 1920s, American farmers owned more than two million automobiles.

While the automobile got us out of the mud and isolation, it was the hissing, lumbering steam engines, followed by the faster kerosene tractors, that really put power into farming. Invented about the same time as Otto's internal-combustion engine, the slow-moving steamers pulled great 12-bottom plows, breaking vast grasslands, and they powered the nation's threshing rigs as well. But it was the small, more efficient kerosene tractor that quickly caught on with the farmers, weary of feeding oats and driving horses. Tight-fisted bankers, however, wouldn't lend money on the first tractors. "They'll make farmers lazy!" they warned. But for the first time in their busy lives, farmers were glad to have a little extra time on their hands with all this newfound power, and by 1920 they owned nearly 250,000 tractors. Farmers own nearly 5 million tractors today.

No more pumping water by hand — often in sub-zero weather! Instead the old pump handle is idled by this electric motor in one of the earliest applications of farm power. — *USDA Photo.*

One trouble with a tractor, farmers used to joke, is that it can't have a colt! But to Father, who loved his horses and raised some beautiful colts, this was no joking matter. He held on to his faithful "oat burners" and might never have surrendered had not my brother Earl virtually threatened to leave the ranch unless we acquired a tractor like the neighbors. Conceding at last, the time and money saved in plowing, planting and seeding a crop earlier, Father finally gave in, and Earl proudly wheeled home a hulking, noisy Titan tractor. My brother wanted to go to a tractor school in Kansas City, but Father couldn't spare him. Undaunted, Earl tore down the whole complicated engine at the end of the season, ground the valves and successfully reassembled the myriad parts. The Titan did the work of three or four teams of horses, but it was still a dirty, exhausting job plowing 8 to 10 hours under a boiling sun, with the wind whipping dust and tractor fumes in your face and eyes. My brother came in from the fields looking almost as grimy as a coal miner. In time, we replaced the Titan with a larger, more powerful tractor

and Father bought a small threshing machine as well. He pensioned his remaining draft horses, putting them out to pasture except for small jobs around the ranch, and our farming was never the same again.

I grew up at just the right time during this period of change to see farmers and ranchers reap the fruits of research at our agricultural colleges, government experiment stations and to benefit from the wealth of practical information pouring out from the farm magazines, the U.S. Extension Service and its county agricultural agents. Our county agent, Evan Hall, induced me to join a pig club, and buy a purebred Duroc sow, for which I was given an impressive sheaf of registered or pedigree papers. I bred my sow to a purebred boar then during gestation, I "scientifically" fed, brushed and pampered her much to Father's annoyance. Came spring: my purebred farrowed three little pigs, while Dad's unpedigreed sows in the next pen had litters of five to eight pigs. "You want production and not pedigree," Father snorted in disgust.

Above. It was a great day when Rural Free Delivery (RFD) came to farms and ranches. Starting in the east, it spread to 32,000 rural routes. Families eagerly awaited the day's mail — including the mail-order catalogs — delivered in horse-drawn carts like this. — *South Dakota State Historical Society. Left.* Once isolated without good roads, or other communication, farmers and ranchers greatly benefited from the telephone and radio. Now they could "ring up" town, their neighbors or the county agent, while the radio brought today's markets and world news. — *USDA Photo.*

But Father was not really antipurebred and unprogressive, as witness his fine crops. He was one of the first farmers to grow the new certified, drouth-resistant Marquis wheat developed by the colleges, and his billowing fields of alfalfa told a dramatic story. Great Plains farmers suffered badly from a lack of winter forage when a Danish-born, South Dakota State College scientist, Niels Ebbesen Hansen, proposed searching the rugged Siberian steppes for acclimated crops of the same latitude. He went there himself, and travelling almost to the Arctic Circle discovered nature had crossed a blue-flowered and a yellow-flowered alfalfa, forming a natural hybrid. Young Hansen, as he told me himself years later, got down on his knees, garnered a teaspooon of seed and gave the West hardy Cossack alfalfa, which my Father was among the first to grow. It saved the farmers.

Farmers and ranchers would now benefit from research and receive this flood of information, thanks to two other vital new means of communication: rural free delivery and the radio. Through the mail came our farm magazines, government bulletins and market reports, and to my great joy, I discovered I could order books, free of charge, from our congressman. No one asked my age. (I was then about 12 or 13.) So boldly, I wrote to Washington, and before long I was getting not only instructive Department of Agriculture Yearbooks, but scientific reports of the Smithsonian Institution, scholarly studies of the Bureau of Ethnology on origins of the American Indian, together with insightful, interesting papers of the American Historical Association—some of them collector's items today.

Unloading a great stack of books one day from his rural carrier cart, our Irish mail man, Johnny Breslin, snorted, "Paul, you must be goin' to start a library," which was precisely what I was doing at taxpayer expense. But Johnny saw no sense whatever in what I was doing. "Look, me boy," he counseled, "instead of taking up all this book larnin' you should be aimin' for somethin' *steady* like bein' a railway mail clerk when you grow up. Now there's a *real* job for a man! You stand there in the baggage car, with a revolver on your hip, sortin' letters for this town and that and travelin' all over the country for free. The country's always goin' to need railway mail clerks." But I stuck with my free government publications, which turned out to be a liberal education. Matter of fact, I've never gotten so much valuable service from Washington since.

Like our neighbors, we bought our first battery set radio in the early 1920s. It came complete with earphones and scratchy static, but we endeavored to get the markets and the news at noon. Our biggest thrill, though, was sitting up late, trying to tune in to the music of the Kansas City Nighthawks or the Cliquot Club Eskimos. We boasted to our neighbors if we got the powerful WLS (Sears & Roebuck: World's Largest Store) in Chicago, or KDKA, America's pioneer radio station in Pittsburgh. Our first Christmas with radio was unforgettable as Mother and Father joyfully sang along with "Hark the Herald Angels Sing" and "Silent Night." We prematurely ran down our storage batteries playing the radio almost constantly. Like Henry Ford's popular "Tin Lizzie," the novel radio sparked a lot of jokes. Whenever anyone bragged about his reception, it was appropriate to tell the story of the old Scandinavian lady hearing the radio for the first time. She was wholly unimpressed about tuning into Chicago or Kansas City or Dubuque. "Why," she scoffed, "I yust tap twice on my snuffbox and I get Copenhagen!" (A then widely used form of tobacco)

And this is how we got out of the mud, shifted into high gear; and through mechanization, research and better communications, our lives were dramatically changed on the farms and ranches of South Dakota.

"Not my will, but thine, be done."

Life on the South Dakota frontier was unsparing and harsh. As evidence, both my grandmother, Mary Frathey Friggens, and my grandfather, John Hosken, died before I was born. Grandma Friggens died in her late 40s soon after coming to America, leaving my grandfather, William Glover Friggens, a hardy farmer who thought nothing of hiking 20 miles cross-country, to live to his ripe 80s. Grandpa Hosken, a lifelong miner, died in his 60s from the then widely prevalent disease, "miner's consumption."

Ailing and without benefit of pension, Social Security or other material means, Grandpa and Grandma Hosken came to live with their daughter on the ranch. This was the era long before society would dream up plush retirement communities and nursing homes; and if you had no close relatives to care for you, your fate—in the words of a then current song—was "Over the Hill to the Poorhouse." Happily, Mother found a place for her parents in our overcrowded, modest ranch house, and with loving care "waited on them hand and foot," as she used to recall. That was the general custom: for the grandparents to spend their declining days with their children, and any other arrangement was virtually unheard of. It's a pity that families so callously ship off their elders to institutional care today.

But not during my youth. Thus it happened that Grandpa Hosken died as he had wished, at home with his daughter, and Grandma continued to live with the family. And what a blessing! A gentle, spirited woman, with an infectious gift of humor and a heart of gold, she endeared herself to family and friends alike. Born and raised in a gray, grim mining town, St. Just, on the stormy Cornish coast, she had little formal education and used to laboriously print her letters in place of writing longhand. But she read her Bible frequently and followed its teachings. Grandma had no concern with theology or disputation. She lived a simple, beautiful faith with charity and love. Whenever there was a family spat or tension in the home, she was invariable the peacemaker. "It takes two to make a quarrel," she would mediate. Handicapped by a breach she had suffered during childbirth, she found it difficult to move about. But on rare occasions when she consented to go to town or attend church at St. Onge, Grandma dressed up in her black, high-collared satin dress, put on her Paisley shawl and gray bonnet and looked positively regal!

But, sad for us, Grandma began to fail and Mother summoned a doctor. Fighting muddy roads and a new-fangled automobile, he finally arrived, but he could do little. It was her heart and general disability, he explained. With the onset of winter, Grandma became bedfast and grew progressively weaker. One day, she was so frail and weak she could scarcely sip her beloved tea or speak above a whisper. "Too weak today, Grandma, to praise your Maker?" Mother asked as she stood by the bedside. Grandma shook her head, "Oh, but a sigh could reach Him," she replied in her abiding faith.

It was a bitterly cold morning in January, and after giving Grandma a bit of breakfast, Mother went out to help the men with the milking. By now, Father had built up a fine dairy herd of about 20 cows to boost our income and help pay for more land; and slogging through the deep snows Mother helped with the chores morning and evening. This morning she left me, a boy of 12, to stay with Grandma.

Now I sat by her bedside, holding her clammy, blue-veined hand. She asked for a sip of water, which I held to her quivering lips. Then I heard, for the first time, the strange gurgling sound in her throat. It grew worse and Grandma seemed unable to clear it. Suddenly, I remembered: this is what I have heard folks talk about—the dread "death rattle." I was terror-stricken and having never before experienced death, I wanted to rush out of the house to call Mother. Grandma made a further feeble effort to clear her throat. Then, pulling me closer, she asked me to fold her hands across her breast. She lay back, closed her eyes and with a barely audible sigh, whispered her favorite scripture—Jesus' prayer in Gethsemane— "Not my will, but thine, be done."

Grandma was gone. Christiana Clemens Hosken went that way on a stormy January day in 1921, at the age of 78 years and three months, and I never expect to experience anything more serenely beautiful or spiritually reassuring again. Grandma had lived every day, as if it were her last, and she was supremely prepared to meet her Maker. Sobbing, I ran out to the barn to tell Mother and Father. They hurried to the house. Grief stricken, Mother smoothed back Grandma's wispy, white hair, patted her folded hands. Then shortly my brother Earl hurried to St. Onge to call the funeral parlors. Grandma would be laid to rest, as she had wished, beside her husband in Mount Moriah Cemetery in famous old Deadwood.

Now, hearing the news, kindly neighbors flocked

to our house, as was the custom, to offer their condolences—and infinitely more. They brought baked goods and meat dishes, jellies, jams and desserts. Moreover, they literally took over the operation of the ranch: milking, feeding the livestock and looking after the place while we journeyed to Deadwood for Grandma's funeral from the home of one of her nieces. Living in a sparsely settled country those early days, people urgently needed each other and they genuinely cared for their neighbors. Too bad that with all of our vaunted affluence, selfish pursuits and indifference, we have lost a lot of this neighborliness today. Yet people yearn for some "sense of community," as we plaintively say now.

Laid out on a lovely pine-crested mountainside, looking down on historic Deadwood Gulch, Mount Moriah Cemetery is a steep, snowy climb in winter, and I marveled at the new motor-driven hearse we followed in the funeral procession. At length, we arrived at the open grave, stood in a raw, biting wind for the brief commital service—"From dust thou art, and unto dust thou shalt return "—and Grandma was reunited with Grandpa Hosken in eternity.

Leaving the cemetery with its sighing pines, we passed a grave just a few yards away from Grandma's, which aroused my interest. Over it stood a red sandstone monument—a sculpture—to "Wild Bill" Hickock. Originally, it had been protected by a fence and netting, completely covering the grave, but now souvenir hunters had ripped apart the netting and vandalized the sculpture. Nearby, over an adjoining grave, there was a monument to Martha Jane Burke—"Calamity Jane"—and I asked Mother about these two curious characters.

"Wild Bill," she said, was a no-good gambler and gunman, who was shot and killed in a Deadwood saloon; and Calamity Jane a rough, tough muleskinner who dressed, drank and cursed just like a man. She had traveled with the freighting outfits to the Black Hills, followed the soldiers and miners, frequented the saloons and died penniless. "She was certainly no lady," Mother let me know.

I left Mount Moriah wondering about all these notorious, fanciful characters, and I suppose my interest in western history was kindled in part the day we laid Grandma to rest, close by Wild Bill and Calamity Jane. Returning to the ranch, we soon realized the tremendous gap that Grandma's death had left in our lives: like a great tree, as someone has written, crashing to earth and leaving an empty place against the sky. But Grandma also left us fond memories and lights to live by—a precious heritage!

"Over the Waves" in Woodman Hall

How did young folks and their elders socialize during my boyhood in the Black Hills? Like corruptive River City in Meredith Willson's delightfully nostalgic box office success, *The Music Man*, St. Onge had a poolhall, which Mother judged a den of iniquity and absolutely forbade me to enter.

"I hear there's gambling going on in there, and I don't want you to cultivate evil companions," Mother admonished. "Don't you ever darken the doors of that foul place." Of course, there was a sign warning NO MINORS ALLOWED. But one day, as a long-legged teenager passing for 18, I slipped into the St. Onge poolhall, musty with stale tobacco smoke and smelly from overfull spittoons. Four or five old codgers sat around a dimly lighted table, puffing on their stubby cigars or rolling their own cigarets from Bull Durham sacks. They were playing some kind of card game and shoving matches into the center of the table. But I didn't see anybody "gambling." A gabby old drummer, or traveling salesman, who had just stopped off between trains, was busy peddling his "prime Havana cigars" to the proprietor, and that was all I saw in the poolhall. Boldly stepping up to the counter, I bought a nickel candy bar and then sneaked out.

Now the poolhall wasn't the principal place for fun and recreation in St. Onge. But it attracted adult males of all ages, and it held a powerful allure for young boys of my time, though I can't recall cultivating any evil companions. What else was there to do for fun in St. Onge? Well, everybody turned out for the Christmas play, Santa Claus and the box socials at the school. We celebrated the Fourth of July by eating gallons of homemade ice cream and shooting off firecrackers (nothing like today's pyrotechnic spectaculars). Occasionally, folks threw a wild wedding shivaree. We picnicked on Labor Day and at the close of school, and we enjoyed socials and suppers at our little Congregational church. I don't recall that the Catholics ever held church socials, but they generously patronized our Protestant church affairs, eagerly bidding up the attractive food baskets as they were auctioned off.

There were a few Masons around St. Onge, who socialized at the lodge meetings, but I grew up somewhat in awe of this secret society. Members of the Masonic Order were reputed to have taken some kind of blood oath to defend themselves against Catholics. I even heard frightening stories that guns were hidden in Catholic churches, awaiting the inevitable war with

Protestants. When that Tammany Hall machine politician, Alfred E. Smith, a Democrat and devout Roman Catholic, ran for president against Herbert Hoover in 1928, people said that someday the pope would rule America from Rome. Feeding on bigotry, the Ku Klux Klan was active that campaign year in the Black Hills, parading in night shirts, hiding behind hoods and burning their fiery crosses. But we didn't become inflamed in St. Onge. Catholics and Protestants continued to break bread together, sent their children to the same public school, and I developed a warmhearted feeling for all kinds of people and a decent respect for their creeds and opinions during my formative years in the tolerant community. Later I learned that all truth is not with any of us.

Our real community center in St. Onge, where we socialized most often, was the local Woodman Hall, built by the fraternal order, Modern Woodmen of America, in the days when lodges filled a vastly greater role in everyday life than now. Picture the unimposing place: It was a two-story, rough-hewn sandstone building with a bank, butcher shop and cluttered general store on the first floor. Upstairs was the mysterious Woodman lodge hall, to which members were admitted only by secret password. "They must have something to hide or they wouldn't be secret," our canny mail carrier warned me against joining when I reached 17. The rest of the Woodman Hall consisted of a huge dance floor where the False Bottom boys (from False Bottom Creek) and the "big bottom girls" as we "smart alecks" used to wisecrack, danced into the dawn.

St. Onge was something to see before one of these dances on Saturday night! Arriving by buggy, horseback and later the automobile, farmers crowded into town to shop at the general store, gossip and maybe pass some time at the poolhall before festivities commenced around nine o'clock at Woodman Hall. Now we climbed the steep stairs to the dance hall: ill-ventilated, lighted by oil lamps and lined with wooden benches along the walls. The single stairway was our only exit, there was no ordinance forbidding smoking, the place was usually jammed, and it's a miracle that Woodman Hall never burned to the ground, trapping us all.

We burned up the dance floor instead. The music was a lively three-piece affair (combo, we'd call it today) consisting of a battered piano, violin or zither and our neighbor rattling the bones. We danced the two-step, Bunny-hug, Bear-dance, Turkey Trot and the waltz. But the waltz was a great favorite, probably because so many older folk liked the graceful, gliding steps and waltzed so well. When the waltz was first introduced in the eighteenth century, with its whirling, embracing couples, polite society was scandalized. But the waltz grew to become the most popular ballroom dance both in Europe and America; and I greatly enjoyed watching my elders swing and sway to the lilting old tunes, such as "Over the Waves" and "Till We Meet Again."

Everybody got out on the dance floor, and in my early teens, I learned to dance, too. I just sidled up to the best-looking girl or beaming matron still seated, asked for a dance, and pumping her arm for dear life, we swung out onto the waxy dance floor. Except for a few men with halitosis ("Even your best friends won't tell you!" the ads warned) and somebody who perspired profusely, almost no one was turned down for a partner at Woodman Hall. While we danced the latest fads, some eyebrows were raised at the bold Bunny-hug, which, after all, was a lot of hugging—and in public, too. In those days it was considered poor taste to hug, caress or display affection openly. Otherwise, Woodman Hall provided wholesome entertainment for the entire family. Outside, there was an occasional fight, but generally drunks stayed off the dance floor. Around midnight, the exhausted musicians stopped playing and everybody paraded to the lodge hall for a box supper. Afterward, we passed the hat to entice the musicians to play longer and returned to dance into the morning hours. The children were left to sleep, curled up and covered with coats, on the wooden benches around the hall.

Infrequently, the community staged a hilarious home-talent play at Woodman Hall, and on one occasion I gave my eloquent oration, "The Wandering Jew," tracing the plight of these persecuted people through the ages. Lamentably, we haven't settled the Jewish issue yet. Another time, my father put up $25,

along with other St. Onge citizens, to underwrite a summer Chautauqua program with lectures and classical music. But some of the entertainers failed to show, the program fizzled and Mother and Father argued for days over the ill-spent $25.

Once country roads were improved, the family frequently journeyed to our neighboring town, Belle Fourche, where one year we went to the circus and got caught in a tornado. We barely escaped as the big center pole crashed to the ground, and we battled our way out before the sprawling canvas collapsed all around us. That was scary, but nothing compared to my first movie, D.W. Griffith's three-hour saga of the Civil War, *The Birth of a Nation.* It was the first Hollywood blockbuster. To the piano accompaniment of martial music and simulated thunder of battle, I watched utterly frozen as the horrors of war were recreated on the screen. Negroes were lynched and the Ku Klux Klan rode roughshod over the vanquished South. There was a story around town that one of the old-time cowboys, violently incensed by the Klan's brutality, whipped out his six-shooter and shot a Klansman dead on the screen. If true, no doubt he was understandably aroused, as was the whole country. People stormed the movie houses, not only to see the blood-curdling film, but to protest its blatant racism and obvious misrepresentation of the true birth of our nation. At that, the movie was a box office success, grossing $10 million.

Probably I was only seven or eight years old at the time, and I didn't see another movie until about 1920, when some 35 million Americans were then flocking to see Charlie Chaplin, Harold Lloyd or Buster Keaton in a slapstick comedy, and I reveled in the exploits of Hollywood's 10-gallon hatted cowboy, Tom Mix. As a treat after the show, we repaired to the ice-cream parlor to indulge in 25-cent luscious banana splits. It couldn't quite match Saturday night with "Over the Waves" at Woodman Hall, but at least we got home before morning.

The day Mother turned on the lights

"Don't talk to me about the good old days." Mother used to say, with feeling, in her sunset years. "I'm grateful now every time I turn on the running water or switch on the lights, and I wonder what I've done to deserve all of these blessings." My mother slaved for over 30 years on the ranch before she enjoyed any of the modern conveniences which we all take for granted today.

While farmers in the United States have made more progress during the past 100 years than all the world in perhaps 100 centuries, the farmer's wife, until comparatively recent times, lagged far behind in labor-saving equipment and everyday conveniences. Mother's work was never done: standing red-faced over a hot cook stove, lugging every drop of water in and out of the house, bending over a back-breaking washboard or "agitating" the clothes with her own woman-power as she cranked one of the first toilsome washing machines.

Mother had to run down the steps to the cool, dark cellar where Father had hung quarters of beef and pork during the winter, and she kept her sausage in two-gallon stone jars. We bought our fresh meat in town during the summer. Until we got an old-fashioned, secondhand icebox, she kept her milk and cream in the cellar, too. She trimmed the wicks, washed the glass chimneys and filled the kerosene lamps daily. She emptied the ashes from two stoves during the winter months. Come spring, the stovepipes had to be taken down and cleaned with extra care so as to avoid shaking out the soot in the house. Picking a quiet day when the wind wouldn't blow the soot about, Mother carefully carried out each length of stovepipe, tapped the soot loose and then replaced the pipe. This was the beginning of a thorough spring housecleaning, during which she took down and washed all of her grimy curtains and also washed the walls and ceiling. Meantime, I reluctantly beat a year's dust out of the parlor carpet which we hung on the clothesline.

It is little wonder that Mother never wished for the "good old days," with their endless drudgery and inconvenience and isolation. To be sure, Father endeavored to lighten Mother's load, and he joined with our neighbors in the 1920s to bring electric lights and telephone to the farm. But local utility companies told the farmers they would have to set their own poles and string their own lines—at prohibitive cost—to receive service at the farm. Lamentably, this was the attitude of most utilities across the country, who figured that the average farmer or rancher wiring his home would use only three or four 60-watt light bulbs, hanging from a cord in the ceiling. The power companies saw no profit in the farmers.

Shortsightedly, American utilities never envisioned the farmer's potential use of electric power, and thus they missed one of the greatest markets in the world. They never conceived of the poor farmer using electric stoves, freezers to store a whole beef, washing machines, electric irons, dishwashers, radio and other home appliances. Neither did they dream of installing electricity in the cow barn and using milking machines, using electricity to auger ensilage into a silo and to heat the hoghouse for farrowing pigs. And who could imagine that someday a farmer, using push-button controls, would run a mammoth cattle feeding operation, mixing feed by computer for thousands of head at a time.

That was the mighty market the power magnates missed. But they didn't know it and farmers didn't realize it either—at the time. Instead, we farmers still used the oil lantern in the barn, while we put up with kerosene lamps in the house until we got something better. One innovation was a new gasoline lamp, which we pumped up with air and then lighted by a match. It worked fine until a flying miller or any little bug struck the delicate double mantle burner, which promptly shattered, leaving us in the dark. Following the gasoline-lamp era, Father dug a big pit in the front yard, installed a tank and we enjoyed carbide lights. But they had an unpleasant odor and the carbide pit had to be cleaned and refilled. Still later, we might have used the new Delco homelighting outfit with a gasoline engine and generator when it reached the market, but it proved too expensive for most farmers in our neighborhood. However, Charley Furois installed a Delco plant in his general store, which brought the first electric lights in St. Onge—quite a novelty!

Meanwhile, getting together with our immediate neighbors, Father and my brother Earl dug the post holes, set the poles, strung the wire and installed our first phone service, connected with a central in St. Onge. Each farm had its own distinctive ring—say, two shorts and a long—and frequently we could hear the receivers click all down the line as neighbors listened in. They weren't necessarily nosy neighbors, but just interested and "visity." There was, for example, a neighbor lady who used to call my mother regularly. "And how are you feeling this morning?" Mother would ask solicitously. "Oh, I'm all right just now," she would sigh, "but I expect to have a splitting headache by afternoon."

After years of isolation on the ranch, Mother greatly enjoyed visiting, too, and gathering considerable community news by phone, she became a country correspondent for the weekly newspaper *The Belle Fourche Post*. She was an enterprising reporter, gathering both news items and features. "I pile up all the words I can," she explained to me. "After all, Paul, I get paid by the inch. It sure beats those damn little cream checks I used to cash." But one time Mother became a little too enterprising. Phoning around for news, she learned that a neighbor was seriously ill. In fact, she was informed that "the man was not expected to live through the night." Since she was now on deadline with her country correspondence, Mother rushed into print and, without checking further, turned in a commendable obituary. Three or four days later, she got a call— from the man himself! Like Mark Twain, he said the news of his death had been greatly exaggerated, but he did like the nice write-up, for which he profusely thanked Mother.

Whenever we cranked our old-fashioned phone, we could be sure of the most personalized phone service available anywhere. We'd put in a call to the bank and helpfully our St. Onge operator, amiable Albina Quillan, might break in with, "No use trying to get the bank today. The Colbys have all gone to the Days of '76 in Deadwood." On the other hand, our phone was operated on dry cell batteries, often the connections were bad, and we had to shout, "Speak up, I can't hear you!"

It was the combined voice of American farmers and ranchers, speaking up to Congress, that eventually brought electric power to rural America, and ironically it occurred under the New Deal during the depths of the Great Depression. Only one farm in ten was electrified in 1935, when Congress created the Rural Electrification Administration (REA). It was given authority to make low interest loans to cooperatives and other rural organizations for the generation and transmission of electric power to unserved rural homes. In a few years, REA had spread across the nation, electrifying most farms and ranch homes in America.

And that's how on a memorable day just before World War II, Mother turned on the lights; and, for her, "women's lib" belatedly began. "I cried," she told me about it later. "Now we've got electric lights, electric stove, refrigerator and, thanks to our electric pump and running water in the house, we can now take a hot bath at the turn of the tap." Mother grew pensive: "I only wish that we had such comforts and conveniences when your Father and I had our serious illnesses and while Grandma was alive." Prudently, Father insisted on keeping the old kitchen range standing for an emergency. And, sure enough, the first time that the REA lines went down during a heavy spring snowstorm, the old cook stove came in mighty handy.

It was a sheer joy to return home and see Mother bustling about her electric stove. "No more corncobs to start the fire!" she reminisced, pushing a button. She turned to plug in the electric pad for Father who was laid up with a bad back. Then, completing preparations for supper, Mother sat down with the family to eat under a cheery electric light. The day that Mother turned on the lights she put exhausting drudgery and inconvenience behind her forever, and it seemed to me that somehow the years fell away and actually she looked younger.

"My son," she remarked, filling her teakettle at the kitchen sink, and flipping the switch to heat it over her prized electric range, "don't ever talk to me about the good old days. *They never were!*"

"At last, the land is ours!"

Drouth is infinitely older than man and it is the most serious threat to crops in nearly every part of the world. Drouths on the semiarid Great Plains are recorded in Indian pictographs, and tree rings testify to a protracted 23-year drouth in the Southwest about 1300 A.D. It forced the Pueblo Indians to move far away, abandoning their cliff dwellings—America's oldest apartment houses. The earliest explorers and travelers encountered drouth and dust storms, long before the Sodbusters and the Honyockers arrived to plow up the virgin plains, and before cattlemen came with their trail herds to graze a sea of grass.

But I hope never again to see another prolonged, disastrous drouth such as devastated the Great Plains country and the Black Hills during the "Dirty Thirties." Unlike other sudden disasters, drouth is stealthy and insidious, and so it was with this ruinous onslaught. Inexorably, day after day, the glare of a scorching sun and the blast of hot winds parched the good earth, withered the field crops and grass, dried up the streams and waterholes. And this was the creeping catastrophe that threatened our ranch, together with most of the Great Plains country, early in 1931. As pastures turned prematurely brown and creeks ran low or not at all that summer, stockmen began shipping their cattle and sheep to market at a sacrifice. Wisely, Father had never overstocked his range and luckily False Bottom Creek continued to run, though just a trickle in some places. So we got through that drouthy year, and 1932 turned out to be slightly better.

But a merciless sun and thirsty winds intensified the drouth conditions the following year, and on Armistice Day, November 11, 1933, a great black blizzard boiled up out of the Dakotas, darkening the skies in Chicago the following day. It was the first of many disastrous dust storms during the next five years that swept the Great Plains from Texas to Canada. I remember driving South Dakota's dust-clouded highways with my lights on at midday, and seeing the topsoil piled in great drifts like snow that buried the wire fences. During the worst storms on the Great Plains, people wore protective face masks and still others were hospitalized with dust pneumonia. Housewives tried to seal up every crack around doors and windows, but still the choking dust relentlessly filtered in. That succession of black blizzards eroded and laid waste thousands of square miles, and left the West with thousands of abandoned farms in what became widely known as the nation's "Dust Bowl".

While the prolonged drouth alone was disastrous, conditions were worsened by plowing up the prairies, which now exacerbated the violent dust storms of the thirties. The whole tragedy triggered the massive migration of the drouthed-out "Oakies" to California.

Although, thankfully, we were spared the black blizzards on our ranch, located so near to the protecting Black Hills, our yields of dryland wheat and other crops were drastically reduced. Trudging through his powdery, burned-out fields, my aging father shook his head in utter disbelief and despair. "In all of my years in South Dakota," he recalled, "I've never seen it so bad as this." That terrible drouth year, he harvested a scant 20 bushels of wheat from over 100 acres! Keeping the precious wheat for seed, Father was eventually to plant it and harvest 40 bushels to the acre when at last the rains returned. But for now, it was overwhelming disaster. Except for a few stagnant pools, False Bottom Creek dried up altogether and we could no longer irrigate our corn and alfalfa. Rangelands burned brown so that we had to cut cattle numbers severely, sacrificing the "culls" under the government's so-called drouth "relief" program for $20 per head. The deepening depression compelled the St. Onge State Bank to close, wiping out savings and a desperately needed source of local credit.

It was an unprecedented ordeal for, by now, western farmers and ranchers battled the drouth, dust storms and the Great Depression—all at the same time. Wheat plunged from between $1.50 and $2 per bushel to as low as 25 cents in some places, hog prices skidded from about $15 per hundred-weight to under $5; and bitter dairymen dumped their unprofitable milk on the highways in futile protest of the times. As the crisis deepened, farmers threatened to strike and in many places they ganged up to halt sheriff's mortgage foreclosure sales. Seeking to save the nation's farms, Congress enacted the Agricultural Adjustment Act, which assisted farmers with some $1.5 billion in direct payments and helped to raise farm prices between 1932 and 1936. But in 1936, the "Triple A" was declared unconstitutional, leading to further distress and chaos until Congress could pass a new farm program in 1938.

As a final blow during the 1930s, one of mankind's oldest enemies, the locust or grasshopper, devastated the Great Plains in a series of plagues that stripped everything clean—wheat, corn, alfalfa, grass, gardens and shrubbery. Voracious hoppers chewed gloves, jackets, clothes on the line, and even pitchfork

Weeks without rain while hot winds blasted the field crops and grass, dried up the streams and waterholes and stripped the land of priceless top toil like this. These were the "Dirty 30s" when farm and ranchers endured drouth, dust storms, grasshoppers and the Great Depression all at the same time. — *South Dakota State Historical Society.*

Farming and ranching on the Great Plains is unending struggle, and over the years grasshopper plagues stripped cornfields and grain like this. During the terrible 1930s, hoppers devastated over $100 million in crops in a single year. — *South Dakota State Historical Society.*

Like all our neighbors, our family experienced good years and bad. But we gloried in the clean, earthy smell of freshly turned sod, the benediction of grass, the beauty of growing grain. To stand in waist-high wheat like this made a man proud! — *South Dakota State Historical Society.*

Following years of devastating drouth and indeed a struggle for survival, South Dakota greened again and farmers harvested the abundance of crops that fed the nation and helped to win World World II. — *South Dakota State Historical Society.*

Once out of the mud, farmers shifted into high gear. Following World War II big-time power farming arrived in earnest, with rural electrification, super plows and planters, costly combines and computerized farming. But the struggle and sacrifice of America's early farmers and ranchers had pioneered the way.—*South Dakota Division of Tourism.*

handles! At their peak in 1936, they destroyed over $100 million in crops. Like our ravaged neighbors, we fought the grasshoppers by spreading poisoned bran bait, flavored with molasses and vanilla extract to induce the insects to eat. While Father's costly control campaign paid off in part, it was a deadly fungus disease that finally decimated the hoppers and saved the farmers. But we all knew that some day the dread locust would return, even as it is recorded in the Bible, "The land is as the Garden of Eden before them ,and behind them a desolate wilderness, yea, and nothing shall escape them."

A combination of drouth, dust storms, grasshoppers and the Great Depression, the "Dirty Thirties" were absolutely the worst years in South Dakota's history, and yet—incredibly—people hung on. Standing in the governor's box at the Tri- State Roundup in Belle Fourche on the Fourth of July, cowboy Governor Tom Berry swept his hand toward the horizon. "Look at these fields," he indicated the drouth and devastation, "and now look at these folks. South Dakota has the greatest *comeback* people in the world!" He doffed his Stetson to the grandstand, amid tumultuous applause, and that day I was even prouder of my people and my goodly heritage.

But with recurrent drouths, hail, hoppers and hard times, our family had always waged a struggle for survival. During nearly 40 years of ranching in the Black Hills, Father and Mother experienced unremitting toil, endless worry and crushing debt. In the worst times, Father borrowed money at 10 and 12 percent in order to pay interest on existing loans. It is a marvel that with poor crops some years, poor prices and distant markets they managed to survive at all.

Consider how we marketed livestock, for example. During the early years, Father received his cattle and hog prices via rural mail carrier, which was quite an advance in communications for those days. But even these livestock quotations were outdated before they arrived, and shipping to the Omaha or Chicago markets was a frightful gamble. Loading his animals on the stock train at a railroad siding, Father climbed aboard to sit up all night in the jolting, smoky caboose. Next morning, he unloaded to feed and water his cattle at the halfway point—Long Pine, Nebraska— after which he journeyed on several hours longer to Omaha. During this hard trip, sometimes in bad weather, the livestock lost considerable weight— "shrinkage", we called it. Turning over his ganted up cattle to a livestock commission house, Father was completely at the mercy of the market—and more often than not lost money.

He returned home utterly dejected and discouraged. "I hate to tell you, Carrie," he'd break the news to my mother, "but I hit another bad market. I'm afraid we'll have to renew our notes at the bank." Mother consoled Father and took the bad news in stride. Later, she would shed some tears, but not for long. She scrimped further on her household spending, went another year without a new housedress and husbanded every cent in order to make ends meet before another season. And taking very little for his share in the ranch, my older brother helped mightily. As a consequence, our family weathered the drouth and Great Depression better than some of their neighbors. My parents were fiercely independent, and when the New Deal shipped in flour, fruit and other food for drouth-stricken farmers and ranchers, they adamantly refused as much as an orange.

"I'd rather be dead than accept a handout!" Mother resolutely disapproved.

At length, the disastrous drouth tapered off toward the close of the thirties; the short grass country greened again; farm prices slowly improved and things began looking up. Meantime, my parents, who had only rudimentary education, fulfilled a dream and saw that I graduated from college. Now Father and Mother pushed on to achieve their lifelong ambition. That was to pay off the mortgage and retire, with over 2,200 acres of choice ranchland gloriously free of debt.

In spite of declining health and the "Dirty Thirties," my determined parents accomplished this miracle and they cleared our beautiful ranch on Lower False Bottom Creek. Father had, indeed, come a long way from the rocky, impoverished bit of soil on which he was born in Cornwall, England.

"At last, the land is *ours!* Now we can face the whole world owing no one," Mother exulted. She held her head high, as if debt all these years had been a badge of dishonor. And looking out on his hard-earned acres, Father was prideful, too. For he had found America good, and together with my mother he had realized his American Dream on the gold-and-grass frontier.

"Bury me beside Wild Bill," Calamity Jane breathed her last—not long after she had stood by his grave in 1903.—*Centennial Archives, Deadwood Public Library.*

PART FOUR
A Gallery of Black Hills Characters

Annie Donna Tallent, one of the most esteemed pioneer women of the Black Hills. "The world is a better place because she lived in it."—*Rapid City Journal.*

First white woman in the Black Hills

She walked over 400 miles, across the perilous prairies, through the desolate Dakota Badlands, forded four rivers and was the first white woman to set foot in the Black Hills.

At age 47, Annie Donna Tallent made this remarkable trek in a wagon train, together with her husband, David; nine-year-old son, Robert; and a party of gold-seekers journeying from Sioux City, Iowa, to the new Eldorado in 1874. The courageous woman wore out two pairs of stout shoes on her rough trip; next, a pair of buckskin moccasins which she sewed up herself; and on the last leg of the 78-day punishing journey in late December she wrapped her feet in gunnysacks to trudge through the deep snows.

While the tourist folders and all too many writers glorify the notorious "Wild Bill" Hickok and "Calamity Jane," lamentably Annie Tallent is almost forgotten. Yet she was, indeed, a memorable character and one of the most esteemed pioneer women of the Black Hills.

The idea for the Black Hills expedition was sparked by a colorful newspaperman, Charlie Collins, Editor of the *Sioux City Times*, immediately after the exciting news of General Custer's gold discovery. Collins had long urged exploiting the Black Hills for their rumored riches, and now he publicly promoted an expedition to search for gold. But this was illegal since, under the Treaty of Laramie, the Hills had been forever set aside as inviolate Indian territory. To enforce the treaty, the army was under orders to seal off the region from all whites and to keep the gold-seekers out.

Undaunted, Collins was determined to run the gauntlet of government troops, and he secretly went ahead with his bold plans. He recruited a party, and just before sunset on the evening of October 5, 1874, 25 men and the Tallent family quietly gathered with their oxen and covered wagons on the banks of the Missouri at Sioux City. They crossed the river on an old ferry and camped that night near the village of Covington, Nebraska. At dawn, October 6, the expedition to the Black Hills set out on its incredible journey. It consisted of six covered wagons, each drawn by four oxen, and loaded with tents, gold pans, picks, shovels, guns, ammunition, personal belongings and enough food—bacon, beans, flour, sugar, canned goods and black coffee—to last eight months. In order to deceive government troops about its destination, the expedition painted "O'Neill's Colony" on the side of one wagon. The struggling settlement was just then getting started in northeast Nebraska. Curiously, organizer Collins did not accompany the expedition, which later became known as the Gordon party, named after John Gordon, who was elected captain and wagon boss.

Deliberately setting out to avoid the army, the Gordon party headed southwest toward the village of Norfolk, Nebraska, then zigzagged up the Elkhorn River Valley to O'Neill's colony. Each morning, Captain Gordon employed a clever ruse to mislead the military. He ordered the wagons to move in circles, first small, then larger, before finally veering off in the direction they were going. Before long, a troop of cavalry did get word of the gold-seekers, but the soldiers were completely baffled by the circles and never located the Gordon trail. A second troop picked up the trail, followed it across Nebraska, and into Dakota territory, but gave up.

Successfully eluding the troops, the Gordon party neared the Niobrara River on October 31 and was only two day's travel from the Nebraska–Dakota boundary, where they would cross over into the Great Sioux Reservation set aside by the Treaty of Laramie. By now, some of the party had grown ill-tempered and a few talked about turning back, but Captain Gordon held them together, except for one man. Probably feigning illness, he abandoned the expedition at Norfolk and returned home. It was now autumn and travel across the prairies was exhilarating. The skies were clear, the weather crisp and sunny. The slow-moving train traveled 15 to 20 miles a day, with occasional stops to rest the footsore oxen. Mrs. Tallent and her wide-eyed little boy, Robert, walked behind the wagons. At night, the party gathered around the campfires where the lone woman led the rough-and-ready crowd in story-telling and song.

Still there was always the gnawing fear of hostile Indians and apprehension that they might encounter the military. Mrs. Tallent tells of her concern in her dramatic account of the trip: "There perhaps was not one of us who did not experience occasional twinges of homesickness as we approached the danger line, and visions of exposure, hardships, sickness and even death rose up before us, and the fierce warwhoop of the Sioux was already ringing in our ears. The outlook was by no means alluring."

Shortly before leaving Nebraska, the expedition met a party of U.S. government surveyors who had been compelled to abandon their work on account of hostile Indians, and now strongly urged the gold-seekers to turn back. But Captain Gordon was determined to press on. By now, however, the footsore, emaciated oxen were beginning to show the effects of their rugged travel, and just ahead lay another hurdle—the treacherous Niobrara River. At 10 o'clock on the morning of November 2, the six heavy wagons began fording the hazardous stream. Ice had formed on both sides of the river, the current was swift and the oxen repeatedly slipped and fell in the shifting quicksands. Annie, her husband and little boy managed to cross the river, but it was a struggle and they were glad to reach firm ground on the other side.

Safely across, the expedition continued north and west along the Nebraska border, and then crossed over into the Great Sioux Reservation. As yet, it encountered no Indians or soldiers. "We were in constant expectation of seeing a troop of cavalry come upon us form the rear, seize our train, burn our wagons and supplies, march us back in disgrace, and possibly place us in durance vile [jail]," Mrs. Tallent recounted. To avoid both military and hostile Indians, Gordon ordered all camp fires extinguished before dusk and he posted an all-night guard. Now, as the party moved into Indian country, it encountered the first winter storms and bitterly cold weather. Since no fires were allowed after dark, the expedition suffered severe hardship. There was further distress when several members of the party, including Mrs. Tallent, were stricken with a painful intestinal ailment, likely due to spoiled food, alkali drinking water and exposure. It would cause the death of one person. But suffering her spasms in silence, Mrs. Tallent kept up with the wagons, until at last she was urged to ride for a day or two to hasten her recovery.

Now deep into Indian country, the Gordon party headed northwest, passing near the sites of present-day Wewela, Okreek and White River in western South Dakota. The party then entered the awesome big Badlands. Traveling through the barren, trackless country, the expedition soon found water extremely scarce and the men chopped blocks of ice from the frozen White River to melt for their own use and to water the oxen. But the chalk-laden water was nauseating and purgative and more people fell ill.

Suddenly the party was plunged into gloom when one of the men, who had been ill for several days, grew acutely worse; and some urged that the wagon train halt to give him time to recover. But the season was late, and wagon boss Gordon feared winter storms might trap them in the terrible Badlands. He ordered one of the wagons emptied, a comfortable bed prepared for the sick man and the trek continued out of the Badlands, probably to the present site of Belvidere or Kadoka. Mrs. Tallent wrote poignantly of her heart-breaking experience along the trail:

All that day I walked along by the side of the wagon with the long agonizing wails of the dying man ringing in my ears; every cry piercing my heart like a two-edged sword, he begging to be shot, and thus relieved from his terrible suffering. This thought no doubt was suggested to his mind by the sight of a gun strapped to the canvas above his head, which was very soon removed. About an hour before arriving at our camping ground his cries ceased, and we all fervently hoped he had fallen asleep. Upon reaching camp and looking into the wagon, it was seen that he, indeed was peacefully sleeping, the sleep that knows no wakening.

Gloom, like a dark pall, hung over our little camp on the dreary, lonely prairie that night. Death was in our midst and every gust of wind that blew down the valley seemed laden with the wails and groans of our departed companion. . . . A coffin of small, hewn timbers was constructed, in which the body was decently laid, then a cover, also of hewn timber was pinned down. A grave was dug on a little grassy eminence overlooking the lonely valley, then sadly and tenderly his comrades lowered him into his final resting-place, there to await the call of the last trumpet on resurrection morn.

A cross, also of small, smooth, hewn timber was erected over his grave. . . . Inscribed: "Died on the 27th November, 1874, on his way to the Black Hills, Moses Aarons, aged 32 years. May he rest in peace."

Leaving Aarons' fresh grave, not far from the present town of Wall, the weary expedition continued westward, and on the morning of December 1, was greeted with a thrilling sight. "We had our first glimpse of the Black Hills about ten o'clock a.m.," Mrs. Tallent recounts. "The Black Hills! The Black Hills! passed from lip to lip. A glad cry of relief went forth at the sight, and every heart sang paeans of joy and thankfulness, that our destination was so nearly reached. We could see plainly, away in the distance, the long line of dark shadowy hills, dimly outlined against a blue sky, and to the right, Bear Butte, standing alone like a huge sentinel guarding the entrance to that unknown land."

Cresting a high, steep bluff on the morning of December 3, the wagon train approached the Cheyenne River, and at first the descent looked impossible. But there was no turning back! The oxen were unhitched, and the sweating men lowered the wagons down the bluffs by ropes. Then hitching up the oxen again, they forded the sluggish river.

Plodding across the prairie, roughly paralleling the route of I-90 today, the party saw the hazy Black Hills take shape as bold, rugged mountains only 40 or 50 miles away. "At length on the 9th day of December," Mrs. Tallent recorded the historic date, "our feet pressed Black Hills' soil, at a point about four miles below Sturgis, where we took dinner in the midst of a howling snowstorm. Here we found a well-defined wagon road made by the heavy supply train, accompanying the Custer expedition on its exit from the Hills. . . . Our first camp was made in a canyon about two miles below where Piedmont now is."

It took the wagon train two weeks winding its tortuous way through the dark canyons and snow-covered glades of the Black Hills to reach its intended destination on French Creek, near Custer. The exhausted, overjoyed gold-seekers ended their long, hard journey on December 23, 1874—just in time to celebrate Christmas in the wilderness. The men went to work building a formidable log stockade, enclosing seven cabins, and then set out that winter to find gold. Life in the stockade was dreary and monotonous for Annie who read and reread Milton's *Paradise Lost* and the light romance, *The English Orphans.* Early in February, John Gordon and another propector, Eph Witcher, "loaded with gold and mail," departed on horseback for Sioux City, which they reached 23 days later. Displaying a sack of gold dust, Gordon created tremendous excitement and, in fact, helped spark the mad, wild rush to the Black Hills. He hastily organized a second wagon train and started back to the Hills, but was intercepted by the military. Gordon was arrested (later released) and all of his goods were confiscated.

On April 4, 1875, two months after Gordon had returned to Sioux City in triumph, the U.S. Army at last caught up with the gold-seekers near Custer. Proclaiming them prisoners, the military gave the remaining members of the party, Annie Tallent and her nine-year-old son, just 24 hours to pack up and leave the region now permanently ceded to the Sioux. Wagons, mining tools, Mrs. Tallent's small trunk with personal belongings—nearly everything was left behind. On April 6, a cavalry troop officially evicted the party and Annie Tallent rode out of French Creek on an army mule!

The entire party was temporarily removed to a cavalry camp in the foothills, from where it was escorted to Fort Laramie. thoughtfully, the army provided an ambulance for Mrs. Tallent in which she made the 10-day journey. At Fort Laramie, the evacuees were released from military control and given free transportation to Cheyenne. Most of the party returned to Sioux City, but the Tallents remained in Cheyenne for nearly a year.

By now the army could no longer seal off the Black Hills, the gold rush was in full swing, and the first white woman to enter the region was eager to return. Together with her husband and son, Annie joined a party of 25 or 30 wagons, well-armed against Indian

attack, and in April 1876, set foot in the Black Hills a second time. Her first stop was French Creek, but finding the mining camp virtually deserted, the Tallents followed the stampede to Deadwood Gulch. While her husband, David, looked for placer claims, Annie and 10-year-old Robert roughed it in a crude log cabin with unfinished roof. During a heavy rain storm, they were soaked. Luckily, the family secured better living quarters, but David found little or no gold.

To feed the family, Annie taught in one-room log schools around the Hills and eventually moved to Pennington County. There she resumed teaching and was elected Pennington County superintendent of schools. The able, ambitious woman served her community well. She was president of the Rapid City Board of Education, taught Sunday school and was a guild leader in the Episcopal church.

Little is known of her early life. Born on April 12, 1827, in the town of York, Livingston County, New York, she received an excellent education for a woman of her day, and it is believed she taught school until she met her husband, who claimed to have legal training. They emigrated West, and she was 38 when her only child, Robert, was born. For a time, David Tallent maintained a law office in Deadwood, after which he apparently deserted his family. He may have died in some western mining camp.

Carrying on alone, Mrs. Tallent raised and educated her son, Robert, and she became a leading citizen of the Black Hills. Retiring from her work with the schools, she plunged into the prodigious task of writing her 713-page book, *The Black Hills, or Last Hunting Ground of the Dakotahs.* It is an invaluable, highly readable guide to Black Hills history from the gold rush to the turn of the century.

Greatly beloved and esteemed, Annie spent her last two years in Sturgis with son Robert. Becoming ill with pneumonia, she passed away two weeks later on February 13, 1901. She was 73. Her funeral services were held at St. Thomas Episcopal church in Sturgis. As a final tribute, a special train was chartered that day in Deadwood, Circuit court recessed and 60 members of the Society of Black Hills Pioneers, together with a host of other friends, came to pay their farewells to a true pioneer. Annie was buried in Elgin, Illinois, beside other relatives.

"A most remarkable woman," eulogized a Black Hills newspaper. Today, beside the highway near Custer, a tall, granite monument honors this "remarkable" lady: the first white woman in the Black Hills. Appropriately, a plaque is inscribed, "The world is a better place because she lived in it."

On Preacher Smith: "While his ministrations were not very effective, it was the fault of the material he had to work with and not due to any lack of zeal or piety on his part."—*Centennial Archives, Deadwood Public Library.*

Sky Pilot who was faithful unto death

Just as that worthy woman, Annie D. Tallent, deserves a foremost place in any gallery of memorable characters, so also does another figure who has greatly fascinated me from boyhood. He was the martyred Methodist missionary, Henry Weston Smith, pioneer preacher of the Black Hills.

I first learned about "Preacher Smith," or the "sky pilot," as ministers were called on the western frontier, when our family motored one day up the mountains to historic old Deadwood. As we climbed a lonely stretch of road through the sighing pines, over which Father had often hauled hay from Centennial Prairie into Deadwood, he remarked, "Not far from here the Indians killed Preacher Smith." A little farther on, we stopped the car to get out and view the new white stone monument which the Society of Black Hills Pioneers had erected to the missionary's memory.

Then an imaginative ten-year-old, I was deeply moved and I could picture the pioneer preacher walking bravely through the dark pine forest alone, while hostile Indians stalked his path. I wondered whether he had been scalped, but Father said no. Later, when I was older, I viewed the missionary's grave in Deadwood's famed Mount Moriah Cemetery, and I was impressed by his selfless life.

Born in Ellington, Connecticut on January 10, 1828, the idealistic young man entered the ministry when he was 23 and became a Methodist "exhorter." This led to his ordination in the Methodist Episcopal church and he served various communities in New England. In 1862, he enlisted in the Union Army where "caring for the wounded may have turned his mind to healing," according to the plaque on his monument. He studied medicine and may have been licensed in 1867. Also, he married, but had the misfortune to lose both his wife and baby at childbirth.

About this time, the Methodist church was dispatching missionaries to the western frontier, and feeling the call to mission, Reverend Smith, at age 49, volunteered to journey to the wilderness of the Black Hills. "In 1876, he joined the great rush to these Black Hills," I read his plaque again recently, "*not to mine gold but to claim lives for God.*" Surely among the horde of gold-seekers, he would find saints and sinners, human hungers and wants aplenty to fulfill his mission. About ten years after his first wife's death, however, the minister had remarried and now supported a second wife and three children. But God called him and he responded willingly. Bidding goodbye to his family,

whom he intended to bring to the Black Hills later, the Reverend Smith left his home in Louisville, Kentucky, destined for Cheyenne, Wyoming Territory. Arriving there on a Union Pacific train, he joined a caravan to Custer, which he reached in the spring of 1876.

Methodist missionaries in those days received scant, if any, financial support, and the sky pilot labored at any job he could find—placer mining, carpentry, chopping wood around Custer—in order to send meager savings to his family and sustain himself. To ease his loneliness, he read and wrote poetry. On Sundays, he preached in the streets. About this time, the gold rush suddenly shifted to Deadwood Gulch, and Smith walked 70 miles beside a bull-train to the northern Hills.

He built a log cabin, furnished with a crude bed and table; worked at odd jobs again, to eke out a living; and preached on Deadwood's Main Street or in the saloons—wherever he could attract a few attentive listeners. His customary pulpit was a packing box, on which he stood, Bible in hand, to exhort the grizzled gold-seekers to lead less sinful lives and to be worthy of their loved ones at home. Miners sometimes dropped a few coins in the hat at his feet, and on one occasion, so the story goes, Calamity Jane passed the hat through the Sunday crowd shouting, "Dig down now, you God damn sinners, for this good man and save your souls." The tall bearded sky pilot was well received and it was said he could command the respect of even the most irreligious. But brawling, bawdy Deadwood was seeking gold and not God.

On Sunday morning, August 20, 1876, Preacher Smith, as was his custom, exhorted the miners gathered in Deadwood's Main Street, and he rejoiced at a bit of gold dust dropped in the hat during collection. He then returned to his lonely cabin, where he tacked a note on his door, "Gone to Crook City to preach, and if God is willing, will be back by 3 o'clock."

It was a 20-mile round trip to the then thriving mining camp, Crook City, and the missionary was warned about hostile Indians on the warpath again, so soon after the "Custer Massacre." He was urged to carry a gun, but refused. "The Bible is my protection. It has never failed me," the missionary responded. So fearlessly he set out from Deadwood, Bible in hand, and sermon notes in his pocket, to walk through the dangerous woods to Crook City.

The pioneer preacher of the Black Hills never returned alive.

The first monument in Mount Moriah Cemetery to Henry Weston Smith, pioneer preacher of the Black Hills. Long since vandalized, only the inscription at the base remains.—*Centennial Archives, Deadwood Public Library.*

About three miles out of Deadwood, he was shot from ambush and killed—supposedly by Indians. He lay sprawled on his back, clutching his Bible. In his pocket were the bloodstained notes for his undelivered sermon. His message was about five ways to "Go ye into all the world" and spread His Word: "First. Without money. Christ sent His disciples forth without purse or script, but he did not intend that they should live without food. Second. By sustaining the social needs of Grace. All can do something here, and are required to do something, every man according to his ability. Third. The Sabbath School. Fourth. By personal efforts to lead men to the Savior. Fifth. By holding up the life of a consistent God as a guide to our own lives." This was his bloodstained exhortation,

which years later Methodist pastors pulled together in a memorial text.

A rancher discovered the body of the slain preacher, spread the alarm, and a party of men went out from Deadwood to haul the body back to town on a hay wagon. A carpenter fashioned a wooden casket, and seemingly all Deadwood Gulch flocked to the funeral, the miners lustily singing the moving hymn, "Nearer My God to Thee." Thus the martyred missionary was laid to rest almost before his soul-saving missionary work had begun. He was buried temporarily in a grave near Deadwood Gulch, but in 1883, reinterred in the new Mount Moriah Cemetery. His family was notified of his death, and at the same time generous Deadwood citizens offered to raise a purse to bring the missionary's wife and children to Deadwood to live. But now in poor health, the widow declined the offer.

Saluting the memory of Preacher Smith, the handful of Black Hills pioneers still alive gathered on August 20, 1914, to unveil the white stone monument that stands today on Highway 85 between Spearfish and Deadwood. On that occasion—38 years after his untimely death—the *Deadwood Pioneer-Times* gave the sky pilot a fitting eulogy. Said the newspaper; "He was highly respected and while his ministrations were not very effective, exhorting miners to abstain from vice and sin, it was the fault of the material he had to work with and not due to any lack of zeal or piety on his part."

Many years ago, a life-size statue of Preacher Smith was sculpted and raised over his grave in Mount Moriah, but like "Wild Bill's" monument, it has been vandalized and destroyed. Today only the inscription at the base remains, but appropriately it reads:

> IN MEMORY OF
> HENRY WESTON SMITH
> PIONEER PREACHER IN THE BLACK HILLS
> FAITHFUL UNTO DEATH

148

Shades of "Wild Bill" and "Calamity Jane"

Growing up in the storied Black Hills, I lived in an aura of lore and legend, peopled with some memorable characters. Two have now become legendary figures, symbolic of once lusty, wide-open old Deadwood: James Butler (Wild Bill) Hickok, and Martha (Calamity Jane) Cannary.

Imagine then my youthful excitement when we climbed to famed Mount Moriah Cemetery one Decoration Day (now Memorial Day) to place flowers on the graves of Grandfather and Grandmother Hosken. Sure enough, just as I had first discovered at Grandma's funeral, my grandparents were laid to rest close by this notorious pair. As we decorated the graves, my mother recalled seeing Calamity Jane on the streets of Deadwood, and of hearing news of her death. Shortly before passing, Mother said Calamity had gasped her last request, "Bury me beside Wild Bill." And sentimental old Deadwood did, turning out in a mile-long cortege to Mount Moriah and staging the largest funeral in the city's history. "Like everyone else," Mother related, "I went to see her laid out at the funeral parlors. She was a swarthy, unattractive little woman, dressed in a buckskin suit like a man. People said she had nursed the miners during a smallpox epidemic, and I suppose she had her virtues along with her vices."

Recently, I climbed to lovely, pine-clad Mount Moriah again and looking down on historic Deadwood in the gulch below, I reflected on the lives of these two legendary characters. Their ghosts still haunt the Hills, and their stories are melodramatic enough without the embellishment of some bad movies and pure fiction produced over the years.

Wearing her fringed buckskin outfit, with a belt of side-arms, Calamity Jane rode into Deadwood one day during the summer of 1876, together with another female sport, "Kittie" Kelly, Wild Bill Hickok and a colorful, character known as "Colorado Charlie" Utter. Then a blue-eyed, auburn-haired, buxom young woman of 24, Calamity was seldom seen in women's apparel. Carousing from saloon to dance-hall in her buckskin garb, the cigar-smoking, tobacco-chewing hellion, who let out wild-animal whoops and was a holy terror when she was drunk, quickly became a brazen figure even for lusty old Deadwood. She had won the name "Calamity," so she claimed, after she had joined the U.S. Army as a scout and showed extraordinary daring and bravado in a skirmish with the Indians at Goose Creek, Wyoming Territory. In the encounter,

the captain of the scouts was shot, whereupon Jane galloped to his side, lifted the wounded man up on her horse and dashed away, saving the scout's life. "I call you, Calamity, heroine of the Plains," the grateful captain bestowed the name that Calamity carried for the rest of her life. But there were also less heroic versions of how she won the name Calamity.

She also claimed to have accompanied a military expedition to the Black Hills in 1875. But these stories, like most about Calamity Jane, are unfounded and now legendary. Moreover, much of her own life story, which she wrote in later years and peddled in her poverty, is largely discredited. The old movies, glamorizing her as a beautiful young girl in buckskin pants, who scouted for the army and had a flaming romance with handsome Wild Bill Hickok, still serve to perpetuate the myths.

The truth seems be to that Martha Jane Canary (or Cannary) was born May 1, 1852, at Princeton, Missouri. Her father, according to one authentic source, was a hard drinker and abusive of his family. So the tempestuous teenager ran away from home leaving her brothers and sisters, and turned up in the "Hell-on-Wheels" railroad town of Cheyenne, where she became a camp follower with the Union Pacific construction crews. Before long, the hell-raising Jane and her dissolute companions were run out of town.

Next, according to her own story, she joined the U.S. Army, but was discovered one day swimming in the buff and discharged. Probably about 1870, she drifted to Abilene, Kansas, where it was said she met and married one James B. Hickok, then a fearless young lawman. She arrived three years later in Montana, where she gave birth to a baby girl she named Jean Hickok. Now separated from Hickok, so it was gossiped, she put her baby up for adoption and was footloose again. This marriage, however, is wholly discredited by most authorities and writers. In Billings, Montana, she shot up a saloon and was escorted to the edge of town. She wandered back to Cheyenne, where on June 20, 1876, she made news in the *Cheyenne Leader* with an item headlined *Jane's Jamboree:*

On Sunday, June 10, that notorious female, Calamity Jane, greatly rejoiced over her release from durance vile, procured a horse and buggy from Jas. Abney's stable, ostensibly to drive to Ft. Russell and back. By the time she had reached the Fort, however, indulgence in frequent and liberal potations completely befogged her not very clear brain, and she drove right by that place, never drawing rein until she reached the Chug [Chugwater] 50 miles distant.

Continuing to imbibe bug-juice at close intervals and in large quantities throughout the night, she woke up next morning with a vague idea that Fort Russell had been removed, but still being bent on finding it, she drove on, finally sighting Fort Laramie, 90 miles distant. Reaching there, she discovered her mistake, but didn't show much disappointment. She turned her horse out to grass, ran the buggy into a corral, and began enjoying life in camp after her usual fashion. When Joe Rankin reached the Fort, several days later, she begged of him not to arrest her, and as he had no authority to do so, he merely took charge of the Abney's outfit, which was brought back to this city Sunday.

Drifting to the Black Hills in 1876, Jane soon became a conspicuous figure in the mining camps around Deadwood. "It is reported from Sturgis City that Calamity Jane walloped two women at that place yesterday," the *Black Hills Daily Times* wrote. "Calamity can get away with half a dozen ordinary pugilistic women when she turns loose, but she never fights unless she is in the right, and then she is not backward to tackle even a masculine shoulder hitter."

Ever on the move, she made frequent long freighting trips to Cheyenne and Ft. Pierre. She swung a 20-foot bullwhip like a man and could out-cuss any mule skinner. Back in Deadwood, she rushed to Wild Bill's side on August 2, 1876, when he was shot in the back of the head and killed while playing poker in Deadwood's wild Number Ten Saloon. The West's celebrated gambler and gunfighter slumped to the floor clutching a full house—aces over eights—known ever since as the "dead man's hand." Thus ended the spectacular career of the 39-year-old Hickok who claimed to have killed 36 men in his brief lifetime. According to Jane, she ran down the killer, Jack McCall, and had him arrested. But this was not so. McCall, however, was later arrested by a U.S. marshal, convicted in federal court and hanged at Yankton, Dakota Territory, on March 1, 1877.

Before coming to Deadwood, Wild Bill had married Agnes Lake, a circus performer. But some sources insist that Calamity still carried a torch for Bill, and drunkenly lurched around town, displaying her grief at Hickok's death. At length, Calamity sobered up to work a stint as a waitress, during which she treated her customers with loud mouthed profanity. "Tea or coffee?" she inquired of a newly arrived eastern "dude" in town. The newcomer requested tea, whereupon Calamity thundered, "You get coffee, you son-of-a-bitch. That's all we've got."

Wild Bill Hickok, the "Prince of Pistoleers." He came to the Black Hills for gold and died clutching a full house: aces over eights, the "dead man's hand." — *Centennial Archives, Deadwood Public Library.*

Yet inside this hellion beat a heart of gold, according to old-timers who knew her well. When she was in the money, Calamity would grubstake a poor prospector, and once she robbed a miner of his gold dust to help pay the doctor bill for a dancehall girl who was ill and down on her luck. In 1878, when a dread smallpox epidemic swept Deadwood Gulch, Calamity was the "angel" who risked her life to carry food to the sick miners and nurse them back to health in a log cabin "pesthouse." She came through unscarred as did most of the stricken miners, who sang her everlasting praises. Although she was a profane, rowdy woman, Calamity had a Christian-like concern for others, and likely at heart was not irreligious. On the fateful Sunday in 1876 that "Preacher Smith," Deadwood's first sky pilot, was killed by Indians, it was Calamity who lamented: "Ain't it too bad that they killed the only man who could tell us how to live. And we sure need the telling."

About 1880, the restless Calamity left the Black Hills and was gone several years, during which time she turned up at army posts and mining camps around the West. Traveling to Texas, she married a hack driver, Charles Burke, and in 1887 she showed up in Montana with a daughter, either her own or adopted. By now,

Wild Bill's fenced but vandalized sandstone sculpture as it once stood in Mount Moriah Cemetery. It now lies broken in the Adams Museum in Deadwood.—*Centennial Archives, Deadwood Public Library.*

Calamity had become perhaps the West's most notorious female character, and she joined Buffalo Bill's famed Wild West Show. She toured eastern United States and journeyed to England. But on her return to the United States, she was fired for excessive drinking. Joining the Palace Museum Show, she was fired for the same reason. She took another job with the Pan-American Exposition and was fired again.

Dissolute, dispirited, down-and-out, the battered Calamity returned to Deadwood in 1895, where she was welcomed as a long lost prodigal. Rallying around her, as if she were a beloved old neighbor, the good citizens of Deadwood staged a benefit on her behalf in one of the town's old dives, the Green Front Saloon. There were laudatory speeches and heartwarming salutes, even from some of the city's most respectable women who saw the inside of the low-down Green Front for the first time. At the close of the benefit, Calamity was presented with a sizable purse, but generous as usual, the old gal invited everybody up to the bar and spent freely. After the homecoming Calamity arranged to enroll her 10-year-old daughter in a Catholic school in Sturgis, and she went on trying to mend her tattered life.

She was hanging out in the high, wild mining camp of Terry, a few miles from Deadwood, when she was taken violently ill in a seedy miners' boarding house and died of alcoholism and pneumonia on August 2, 1903. From the funeral parlors, her body was taken to Deadwood city hall and old-timers asked the Reverend C.B. Clark to say a few words over her coffin. But the minister did even better. "Bring her to the Methodist Church and we'll give her a real funeral," he offered. So Calamity came to church, and Reverend Clark preached a moving sermon on her neighborly virtues that had won the hearts of old Deadwood.

The First Methodist church was crowded, people stood respectfully outside, and a long line of horse-drawn carriages joined the funeral procession to Mount Moriah. Just as she had wished with her last breath, Calamity was buried beside Wild Bill and so became a legend. Every year now, thousands perpetuate this legend as they flock to Deadwood to celebrate the colorful Days of '76 and to gaze on the graves of Calamity and Wild Bill on Boot Hill.

Among those respectable Deadwood ladies, who welcomed Calamity back and understood her best was Estelline Bennett, daughter of a pioneer federal judge. Miss Bennett paid Calamity a fitting tribute in her rare book, *Old Deadwood Days.*

"More than anyone else who lived in the twentieth century," wrote Miss Bennett, "Calamity Jane was symbolic of old Deadwood. Her virtues were of the endearing sort. Her vices were the wide-open sins of a wide-open country—the sort that never carried a hurt. Some one has said of her once that she was a contradiction of 'The Evil men do lives after them. The good is oft interred with their bones.' Whatever there was of evil in Calamity's life has been long since forgotten. The good she did will be on men's tongues until the old stagecoach aristocracy is gone. It is not lost in the dust of the grave beside Wild Bill."

151

During its early years, the Black Hills Stage and Express was attacked or held up almost daily. It operated for 11 years, from 1876 to 1887.—*Western History Department, Denver Public Library.*

They rode "shotgun" on the treasure coach

"He used to ride shotgun on the Deadwood treasure coach!" People spoke about Jesse Brown with a certain awe when I was a boy in the Black Hills. Brown had freighted on the Bozeman Trail, fought Indians and road agents and then took a death-defying job as a shotgun messenger guarding the gold bullion shipped weekly from the Hills' mines. Father knew Brown, as he did one or two other surviving stagecoach drivers, and on occasion we saw the old-timers at Fourth of July or Labor Day celebrations. Thus I grew up with an abiding curiosity and wonder about these audacious characters, who sometimes guarded from $100,000 to $300,000 in gold bars and delivered it safely to Union Pacific Railroad gunmen in Cheyenne for shipment East.

I never forgot those white-haired old shotgun messengers and stage drivers, but it was many years before I was privileged to learn their whole incredible story from a man who knew them intimately. He was Russell Thorp, Jr., pioneer Wyoming cattleman and western history authority, whose father, Russell Thorp, Sr., had owned and managed the famed Cheyenne and Black Hills Stage and Express. Operating 11 years, from 1876 to 1887, the stage during the early days was attacked or held up almost daily. A U.S. cavalry escort was required at one time from the Jenney Stockade near Custer to the Hat Creek stage station in Wyoming, and it was worth anyone's life to ride on the line.

"Two weeks after the stage line was established," Thorp recalled, "the coach was attacked by Indians and the driver was killed. During the following summer the redskins continued to attack the line, burn relay stations and run off the stock. Six employees of the company were killed and 98 head of horses were stolen. Finally the Indians were brought to order by the troops, but now a new foe confronted the stage company and its fearful passengers: desperate road agents and outlaws who flocked into the country endangering each journey from Cheyenne to Deadwood and back. Two stage drivers were heartlessly shot down and much property seized by the outlaws."

It was a jolting, 320-mile journey on the Black Hills stage from Cheyenne to Deadwood, with seven-minute stops to change horses and grab a bite to eat at "swing stations" located roughly 14 to 16 miles apart. In September 1876, the stage, traveling continuously day and night, made a record run in 47 hours, a remarkable achievement in overland transportation.

The driver, who seldom carried on a conversation but concentrated on reining his spirited six-horse team, rarely left his seat until the end of his run. Expertly handling his prancing steeds, a good stage driver earned $60 to $100 per month, plus food and lodging; and he proudly wheeled over the rutted trails in a rugged Concord coach, recognized at the time as "the only perfect passenger vehicle in the world."

The Concord was designed and built in Concord, New Hampshire, by the Abbot-Downing Company, expert New England wagon makers. They did a tremendous business. The coach used on the Cheyenne-Deadwood line cost $1,800 at the factory and at one time the company shipped these beautiful maroon coaches (wheel and running gear were painted canary yellow with black stripes) much as we ship automobiles by rail today. Imagine a string of Union Pacific flatcars loaded with these gleaming Concords headed West. Built of well-seasoned, selected ash, the Concords were designed to carry heavy loads over rough trails, deserts and mountains. The body was attached to rockers which, in turn, were attached to "thoroughbraces" or tough leather straps. These allowed the coach body to rock back and forth, providing a more comfortable ride for the passengers jouncing over the prairies. Hand made, the Concord was a thing of grace and beauty and carried 17 passengers, inside and out, beside the driver. In addition, the coach carried mail and baggage in the front and rear boots, and there was a treasure box.

This was a steel-lined, 16-by-30-inch chest or safe, bolted to the floor and guaranteed to be burglar-proof for at least 24 hours. And in this treasure box, the stage line commenced hauling $25,000 and $30,000 shipments of gold dust from the Hills to Cheyenne. At first, the company carried gold dust right along with the passengers, but soon it was plagued with road agents and outlaws and abandoned this practice as too dangerous. Instead, it introduced the steel-plated treasure coach—"Old Ironsides." No passengers were allowed and in their place rode the fearless "shotgun messengers."

The Deadwood treasure coach was a tempting prize and on the afternoon of September 19, 1878, a band of highwaymen held up the stage in a brazen robbery. Years afterward, my good friend Russell Thorp, Jr., whose father had operated the stage line, interviewed some of the shotgun messengers guarding the gold on this trip, and from his carefully preserved notes and personal recollections, he told me this story:

"In September, 1878, at Canyon Springs station [located on the western edge of the Black Hills] occurred one of the most thrilling robberies in the history of the line," Thorp recounted. "The treasure coach sometimes carried as much as $100,000 at one time in the steel box bolted to the floor. On this trip, the gold bars and bullion amounted to about $37,000 and was guarded by shotgun messengers Scott Davis, captain of the guards, Gale Hill, Donald Campbell and a Captain Smith.

"Often the robbers staged their holdups at night, but this was broad daylight and Captain Davis wasn't expecting trouble. Gale Hill rode up front with the driver. Inside the coach, by the treasure box, Davis rode with Campbell, who was on his way to take charge of the telegraph office at Jenney Stockade. About three o'clock in the afternoon, the driver pulled up in front of the barn where the stock tender should be standing ready to unhitch the six horse team and change to six others—usually done in seven minutes!

"The stock tender not being in sight, Gale Hill jumped down to see what had happened. At this point, the road agents who had captured the stock tender and bound him hand and foot, opened fire through a hole in the chinking between the logs of the stable. They hit messenger Hill, seriously wounding him, and they grazed Smith's scalp. Campbell was killed instantly. Captain Davis now jumped out of the coach, on the opposite side from the barn, and made a run for a big pine tree. Getting behind the tree, he shot it out with the four bandits, badly wounding one. The leader of the gang called out to Davis to surrender, but he retorted: 'Surrender never! I'll see you in hell first!'

"But now seeing he was badly outnumbered, Davis backed away through the woods until he was safe. Then he walked for two hours to the next stage station where shotgun messengers Jesse Brown, Boone May and Billy Sample were awaiting arrival of the treasure coach. Mounting their horses, the messengers hurried to the Canyon Springs station to find that the robbers had opened the 'burglar-proof' treasure box and escaped. First taking care of the wounded Hill, the shotgun messengers then hit the trail in pursuit of the bandits. They followed so closely the robbers dropped most of the heavy treasure so they could make better time getting away. Eventually, nearly all of the gold shipment was recovered and later two robbers were captured and strung up."

There were repeated holdups of the Black Hills stage, and attacks on stations and men. But, unbelievably, no major loss of gold occurred, and usually the fearless shotgun messengers ran down and got their man.

The country was now free of Indian attacks, the road agents were gone, the railroad had come and this was the last Deadwood stagecoach.—*Grabill photo. South Dakota State Historical Society.*

Thorp recounts another exciting chase and capture by intrepid Scott Davis. One day in 1877, road agents waylaid the treasure coach, secured considerable bullion and stole some stage horses in the vicinity of the Cheyenne River. Davis telegraphed officials at Cheyenne for authority to pursue and capture these men. The commanding officer at Fort Laramie ordered a detail of four men and a noncommissioned officer to accompany Davis. They trailed the desperadoes across Wyoming and up the Sweetwater. Heavy snows then fell and the cavalry escort, whose horses had played out, refused to go any further.

The incredible Davis went on alone. He continued, Thorp told me, over South Pass and caught up with the outlaws at a stage station on the Big Sandy, west of the Continental Divide. It was midnight—a moonless night—when he found the two men asleep beside a haystack. He ordered them to throw up their hands.

"When they came up, they came up shooting," Thorp related. "Davis wounded one and captured the other. He recovered the bullion and the horses, and leaving the wounded bandit behind, proceeded with his prisoner, horses and the gold to Green River City. He wired Cheyenne that he was there with the recovered property. The carload of horses was attached to a passenger train, and guard Davis arrived in Cheyenne where a crowd of people came down to the railroad station to see the man who had made this remarkable capture."

One of Thorp's more delightful recollections is the account of Mrs. Thomas Durbin's first stage trip from Cheyenne to the Black Hills. "Her husband had preceded her, leaving her a package to carry for him. Not until after she had started on the journey did she discover that she had $10,000 which was to be used in operating the first bank in Deadwood. Mrs. Durbin carried the money in a small bag with her baby bottles. Her coach passed through Red Canyon within a few hours after a killing there."

Over its 11-year-operation, the Black Hills stage carried millions of dollars in gold, together with the U.S. mail and thousands of passengers at 15 cents per mile. Then on Saturday morning, February 19, 1887, the Cheyenne *Daily Tribune* carried this headline:

THE LAST COACH OUT

The stage line from Cheyenne to Deadwood has been compelled to give way to better and more substantial improvement. The last stage has departed from this city. It was like bidding adieu to an old and cherished friend, as attested by hundreds of people this morning who filled the streets in the neighborhood of the Inter-Ocean Hotel.

One of the fine and substantial coaches recently built by Mr. Russell Thorp, the genial stageman and proprietor of the line, rolled down the street with the oldtime sound. Geo. Lathrop, one of the oldest and best stage drivers in the West, was upon the seat holding the reins over six as fine horses as were ever headed towards the gold fields of the Black Hills over 300 miles to the north.

A stop was made in front of the Inter-Ocean, when Mr. Thorp made the announcement that the coach was ready to depart. At this, a general rush was made to secure choice seats, and within minutes the stage was crowded and some six or eight gentlemen occupied places on top. Trunks were strapped upon the boot and there was every evidence that the parties so seated were prepared for the long journey to Deadwood.

The trip would be historic, the newspaper noted. "The country north is now free from the Indian, road agents are no more, the railroads are pushing through and the country is being settled up with happy, prosperous people. Such is the change of a few years."

After his father's death, Russell Thorp, Jr., presented one of the original Cheyenne-Deadwood stages to the Lusk, Wyoming, museum; and passing through the town (near where Thorp was raised at Rawhide Buttes station) I dropped in to see the beautiful old Concord vehicle again. Standing beside it, I could almost imagine the ghosts of Jesse Brown, Scott Davis and the others climbing aboard once more to ride "shotgun" on the Deadwood treasure coach.

Except for the rifle, this is how a typical cowboy was garbed in the 1880s to ride the range for the big cattle outfits.—*Grabill photo. South Dakota State Historical Society.*

156

My high-heeled heroes: the old cowboys

*I believe I would know an old
cowboy in hell with his hide
burnt off. It's the way they
stand and walk and talk.*
 —*Teddy Blue*, We Pointed Them North

They've now all gone to their last roundup, to a far range, across the Great Divide. They were my boyhood heroes, those old-time cowboys I knew so well, and I have cherished memories of them ambling about the lively old cow town, Belle Fourche. My favorite recollection is of seeing them sitting and chatting outside the town's livery stable. Or they were dozing in the lobby of the cattleman's hangout, the Hampton House, their high-heeled boots cocked up indifferently in the plate-glass windows on State Street.

When they weren't dozing, they would chew and spit Horseshoe cut-plug tobacco and reminisce by the hour: about the time, for instance, that Billy Clanton, using six horses, single-handedly roped 4,200 head of Texas steers in four and one-half days; or how Abe La Duke broke hundreds of wild horses, bragged he never once was thrown.

As a young newspaperman in Belle Fourche, I relished the opportunity to talk with colorful Ed Lemmon, "Dean of the range." Ed's life story was really the saga of the whole northern range cattle industry, and it was said that Lemmon, from about 1880 to the turn of the century, handled more cattle than any other man in the world. At one time, Ed ran cattle on more than 850,000 acres of leased Indian lands, he was a power in the South Dakota Stockgrowers Association and he had a town named after him—Lemmon, South Dakota. Badly crippled when I knew him, and hobbling about on a cane, energetic Ed reluctantly retired "after 53 years in the saddle."

Another of my heroes was a soft-spoken, six-foot-three Texan, Sam Moses. Sam first came up the Texas Trail with a herd of Longhorns during the Black Hills gold rush. He made repeated trips up the long, lonesome trail, then became boss of the famous TOT outfit when the foreman was killed in a poker game. But when cattle thieves commenced slapping their running iron on the unbranded calves during the spring roundups and rustled from the big cattle outfits, Sam took on the dangerous job of stock detective. Soon after, the foreman of one of the big ranches was shot off

his horse by a gang of five men, and Sam Moses, deputized as a special agent of the Department of Justice, went after the gang. Incredibly, Sam trailed Hank Smith, one of the killers, for 90 days through the wilds of the Southwest, into Mexico and back again, capturing him finally in Indian Territory. He returned Smith to Wyoming for trial at Cheyenne. Moses, who once was credited with 13 convictions in two years, was "tops" of all the stock detectives, but he rarely talked about his exploits. "I jest did my job," he'd say laconically.

Those gun-totin', bronc-bustin', honest-to-God old cowpunchers were rugged and they were individual and we shall not see their breed again. I was fortunate to see some of the old-timers in their familiar Stetsons and high-heeled boots, gathered for a cowboy's reunion at Hot Springs, South Dakota, in 1947. They called themselves "The Last Round-Uppers"; and although now a bit short-winded, they were mightly long on reminiscence, and they celebrated late into the night. Leaving a bar about two o'clock in the morning, a couple of cowmen found one of their cronies sound asleep and snoring in the hotel lobby. Kicking his boot, one of the celebraters inquired: "What's a matter, Ed? Can't you get a room?" To which the Last Round-Upper replied, "Hell, what do I want a room for? Only goin' to be here two or three days."

These old cowboys were salty, they had made history, and I delighted in their unvarnished tales, which I heard for the first time when I attended Belle Fourche High School and saw them regularly around town. I found one of my heroes right in Belle Fourche High: Billy Hubbard, the graying, friendly custodian who had been a roundup cook with one of the big cattle outfits. "Cookie" used to tell us about running the old chuck wagon, when his day started about three o'clock in the morning, getting his fires going and fixing breakfast so that the cowboys could be on their horses and working cattle by daybreak.

Just what were the old cowboys like? Annie Tallent, who saw them frolicking along dusty, rip-roarin' "Saloon Street" in Belle Fourche at roundup

Dinner on the rounup: bacon, beans, baking powder biscuits, jam, canned goods and plenty of Arbuckle's strong coffee.—*Photo by J. H. Bratley, 1895. South Dakota State Historical Society.*

time, gives us an honest picture. "I must confess to something of an admiration for cowboys despite their faults," she admitted.

"Of course, they have been known to fire random shots as they dashed along the streets of Hills towns in the early days, and to ride their bronchos, roughshod, through the doors and up to the bars of saloons, and such playful pranks, but, after all, they are in many respects, very manly fellows. They are perfect types of muscular development, endure hardships that would kill an ordinary mortal, are dead shots and the most expert horsemen in the world. The average cowboy is honest, kindhearted, generous to a fault, and, in short, is not half so bad as he is painted."

The cowboy, as a class, probably has been less understood and more maligned than any character in our country. To be sure, when the roundup was over, the dusty, sweaty cowpunchers raced into Belle Fourche; got all prettied up at the barbershop with haircut, shave and bath; then strutted about in the fanciest new trappings money could buy. There was a little carefree shooting as the boys made the town. But nobody was hurt much, and a lot of the old boys would pass up a drink of whiskey for ice cream—or the rarity, oysters—any time. Perhaps America has never developed a more courageous, capable and self-reliant class than the cowboy. Almost invariably, these old-timers were hard working, faithful to their employers

and honest as the day is long. The country could well use more of their spine and starch today. They were a law unto themselves but they dispensed fair justice. They were gentle with their horses and respectful to women. Even the cowboy songs, which the old hands used to hum to quiet their night herds, extolled home, mother, love of chivalry. Those old cowboys, cocking their heels up in the Hampton House windows, were light hearted and friendly and they had a song:

> I'm one of the boys.
> I can take a smile or sing a song
> With any good friend that comes along.
> I can tell a story or crack a joke
> And never refuse to drink or smoke;
> I'm a gay old sport you'll all agree,
> And I feel as young as I used to be.

Those were my heroes—the real American cowboys—and, significantly, they were President Theodore Roosevelt's heroes, too. Journeying to the West for his health in 1883, young Teddy Roosevelt took up ranching in Dakota Territory, where he made firm friends of many cowboys and westerners, including Captain Seth Bullock of Deadwood. Thus it happened that at Teddy's inaugural on March 4, 1905, Bullock conceived the idea of taking 62 rollicking Black Hills cowboys—with their horses—2,000 miles to Washington to salute the president. Henry Roberts of Belle Fourche, who was 15 at the time and went along as a mascot, told me the story in his late years; and judging from his sheaf of newspaper clippings of the event and personal recollections, Washington has never seen another inauguration like this one in 1905.

"We were up early," Hank recalled, "but we didn't saddle up till noon. Then we rode down back of the hotel and waited in front of the Police Court for our turn to fall in line. A lot of the old boys had fun roping Washington policemen and the first Negroes we had ever seen.

"We swung into the procession at four o'clock," Roberts went on. "It was great. When we rode by the President's stand, he took off his hat and hollered and I took off mine and hollered right back. After the parade, we all rode up to the White House and shook hands with the President. He says to me, 'I'm glad to meet you.' I says, 'Same to you.' He says, 'Don't mention it.'"

Following a private dinner given by the president, the ebullient cowboys went sight-seeing in Washington. Having nothing better to do on one occasion, they rode out Pennsylvania Avenue to a palatial foreign embassy, surrounded the grounds, and commenced shooting. The distraught diplomats, fearing no doubt that they would be captured and perhaps scalped alive, pulled the shutters and summoned Washington police. Washington would never forget the Dakota cowboys, and a few days later, when the hell-for-leather visitors started roping pedestrians from the top of Fifth Avenue coaches, New York was pop-eyed, too.

Writing in a New York newspaper, a reporter assigned to accompany the cowboys, described their memorable visit:

Seth Bullock's cowboys, who assisted in blazing the trail from the White House to Capitol Hill for Chief Ranger Roosevelt on Saturday last, arrived in New York last night. They rode on the cars, spilled soup on the train, joked with the conductor, played seven-up with the train butcher, marvelled at the wonders of New York and finally were corralled at the Union Square Hotel. The boys, who sold their horses in Washington and put up their guns before they got here, will take in Wall Street, the subway, and the theatre before heading back for the wide open ranges across the Missouri River.

The last time any of the surviving cowboys greeted a president was in 1927 when Calvin Coolidge vacationed in the Black Hills and attended the famed Tri-State Roundup at Belle Fourche. He had intended to stay for only a little while, but that day world champion bronc rider, Earl Thode (another of my heroes, who was as colorful as the Dakota Badlands from which he hailed) was scheduled to do an exhibition ride on Tipperary, then the world's only unridden bucking horse. Raking the sun-fishing, nasty bronc from stem to stern, Thode stayed on for six bone-bruising pitches and then was ignominiously bucked off—before the president of the United States! Apparently, the president enjoyed his first rodeo, for at this point he took out his watch and in his twangy New England voice announced he'd stay for the whole show. The cowboys named a bucking bronc "Cal Coolidge," the President thanked them and laughed dryly. That was about as much as the Vermonter ever said on the subject of cowboys. But everybody knew that the East had met the West; and as one of the old cowboys quipped, "It was a damned fine thing for the country!"

And I've often reflected, what a fine thing it was for me, growing up with my high-heeled heroes: the old cowboys.

"Potato Creek Johnny," who found one of the biggest gold nuggets ever seen in the Black Hills. Panning the streams until he got too old, he never found another, but he became a beloved character. — *South Dakota Division of Tourism.*

"Potato Creek Johnny" and his gold nugget

He was a pint-sized, picturesque character, only four feet, three inches tall, and the perfect image of the old prospector. As he bent over his gold pan on Potato Creek, for which he was nicknamed, his straggly white beard and long tangled hair reached down to his chest. He wore hip boots, a battered slouch hat, the sleeves of his longjohns showed beneath his light jacket; and he squinted through old-fashioned, rimless glasses looking for any elusive flecks of the precious yellow metal.

As he panned for gold, he reminisced about the "good old days" when nearby Tinton, in the Spearfish Canyon area, was a bustling mining camp and a man could sluice maybe $35 or $40 a day out of the gravel in Potato Creek. "But gold huntin' ain't what it used to be," he grumbled. "The Black Hills is full of them tourists, we've got too many fishermen riling the streams and a fellow's lucky anymore to make a livin.'" The old prospector waded out of the stream up to his rustic cabin in the pines. On the way, he stopped at a moss-covered whiskey barrel which he had sunk just below a spring and drank from a tin dipper.

"I call it 'The Last Chance Saloon,'" the genial prospector joked about his whiskey barrel, into which spring water was piped. "Here, have a drink on the house," he invited. Then, resting outside his cabin, he fed his fellow creatures of the woods, chipmunks and squirrels, from his hand while birds gathered unafraid to eat at his feet.

This was the Potato Creek Johnny I remember well, panning gold in Potato Creek where long ago a party of marooned prospectors was saved one winter from starving by existing on potatoes. His real name was Johnny Perrett, and he became a popular character not only because he was the last of the old-time prospectors, but because on a lucky day in May 1929, he had found one of the biggest gold nuggets ever seen in the Black Hills. Measuring 5 inches long and weighing 7¾ troy ounces, the nugget was worth $139.25 in those days, but would bring many times this amount at current gold prices.

Johnny sold his nugget to the Adams Museum in Deadwood for $250, and confidently went panning for another like it. There was something poignant about this dyed-in-the-wool aging prospector, working the streams alone, ever hopeful of striking it rich. He never found another sizable nugget, but his first one changed his life. Johnny became a local celebrity and until his death at age 77, he was one of the best-known tourist attractions in the Black Hills. Tourists, writers and photographers sought him out at his cabin on Potato Creek, and he was a star attraction during the annual "Days of '76" celebration in Deadwood. The little old prospector had come a long way since he had immigrated from Wales when he was 17 to seek his fortune in the Black Hills. Johnny worked on farms and ranches, carried the mail and even tried barbering before he settled down to the freewheeling life of a prospector. It was rumored that he had been married briefly and divorced.

Growing a bit weary in his later years of climbing the canyons, panning the streams and sifting his 100-foot sluice boxes for gold, Johnny accepted an offer from the Deadwood Chamber of Commerce. During the summers, he panned gold in Deadwood Creek and spun stories to the delight of fascinated tourists. Children in particular loved the elfin figure with the white beard, who reminded them of the Seven Dwarfs in Disney's Snow White. Johnny danced a little jig in the street, shot off his toy cap pistol and was such a hit in the "Days of '76" parade that the chamber of commerce decided to send him as a goodwill ambassador to travel and talk shows in Chicago and New York. This led to my most memorable experience with Potato Creek Johnny.

One day, long after I had left the Black Hills and was a newspaperman in New York, I got a call from Nell Perrigoue, able secretary of the Deadwood Chamber of Commerce. "Paul, I'm right here in New York," Nell phoned, "and guess who I have with me?" It was Potato Creek Johnny, who had been invited to appear on the then popular radio show, "We, the People."

Nell urged that I come over to the broadcast studio to renew acquaintance and to watch Johnny's rehearsal for the evening show. I met Nell and Johnny at their hotel, and as we tried to shepherd the tiny, buckskinned, long-haired character across busy Broadway, to the studio, we were mobbed by curious New Yorkers. Back at the hotel, Johnny had fortified himself at the bar; and now, arriving at the studio, he stepped onto the stage unannounced to dance a little jig and shoot off his pair of cap pistols. The audience howled, and the pint-sized prospector danced some more, delaying the tightly scheduled rehearsal.

At last, Johnny was calmed down and seated facing the announcer across a table with the microphones. He was handed a script as a prompter, the orchestra struck up the musical cue and the rehearsal began. But Johnny wasn't ready. Fumbling about in his white beard, he blurted out, "Hell, I cain't find my glasses." Undismayed, the announcer went on to introduce the celebrated character from the storied Black Hills. Johnny, at length, managed to untangle his glasses from his beard and long hair and the show got underway.

It went well enough, Johnny discoursing on the Black Hills gold rush, the story of his gold nugget and the life of a prospector. In closing, the script called for discussing Johnny's rugged outdoor life and his remarkable vigor in his 70s. By now the garrulous guest was warming up to his subject and tossing aside the script, he chatted freely before the microphones. "And to what do you owe your longevity," the announcer asked, whereupon Johnny looked him straight in the eye and replied, "Well, Sir, I always kept my bowels open!" The rehearsal ended abruptly, and the studio hastened to coach Johnny further before he really would be aired on "We, the People" later that evening.

Not long after his trip to New York, the old prospector was taken seriously ill and died in St. Joseph's hospital in Deadwood on February 21, 1943. In his honor, Deadwood businesses closed shop during his funeral, and as his cortege passed the Adams Museum, where his gold nugget was on display, the carillon chimes tolled 77 times for his 77 years of age. The old-timer's body was escorted to Mount Moriah Cemetery where it lies today beside the graves of Wild Bill and Calamity Jane.

Like a host of people, I was saddened at the passing of this kindly, genial pioneer, and I was touched to learn that during the "Days of '76" the following summer the crowd had stood for a few moments of silent tribute to this last of the grizzled old gold-seekers.

Hard-rock men: the curious Cousin Jacks

Lured to America, the land of opportunity, the Irish, Italians, English, Finnish, Slavic people and other nationalities streamed into the Black Hills to work in the mines. And of all these immigrants, the curious Cornish from Cornwall, England—land of my forebears—earned the reputation of being the most competent and colorful of the hard-rock miners.

There is an old saying that "wherever there is a hole in the earth, you will find a Cornishman at the bottom of it." Indeed, the Cornish have long ranked among the world's greatest hard-rock miners, and they have made a monumental contribution to mining in South Africa, Australia, New Zealand, Canada and the United States. "The Cornishmen," says Thomas A. Rickard in A History of Mining in America, "knew better than anyone else how to break rock, how to timber bad ground, and how to make the other fellow shovel it, tram it and hoist it."

Hailing from the ancient tin and copper mines of Cornwall, which tradition says were worked even before the time of Christ and may have supplied the metals used in the Temple of Jerusalem, the hardy Cornishmen were welcomed in the Black Hills. They were experienced hard-rock miners, gifted with an uncanny "nose for ore" and were expert at sinking shafts and striking illusive pay dirt. For centuries, Cornwall was famed as the tin and copper capital of the world. But in the 1800s, the most accessible ores began to peter out, water flooded the deepest mines, rich ores were discovered overseas and Cornwall was gripped in a disastrous depression. Thus hordes of Cornish swarmed to other mining areas of the world, including the Black Hills.

Immigrating to America by the thousands, the Cornish quickly won the derisive sobriquet, "Cousin Jacks." It appears that whenever men were wanted in the mines, or for any work, the eager Cornishmen always volunteered that they knew somebody back home—a Cousin Jack—who could do the job. Thus was coined the name Cousin Jack, and later, their quaint womenfolk, dressed in their "dust ruffle" skirts, leg-of-mutton sleeves and ostrich-plume hats, became known as "Cousin Jennies."

Fresh from Cornwall and speaking an almost unintelligible dialect, the rough-and-ready Cousin Jacks were considered peculiar, indeed. Physically, they were of small stature, but with top-heavy shoulders and chest (quite possibly developed from drilling and mucking in the mines), which appeared disproportionate to their slender hips and legs. Altogether, a strange new breed with a speech people considered odd and even laughable, the Cornish soon became the butt of crude mining camp ridicule and humor. Intrigued by the colorful Cousin Jacks, a Yankee shift boss decided to bring home Jan and Bill after work to meet his wife, so the story goes.

"Dearie," the shift boss called upstairs to his spouse, "I've got a pair of Cousin Jacks down here for you to see."

But it was already past bedtime, and the woman had retired. "Put them in the barn, give them some hay, and I'll look at them in the morning," she called back.

These immigrant Cornish were a distinctive people: curious, clannish, superstitious, generous, humorous, with a lusty interest in life and the opposite sex, and they were soon famed for their strange tongue and even stranger customs and food. Consider their curious language. Using a mixture of Celtic and local dialects, the Cornish developed their own peculiar tongue much like their closest neighbors, the Welsh. Indeed, the genuine Cornish language was spoken until about 200 years ago when it gradually became anglicized. But the Cornishmen gave it their own distinctive touches. Characteristically, they dropped their "h's" on many words and added them on others. Thus the Cousin Jack said 'ome for home and "Hearl" for Earl. And invariably, they used the word "thee" for you, together with such endearing terms as "My son," and "My 'andsom." Their common swearword was "damme!" and their favorite descriptive, "bloody." Thus the Cousin Jack might say of an injury or pain, "my bloody old leg is killing me."

But they were virtually unintelligible whenever they mixed original Cornish with English. Take the Cousin Jack who went to a doctor's office in Lead and tried to explain his trouble to an American nurse.

"Look 'ere thee," complained the hard-rock miner. "Es 'ave a sore ouzel and can't clunk."

Flabbergasted, the poor nurse pressed for a translation. But the Cousin Jack kept repeating, "Sore ouzel and can't clunk," and was obviously becoming irate. At this point, the doctor stepped out of his office, and being familiar with Cornish dialect, got right to the trouble.

"You say you've got a sore ouzel and can't clunk?" he said to the patient. "You mean you've got a sore throat and can't swallow?"

"Es can 'ave im that way if thees a mind to,"

"Wherever there is a hole in the earth, you will find a Cornishman at the bottom of it." A typical Cornish miner with lunch pail on his way to work.—*Western History Department, Denver Public Library.*

smiled the relieved Cousin Jack.

Stories of the Cousin Jack in the Black Hills are legion, and out of a lifetime of listening and laughing with my Cornish people, I treasure these gems:

Passing a meat market in Deadwood, a Cousin Jack was fascinated by a huge stuffed owl in the window. Entering the shop, he inquired of the butcher: "Ow much dust thee want for thy broad-faced chickon?"

"That edn' no chickon," said the butcher. "'Es an owl."

"Damme," swore the Cousin Jack, "I dusent care ow auld it is. What thee want for hit?"

Illiterate, but proud, the newly arrived Cornish miner did his best to conceal that he could neither read nor write. Picking up a newspaper one day in a Central City boarding house, a Cousin Jack blurted out, "Damme, some bloody wreck 'ere!" The illiterate miner was looking at a picture of a train, but holding the newspaper upside down!

Two Cornishmen went shopping for a hat. First Jan tried one, size 6⅞. It fit and he bought it. Now the clerk turned to Bill. "And what's your size?"

Puzzled, the Cousin Jack said, "Jan, thee took 6-7-8? Well, damme, my 'ed's bigger. I'll take 9-10-11."

Holding out his clenched fist, a Cornishman said to a schoolboy, "Look 'ere, my Son. If thee's can tell me 'ow many pennies 'es got in my 'and, thees can 'ave all five of 'em."

"Five," said the boy.

"Damme, take 'n," said the Cousin Jack. "Thee'rt a wizard."

Though they may have lacked education and good manners, the Cousin Jacks were usually warm-hearted and good family men. On arriving in the Hills, one endeavored to correspond with his sweetheart back home in Cornwall. But unable to write, he dictated his letter to another man in the boarding house, pouring out all his loneliness and love.

"Now pardner, you readen' back," he ordered the Cousin Jack. But first he clapped his hands over the other man's ears so he wouldn't hear all of the endearing things he had confided in the letter.

Although they were highly skilled hard-rock miners, the Cousin Jacks faced bitter competition from the Irish, Italians and other immigrants, some of whom worked for less pay than the Cornish. Naturally, this aroused fierce jealousy, frequent fist fights, and a story illustrates the racial tension.

Making the rounds one morning, a mine foreman talked to a pair of Cousin Jacks who were drilling and blasting in a stope.

"Ow art e gettin' 'hon, my sons?" he inquired.

"Bloody 'ard. She's bloody 'ard," the sweating miners relied.

"Well, never mind you, patience and perseverance will do the job," the foreman encouraged and went on his way.

After he was out of sight and hearing, one Cousin Jack turned to the other. "Dost thee ever 'ear of these two, Patience and Perseverance?" he inquired.

"God damme not," said his partner. "They must be some of them bloody Eyetalians they're bringing in 'ere to work."

Nurtured in a land of myth and legend, the Cornish miners were naturally superstitious. They considered crows a symbol of death, as were red-headed women. They believed that women would bring bad luck or disaster to a mine, and no woman was ever allowed underground. (Many mine and tunnel workers hold this belief to this day.) The Cornish believed that if a miner's candle went out three times or fell off the wall, somebody was at home romancing with his wife.

164

They were avowedly religious, gifted musically and like their Celtic kinfolk, the Welsh, they gloried in church choirs and hymn singing. The Cousin Jacks not only attended church, but they turned out, too, for fervent religious revivals such as held by the Salvation Army, and my mother told a memorable story.

One night after a stirring revival, when the crowded hall had been emptied, a Salvation Army lass found a lone Cousin Jack on his hands and knees between the seats. Touching him gently on the shoulder, she softly inquired, "My good man, are you seeking Jesus?"

"No my dear", the explosive Cornishman replied, "I'm 'untin for my bloody 'at!"

A curious, clannish people, who evolved their own peculiar language and culture, the Cornish also developed their distinctive "mait and drink" as they called it—or some of the oddest fare in the world. The original Cornish were a hardy folk who ate a coarse, heavy diet. Today they still delight in "herby" (herbs and bacon) pie, kiddley broth, "figgy pudden," toad-in-the hole (dumpling), scalded or "Cornish craim" and—favorite and indispensable—the pasty (pronounced pass-tee).

Some say that the pasty originated with a Cornish housewife who for years had been providing her miner husband with stale, unappetizing lunches to be eaten underground. But seeking to satisfy her grumbling spouse, she hit one day on a tasty replacement in a perfect package. She rolled her "beef and tetty" (potato) into a pie crust, folded it over and crimped the edges, producing a tightly sealed and nutritious meal which fitted conveniently into a miner's coat pocket. Thanks to my Cornish heritage, our family enjoys pasties frequently.

Inheriting the ancient food additve, saffron, from the Phoenicians, who long ago, bartered the substance for Cornwall's tin, the Cornish baked a pungent saffron cake. It was light yellow, heavy and tasted like medicine. Saffron cake tastes the same today, but you learn to like it. The Cornish are heavy-handed cooks, as witness the "fuggan"—a kind of poor man's cake that was as heavy as lead. The Cousin Jacks carried fuggan in their coat pockets, like pasties, but not safely. There's a story that one day as a miner descended a shaft to work, a chunk of heavy fuggan slipped from his pocket, ricocheted to the bottom and killed three men. Another coveted Cornish dish, even more loaded with calories, is scalded or clotted cream. Bringing the fresh milk to a boil, the Cornish then skim off the rich cream, which rises to the top as it cools, and spread it thickly on their bread, together with "treakle" or syrup. My Grandmother Hasken used to serve clotted cream to her miner boarders in Lead as a Sunday treat, and on one occasion a hearty Cousin Jack lapped up the whole bowl of dessert. Grandma was aghast and protested. But, undismayed, the Cousin Jack replied, "Why Missus, I could eat enough of this bloody craim to lather the Open Cut!"—that mammoth hole in the earth, that was once a mountain, where the fabulous Homestake Ledge was first discovered.

Such were the curious Cousin Jacks: truly memorable Black Hills characters.

Badger Clark, the celebrated cowboy poet who dared to live as free as the wind and the hawk that circles down the breeze.—*Rapid City Journal.*

Badger Clark: the carefree cowboy poet

He cut a handsome, striking figure striding across a college campus or delivering a commencement address. A six-foot-two, lithe man with graying, trim goatee and flashing dark eyes, he dressed distinctively, wearing polished riding boots, forest-green whipcord breeches, a military-type tunic and a gay-colored, checkered shirt with flowing silk tie.

Charles Badger Clark was the carefree cowboy poet, and I first heard him read his poems in his rich, sonorous voice at Spearfish Normal School (now Black Hills State College). As always, he recited "A Cowboy's Prayer"—his most popular, and some say immortal, verse. "I wrote it," the poet explained, "although I never heard a cowboy pray. But I know that when one did, it would be simple and straightforward." Later, as I became better acquainted with this uniquely individual man, I felt that this poem, which was a favorite of the cowboys themselves, pretty well reflected the poet's own philosophy of life. Listen to these lines from "A Cowboy's Prayer:"

> Just let me live my life as I've begun
> And give me work that's open to the sky;
> Make me a pardner of the wind and sun,
> And I won't ask a life that's soft or high.
>
> Make me as big and open as the plains,
> As honest as the hawse between my knees,
> Clean as the wind that blows behind the rains,
> Free as the hawk that circles down the breeze!
>
> Just keep an eye on all that's done and said
> And right me, sometimes, when I turn aside,
> And guide me on the long dim trail ahead
> That stretches upward to the Great Divide.

At the Tri-State Roundup in Belle Fourche on July 5, 1927, I heard the poem read again by rodeo announcer Warner Putnam to some 30,000 people, including President Calvin Coolidge, and the grandstand was hushed at this fitting tribute to the cowboy. Back of the chutes and around the corrals, the callused rodeo hands were quiet, too, respectfully standing, hat in hand.

Badger Clark knew cowboys and ranch life firsthand, but curiously he became a cowboy poet by chance. Son of the pioneer Methodist preacher, Charles Badger Clark, who had conducted the funeral service for the notorious character Calamity Jane, the poet was born in Albia, Iowa, on January 1, 1883. (His ancestors on his father's side were of Puritan stock and

his mother's people were Pennsylvania Quakers.) Shortly after his birth, the family emigrated to frontier Dakota Territory where the child had a harrowing experience. He was alone with his mother when a sudden prairie fire threatened their home. Carrying her six-month-old baby and driving a team, his courageous mother plowed a strip of sod around their shack to save them from the fire.

Following pastorates at Huron and Mitchell, Dakota Territory, Reverend Clark moved with his family by ox-team to Deadwood, where he endeavored to evangelize in the wide-open mining camp with five struggling churches, two dance-halls and 26 saloons. The bawdy environment must have had a lasting effect on the preacher's son, for he grew up a teetotaler. Graduating from Deadwood High School, where he was more of a dreamer than student, Badger Clark attended Dakota Wesleyan University at Mitchell, but only for one year. He was kicked out of college for smoking—an embarrassing episode for a Methodist preacher's son, but one which he never glossed over. A searching, restless young man, Badger left his home in Deadwood to spend the next two years with an unsuccessful colonizing scheme and adventuring in Cuba. While in Cuba, he was stricken with tropical fever. He had the further misfortune to be mistakenly arrested and jailed after he had innocently witnessed a shooting fray in the streets. Returning to the Black Hills when he was freed, the 22-year-old Clark worked at odd jobs and then became a reporter for the *Lead Daily Call*. But the after effects of the tropical fever had so damaged his health that a doctor "exiled" him to Arizona to recover from tuberculosis. Some of Clark's close relatives had died of the dread TB.

Happily, Clark's "exile" to the high, dry air of Arizona greatly improved his health and also changed his life. The young man went to work on a cattle ranch near storied old Tombstone, where he learned to ride and rope, picked up cowboy lingo and made genuine friends with the old-time, colorful cowmen. Cowpunching and the open range made an indelible impression on the sensitive youth. As he recovered from TB, he commenced writing poetry about cowboys and ranch life and one day he sent a new poem, "Ridin'," home to his stepmother in Deadwood. (His own mother had died when he was 15.) She thought it was so good that she sent it off to the old *Pacific Monthly*. Promptly the magazine purchased the poem, and to Clark's astonishment sent him a check for $10.

"That check," he used to recall, "wrecked any plans I had for a decently conventional career like selling insurance or being a doctor. If they paid for stuff like that, I figured, I was fixed for life."

Thus, by accident, Clark decided to become a poet and in 1910 he returned to the Black Hills and settled down to the writing which produced his first little book of poems (only 56 pages) *Sun and Saddle Leather*. It contained "A Cowboy's Prayer" which was warmly received. Flushed with his new-found success, Clark had dreams of becoming a major poet and author. But then after meeting several successful writers, such as the then best-selling novelist Harold Bell Wright, he became wholly disillusioned. "I found that they had more money than they could spend, but no privacy, no peace and quiet," the poet later recalled. "Their careers were charming little tiger kittens which they assiduously raised on a bottle until they grew so big they ate them up, and there was really nothing left but career."

The price for this kind of success was altogether too high, Clark decided, and he boldly determined to lead a *career-less* life: to live as free as the wind and "the hawk that circles down the breeze." The absolute antithesis of the organization man, the poet deplored bosses and time clocks and jobs, routine and responsibilities, and he wanted no part of the old rat race. "No wonder individualism is declining," he lamented. "We're killing it with ambition and overorganization, and people no longer have time to lead the good life."

Although he was a minister's son, the poet had little patience with organized religion, and indeed once confessed he wasn't sure whether he was a church member in good standing. He was attractive to women, but never married. He used to comment, "If a woman ever found out how much money I make, she'd never have me." He was determined to be the carefree cowboy poet; and to insure the tranquility that millions seek in vain today, he secured permission to build a cabin near the shores of Legion Lake in Custer State Park. Appropriately, he named the hideout from distractions and hurry, which he built himself, the *Badger Hole*—"four rooms and a path," the poet joked about his humble home. But it suited his simple needs, and there in his book-lined living room, by the light of a kerosene lamp, he continued to write both prose and poetry. He published two volumes of prose: *Spike* and *When Hot Springs Was a Pup*. His more important work was two volumes of prose: *Grass Grown Trails* and *Skylines and Wood Smoke*. But like his first collection of poems, these books netted him little, as the poet himself confirmed. Inscribing one of the volumes for a friend, he wrote:

Just a-writin'
  Nothin' I like half so well
As a-slingin' ink and English —
  If the stuff will only *sell*
When I'm writin'.

But sale or no sale, Badger Clark appeared to be the perfect image of contentment. For one thing, he had no income tax worries since he never wanted to make any more money than was necessary to buy his food, books and clothing. "I've never made more than a bare living, but I've always had enough for necessities and to pay my bills," he philosophized, "and luckily I don't crave luxuries." The poet augmented his meager income from writing by lecturing and reading his poems to clubs and conventions. He was a good speaker with a lively wit. His speaking fees were modest and obligingly on occasion he asked only that someone pick him up, return him and throw in a free meal. Though he generously accepted speaking engagements, he shunned serving on "prominent citizen committees." His trumped-up excuse, as he once wrote the governor of the state: "Really, I can't go anywhere for meetings. It's not practicable for me to leave home unless I'm paid for it." He was a widely popular commencement speaker and probably addressed more graduates and inspired more young people than any other citizen in the state's history. Fittingly, in 1937, he was named South Dakota's first poet laureate, or "Poet Lariat," as he was sometimes called.

Like another gifted loner, Henry David Thoreau, Badger Clark lived a spartan life in the Badger Hole. Scorning today's conveniences, he had no telephone, radio or electricity. He cooked his two meals a day on an old-fashioned, wood-burning kitchen stove, lugged water from a spring up the hill and lived on about $600 a year.

But the poet was no hermit. He loved people and was deluged with visitors. A greeting carved over his glowing fireplace in Spanish said simply, "My house is yours," and visitors were assured of a warm welcome. In 1927 when President Coolidge spent his summer in the Black Hills, he sent for Clark and asked him to read "A Cowboy's Prayer." The chatty, articulate poet visited with the delighted president most of the afternoon. When it was first announced that Coolidge would vacation in the Hills, everybody had an idea about how to entertain the President. Suggested Clark, "Let the Hills entertain the distinguished visitor—they have been associated with God for millions of years and are well endowed to handle a President."

The poet relished chatting with his many visitors, and he also enjoyed a heavy mail, which he faithfully answered. I know because one of my treasured possessions is an autographed, personally typed copy of the poem, "The Job", which the poet considered his finest work. (He was disappointed, however, that it never received the recognition of "A Cowboy's Prayer.") I had written requesting a copy of the then unpublished poem after I had heard it delivered at Belle Fourche High School, and obligingly Clark typed it on his battered machine and mailed it to me.

"The Job" is philosophical verse about how often a man's ideas, his dreams and schemes just won't come right. But then on reflection, he sees that God also has his struggles, as with infinite patience He goes on to create a better world. But man just won't come right! The poem concludes:

O God, forgive my pettish row!
I see your job. While ages crawl
Your lips take laboring lines, your eyes a sadder
  light,
For man, the fire and flower and center of it all —
Man won't come right!
After your patient centuries,
Fresh starts, recastings, tired Gethsemanes;
And tense Golgothas, he, your central theme,
Is just a jangling echo of your dream.
Grand as the rest may be, he ruins it
Why don't you quit?
Crumple it all and dream again! But no;
Flaw after flaw you work it out, revise, refine —
Bondage, brutality, and war, and woe,
The sot, the fool, the tyrant and the mob —
Dear God, how you must love your job!
Help me, as I love mine.

And so this inspiring bit of verse has hung above my desk now for many years, giving me the courage to try again when things won't come right, and helping me, too, to love my job.

The poet passionately loved his Black Hills, hiked its myriad trails, camped, studied its wild life and was on speaking acquaintance with a half dozen deer that hung around his cabin in the woods. He didn't fish and only on one occasion was he persuaded to go hunting. On this venture he tracked a buck upwind and had him in plain sight, right under his trigger. But there he stood, Clark wrote sentimentally, "his big eyes searching the ground" and "black nose sampling every breeze." It got the better of the nature-loving poet and he let the buck go free.

Badger Clark dearly loved the wild life of the Hills, and in a letter to a local newspaper once wrote scathingly about the hunter: "He is responding to the call of the primitive, the rich red blood of his caveman ancestors, and he must always go hunting to enjoy Gawd's Great Outdoors. . . . On mature reflection, I've concluded that going out with an irresistible weapon and inflicting terror and pain and death on harmless things that can't possibly fight back is not an especially manly pursuit. It is more satisfying to have a friendly fellow feeling for every creature that shares with us this mysterious and marvelous thing called life."

Apparently, his simple, outdoor life, together with the peace and solitude of his abode, kept the poet in excellent health. "I've only seen a doctor once or twice in about 40 years," he used to boast. "Oh, I had a little psychological heart trouble once, but the doctor just laughed at that." Unknown to the public, however, the poet was suffering from lung cancer. Ten days after he entered a Rapid City hospital, he died on September 26, 1957, at age 74. His only close relatives were nieces and a nephew.

Today his picturesque retreat, the Badger Hole, is maintained as a memorial, looking just as it did the night he last lowered the American flag before going off to the hospital. As I visited his book-lined living room again and stood over his desk, where he wrote under a kerosene lamp, I recalled his advice to an aspiring young journalist. "Young man," he urged me, "read everything you can lay your hands on. For reading will introduce you to the whole world and make you at home among men. At meal time, I take a good book to the table and I always have good company."

And leafing again through my well-worn copy of *Sun and Saddle Leather*, I find good company, too, in this carefree cowboy poet who dared to live as free as the wind and the hawk that circles down the breeze.

The Mount Rushmore National Memorial enshrining four presidents. "They personified America at its best!" declared Borglum.—*South Dakota Division of Tourism.*

Epilogue

The discovery of gold and grass first opened the Black Hills country to exploitation and settlement and made the nation aware of this remote, bountiful region. A half century later, a taciturn New Englander, President Calvin Coolidge, put the Hills on the map again when he vacationed there during the summer of 1927.

Coolidge occupied the State Game Lodge in Custer State Park and maintained offices in the high school at Rapid City, where he made his famed surprise announcement, "I do not choose to run for President in nineteen twenty-eight." The president's sojourn in the summer White House was a priceless publicity boon for the Black Hills. He was pictured in the nation's press and on newsreels with a good-sized catch of trout. On his fifty-fifth birthday, July 4, Coolidge wore a fancy cowboy outfit, that had been presented to him, with C A L embossed in big letters on his "chaps," and he was adopted as a chief by the Sioux Indians who named him Leading Eagle. In honor of the president, Deadwood staged an elaborate historical pageant, complete with the shooting of "Wild Bill" Hickok by Jack McCall in the infamous Number Ten Saloon, and reenactment of the Battle of the Little Bighorn. Wearing his cowboy boots and Stetson hat, "Cal" saw his first rip-roarin'-rodeo at the Tri-State Roundup in Belle Fourche, and I saw my first President—we sat only a few seats away from the presidential box in the grandstand.

The president's visit generated nationwide interest in the then little known Black Hills and attracted thousands of tourists. I recall seeing out-of-state license plates for the first time, and wondering how on earth people had the time and money to stop work, leave home and travel across the country. Ranchers could never do this. Today the lucrative tourist trade has turned out to be another bonanza for the storied Black Hills.

Visiting the Black Hills at the same time as Coolidge, the renowned sculptor, Gutzon Borglum, chose rugged Mount Rushmore as the place to carve his massive likenesses of four great Americans—Washington, Jefferson, Lincoln and Theodore Roosevelt—who personified "America at its best." "American history shall march along that skyline," Borglum declared. Donning his Stetson and cowboy boots once more, President Coolidge rode horseback over a rough trail to the imposing site, where on August 10, 1927, he dedicated the Mount Rushmore National Memorial; and sculptor Borglum raised the American flag over the granite mountain.

The creation of this shrine of democracy was as dramatic as it was monumental. Swinging in leather harnesses across the face of the 6,000-foot mountain, miners blasted and drilled for 14 years, removing some 450,000 tons of rock. I shall always remember my thrill at first viewing the world's most colossal sculpture. Colorful, flamboyant and absolutely fearless, Borglum climbed the mountain, a mere flyspeck against the great rock, and, dangling 250 feet over the cliff in midair, personally directed the daring operation.

It was hard, hazardous work, and the project was continually plagued with financial difficulties, but the first roughed-out head—that of George Washington—was dedicated with fireworks and oratory on July 4, 1930; the second—Jefferson—six years later, and Lincoln the following year. Borglum, now 70, could at last foresee the realization of his bold dream. In July, 1939, the figure of Teddy Roosevelt was dedicated. (Visitors often inquire about adding other Presidents. Unfortunately, there is no more suitable granite on Rushmore.)

Sadly, on March 6, 1941, Gutzon Borglum died of a heart attack, just a few months before the great sculpture was finished. His son, who had worked with him, completed it. Today the breathtaking Rushmore National Memorial is another tremendous boon for the Black Hills, and millions now come to gaze in awe at the shrine of democracy.

It is interesting to observe how differently people react to their first view of Mount Rushmore. Overwhelmed by the gigantic carvings in ageless granite—the heads are 60 feet tall, and larger than the Eyptian Sphinx—a graying Illinois farmer is misty-eyed. "I never thought I'd live to see this sight," he exclaims. "It makes me proud to be an American!" Overcome with emotion, a grateful young couple, refugees from behind the Iron Curtain, cling to each other in tearful embrace before this newfound shrine of freedom. The crowds, for the most part, are quiet, contemplative. Many stand in respectful silence. I recall one fellow who gazed up at the colossal carvings in wonder and amazement. Finally, turning to me, he pondered: "She's a lot of *chiselin'*, a lot of *chiselin'*!"

I have often pondered those great stone faces, too. And words the men used in their lifetimes come rushing to mind, words that have special meaning for our times. Washington, "Let us raise a standard to which the wise and honest can repair." Jefferson, "I have sworn upon the altar of God eternal hostility against every form of tyranny over the mind of man." Lincoln, "Let us have faith that right makes might and in that faith let us to the end dare to do our duty as we understand it." Roosevelt, "The first requisite of a good citizen in this Republic of ours is that he shall be willing to pull his own weight."

Like the Illinois farmer and the tearful refugees, I never fail to feel at Mount Rushmore a new fervor for our American freedoms—and for the only country, as author John Gunther said, that was deliberately founded on a good idea.

Back in 1948, not far from Rushmore, the sculptor Korczak Ziolkowski began carving a fitting memorial to the great Indian chief, Crazy Horse, whose warriors wiped out Custer. Ziolkowski conceived the heroic figure of the Indian on a horse, one outstretched arm pointing to the horizon. The sculptor spent 34 years carving the colossal monument, which would dwarf Rushmore, and had blasted over 7 million tons of rock from the granite mountain when he died in 1982 at the age of 74. It is high time that the Indian should be equally memorialized in the Black Hills, and happily the sculptor's family plans to continue the work which will take many more years to complete.

So, understandably, the tourists now flock to my native Black Hills, which offers many attractions. One of the finest is the Black Hills Passion Play, that a refugee from Nazi Germany, talented actor Josef Meier, brought to the lovely little city of Spearfish in 1938. It is a heartwarming story. Spearfish citizens raised $38,000 to develop the grounds, and build a huge outdoor stage looking up to the mountains, and townspeople volunteered to take part in the mob scenes leading up to Jesus' Crucifixion. News of this "Gethsemane in the Black Hills" spread and every year now thousands come to witness this deeply moving religious drama. I have seen a hushed audience sit through a rainstorm completely absorbed. Thus a 700-year-old Passion Play, driven out of Hitler's Germany, is now fittingly rooted in the "sacred" Black Hills. (The historic Passion Play at Oberammergau, Germany, is still seen every 10 years.)

Just as the mining industry boomed the Black Hills, so has the thriving tourist trade, but likewise it has created some scars: tawdry tourist traps and shoddy roadside "attractions" utterly out of character with the lovely mountains; a jumble of flashing neon signs that at night make the streets in some towns look like honky-tonks.

Time has tamed many of the old haunts and taken its toll in the Hills. Looking down on Deadwood from Mount Moriah Cemetery today, I find the town appears much as it used to be, except for a few aged, burned-out landmarks, now turned into parking lots. The puffing steam trains are gone and the city has created a new street in the narrow gulch by laying pavement over the once polluted, murky creek which runs through Deadwood. Virtually all of downtown Deadwood is now designated a National Historic Landmark.

The big change though is the work of federal and state lawmen. As I write this, they've closed and padlocked the storied bawdy houses, "the girls" are nowhere to be seen and wicked old Deadwood has lost its main claim to sin. "The do-gooders done this!" snorted a 95-year-old Deadwood character I knew well. "It's a damned shame. A little sinnin' is a necessity."

And what about the Indians?

This is the real tragedy. Caught up in a devastating culture clash, they have never really recovered from loss of their beloved buffalo-hunting country and their sacred Black Hills. The Indians today are a people in transition, between a time lost forever and a still-clouded future. Like Ziolkowski's roughed-out, unfinished sculpture of the great Crazy Horse, the ultimate destiny of the Indian is yet to take shape.

But it is beyond the scope of this book to ponder the complex question of the culturally displaced Sioux. Our aim was to tell the Black Hills story. We have found it immensely satisfying to write this book, and we trust the effort has been rewarding for you, the reader, as well.

Wearing his fancy cowboy boots, President Calvin Coolidge dedicated Mount Rushmore National Memorial on August 10, 1927 as sculptor Gutzon Borglum (in knickers) and other dignitaries looked on.—*National Park Service Photo.*

Sculptor Borglum raises the Stars and Stripes over Rushmore. "America shall march across that skyline," he vowed.—*National Park Service Photo.*

"Father into thy hands I commit my spirit." Crucifixion scene in the famed Passion Play at Spearfish: Gethsemane in the Black Hills.—*Black Hills Passion Play Photo.*

The U.S. Supreme Court has decreed the Black Hills were illegally taken from the Indians and it approved a $122.5 million settlement. Spurning this award, many Sioux, like this one in Rapid City, are demonstrating for return of their sacred Paha Sapa. — *Rapid City Journal.*

Just as the red men had dreamed of long ago, the great, shaggy buffaloes are back. But never again to provide food, clothing and shelter. Instead, this protected Black Hills herd, braving a winter storm, thrills the visitors to Custer State Park.—*South Dakota Division of Tourism.*

Suggested Reading

Brown, Dee, *Bury My Heart at Wounded Knee*; Casey, Robert J., *The Black Hills and Their Incredible Characters*; Clowser, Don C., *Dakota Indian Treaties*; Fielder, Mildred, *The Treasure of Homestake Gold*; Hyde, George E., *Red Cloud's Folk*; Lee, Bob (Editor), *Gold, Gals, Guns, Guts*; Parker, Watson, *Gold in the Black Hills*; Parker, Watson, *Deadwood's Golden Years*; Peattie, Roderick (Editor), *The Black Hills*; Rezatto, Helen, *Mount Moriah*; Sandoz, Mari, *Crazy Horse*; Smith, Rex Alan, *Moon of the Popping Trees*; Stewart, Edgar I., *Custer's Luck*; Tallent, Annie D., *The Black Hills*; Thomson, Frank, *The Thoen Stone*; Utley, Robert M., *Custer and the Great Controversy*; Utley, Robert M., *The Last Days of the Sioux Nation*; Vestal, Stanley, *Sitting Bull.*

Index